# THE SPIRITUAL EXERCISES OF ST. IGNATIUS

# EXPOSITION AND INTERPRETATION

by
William A. M. Peters, S.J.

Published by
THE PROGRAM TO ADAPT THE SPIRITUAL EXERCISES
144 Grand Street
Jersey City, N. J. 07302

Cover photograph by Reverend Algimantas Kezys, S.J.

*Imprimi potest* Walter L. Farrell, S.J., Provincial of the Detroit Province, September 21, 1967. *Nihil obstat* James J. McQuade, S.J., *censor deputatus*, September 27, 1967. *Imprimatur* Most Reverend Joseph M. Breitenbeck, Vicar General, Archdiocese of Detroit, October 5, 1967. The *nihil obstat* and *imprimatur* are official declarations that a book or pamphlet is free of doctrinal or moral error. No implication is contained therein that those who have granted the *nihil obstat* and *imprimatur* agree with the contents, opinions, or statements expressed.

MY DEAR BROTHER JAN

1908 - 1967

and

E. BEUKERS, S.J.

1870 - 1965

In piam memoriam

Table of Contents

## EDITOR'S FOREWORD

Among the great contemplatives of the Church, St. Ignatius of Loyola chose a unique way to communicate his mystical experiences to his followers. He destroyed nearly every page of his *Spiritual Diary* and left his *Spiritual Exercises* as the legacy of his prayer—seemingly in the hope that this little book would guide others to a prayer-life roughly similar to his own. These Exercises, when experienced under proper direction, will lead to singular advances in union with God.

Inevitably, the book of the *Exercises* found many interpreters. Several of these, in the early years of the Society of Jesus, wrote companion volumes called Directories which were intended as guides for the retreat master. We may note that the latter term, in the sense of a man who "preaches a retreat" to a few dozen or a few hundred religious, would have been meaningless to St. Ignatius. In his day, the Exercises were given to one retreatant or to a very few at a time; and the director was a "resource person" who briefly explained the subject on which the prayer was to be made and who offered counsel and guidance in the discernment of spirits.

There are many good modern translations of the *Spiritual Exercises* (Moore, Mottola, Rickaby, and Puhl are frequently referred to by the author), but few modern Directories properly so-called. In the present volume Reverend William A. M. Peters, S.J. provides a Directory for the long retreat, i.e., for the Exercises made by one who is "desirous of making as much progress as possible" and who withdraws from his work and other duties for a period of thirty days of prayer. With a few adjustments, however, the guidance Father Peters gives is almost equally applicable to a retreat of eight days or even less.

Father Peters' book is based upon a careful reading and literary analysis of the Spanish text with which he is thoroughly familiar. An accomplished linguist, he studied at the Jesuit colleges of Roehampton and Heythrop (1931-1935) in England and subsequently taught English in his native Holland. During this period, his book, *G. M. Hopkins: An Essay Towards the Understanding of His Poetry,* was published by Oxford University Press in 1948. He also wrote a number of articles on leading modern writers, including Waugh, Greene, Carey, and Faulkner.

Since 1953 Father Peters has given numerous retreats to English-speaking priests and religious in Canada, the Philippines, the United States and elsewhere. His reflections on the original text and his experience in the guidance of souls have helped him to develop an interpretation of the *Spiritual Exercises* which is original, penetrating, and psychological in a very sound sense. He has presented his views in ascetical institutes in Toronto, Cleveland, London, Dublin, Manila and New York. Reports on these institutes have fostered a demand for a total presentation of his interpretation.

His initial premise is his contention that the Exercises are first and foremost a school of prayer—and especially of contemplation, since it rather than discursive meditation is the species of prayer to which Ignatius gives greatest space and dominant importance in his book. This stress on the Exercises as a school of contemplation is indeed a unique feature of the present book, one which alone would make its publication highly desirable. For too many commentators, especially within the last century, have unfortunately all but overlooked the fostering of contemplation as a prominent Ignatian purpose in the Exercises. Instead, they have presented them as chiefly a "manual of arms," a collection of ascetical maxims, or a series of logical reasonings on spiritual living. Hence many readers and retreat masters may at first blush deem Father Peters' book a departure from the tradition to which they were accustomed in preached retreats. But in reality this book is a return to a more ancient tradition in the Society, one begun (we believe) under the Founder himself. Although it suffered eclipse through unfortunate historical developments within the century after his death in 1556, it reappeared in distinguished Jesuit writers such as La Puente (d. 1624), Lallemant (d. 1635), De Maumigny (d. 1918), and Louis Peeters (d. 1937), and it is worthy of fresh discussion today.

Ever since the first publication of Ignatius' *Exercises* in 1548, its compressed character has evoked numerous questions and controversies about its use and interpretation. Many a writer has erred in some details but nevertheless contributed insights of great value on others; and it would be a great pity if publication of their works had been sacrificed for fear of criticism or of some error in details relatively unimportant. Bushels of wheat which are altogether free of cockle are rare. Father Peters too must expect that some of his views, including his interpretation of some Spanish words in Ignatius' text, will be challenged by scholars. Even if these criticisms are right, his main contention will retain its value, especially in our times. One Spanish-speaking reviewer of his work has observed that Father Peters' interpretation has psychological validity, even though the reviewer could not agree with every argument deduced from the text itself. The present writer thinks that this sound observation is one more reason why Father Peters' book ought to be published.

As he indicates in his Preface, Father Peters follows the numbering of the Marietti edition of the *Exercises* in 1928 when he refers to the text. A copy of this edition or of a translation which uses that numbering (such as Puhl's) should be near one who reads the present book. Footnotes to each chapter are collected at the end of the volume. A full bibliography is not given, though the author has read widely in this specialized field—as his footnotes amply reveal.

Father Thomas A. Burke, S.J., Director of the Program to Adapt the Spiritual Exercises, has generously undertaken the publication of this timely book, and Father George E. Ganss, S.J., Director of the Institute of Jesuit Sources, Loyola University Press, Chicago, Illinois, has given much helpful advice and technical aid. To these men, for their patience and understanding, the editor is profoundly grateful.

Miss Helen Dougherty prepared the copy and the Sisters of Saint Joseph of Cleveland, Ohio, made the work of the editor vastly easier with their generous assistance.

Reverend Henry F. Birkenhauer, S.J.
Instructor of Priest-Tertians
Colombiere College
Clarkston, Michigan 48016
January 2, 1968

# PREFACE

Ignatius of Loyola did not write a short treatise about the nature of spiritual exercises; he composed a book, or even better, a series of spiritual exercises. At the same time, he gave advice and laid down rules designed that such exercises should be effective. He had experienced them first in his own person. He was firmly convinced that God Himself had inspired him to make these exercises and that God intended this grace for others as well. Hence, he urged many persons to make his exercises; hence too, his desire that his book of spiritual exercises be officially approved and recommended by the Church.[1] It explains why he and his first followers insisted that the exercises be made *exactamente*.[2]

The simple fact is that Ignatius was not engaged in theology, liturgy, or biblical exegesis. It is unfair criticism of the *Spiritual Exercises* to argue that this book does not give the exercitant a clear insight into the Church as Christ's Mystical Body or bring him to a true appreciation of the riches of the liturgy. The director who uses the Spiritual Exercises primarily as a vehicle for the latest theological opinions or in order to shed new light on the composition and contents of Holy Scripture has moved away from St. Ignatius' book and does not give an Ignatian retreat; he is doing something altogether different.

The Spiritual Exercises have not always been approached as a series of *exercises*. There has often been a great deal of explanation, argumentation, and marshalling of reasons and proofs to convince the exercitant and persuade him to serve and worship God. But this is not the same thing as serving and worshipping God here and now. Moreover, commentators and directors of retreats have not always given the text the attention it deserves and demands. As a result, words and phrases have been carelessly read, at times the stress has been placed on the wrong word, quite frequently the structure and purpose of an exercise have not been accurately assessed, and the connection between succeeding exercises and succeeding weeks not studied closely enough.

These two shortcomings explain why this study came to be written and why it is presented in the present form. We shall be much concerned with the Spiritual Exercises as exercises, and the starting point of our exposition will always be a careful reading and literary analysis of the text. This implies, for reasons to be considered in the second chapter, that we shall be occupied with the exercitant of the twentieth annotation, that is, with the exercitant who makes the thirty days' retreat. A close study of the text will answer many questions that are nowadays being asked concerning these exercises, and it will preclude the posing of false problems. Hence, objections against the Spiritual Exercises as being Pelagian or at least semi-Pelagian, individualistic, methodical, and so forth, will not be mentioned, although we are very much aware of them.

Misreading clearly breeds misinterpretation. But a second source of misinterpretation has been the fact that only too often the text has been considered as supra-temporal; it has not been approached as a book written in the sixteenth century. So exposition of the text will be accompanied by interpretation where this is necessary or desirable.

When we quote the text of the *Spiritual Exercises*, the Marietti edition of 1928 has been used, and the marginal numbers there introduced and now generally accepted have been adopted. The official edition of the text as published in the *Monumenta Historica Societatis Jesu*, together with the early *Directories*, is referred to as *Ex. Sp.*, and the *Directoria Exercitiorum Spiritualium* 1540-1594, in the same series, is referred to as *Dir.*[3]

Shorter quotations from the Spanish so-called autograph text will not cause any great inconvenience to the reader. We have not confined ourselves to one English translation. We have made frequent use of the translations of Morris, Rickaby and Puhl, while we have constantly consulted the more recent translations of Moore, Mottola and Corbishley. Courel's rendering into French and those of Raitz v. Frentz and Urs von Balthasar into German have also been of help.[4]

When quoting the autograph text, we have adhered to the spelling of Ignatius and not made any corrections. It accounts for "pecado" by the side of "peccado," of "fe" and "fee", of "cognoscimiento" and "conoscimiento," of "caridad" and "charidad," etc.

The reader will look in vain for a bibliography, and only a few books are referred to in the text of this study. It does not mean that what I owe to others is negligible. Quite the opposite. I acknowledge my great indebtedness to the many who contributed to the contents and shape of the book, both living and dead. The dead: from Ignatius' companions and first commentators down to men like Roothaan, Nonell, Hummelauer and others, and the great men who began the *Monumenta Historica S.J.* The living: those whose published or unpublished studies, lectures, and articles I have been privileged to read, the translators, and among these, in a special way, Louis Puhl, S.J. for much-appreciated help, and the many fellow-Jesuits, young and old, who in various parts of the world have listened to my lectures and have been good enough to place before me their doubts and questions concerning the Spiritual Exercises. They go unnamed, except for John Wickam, S.J., D.Lit. for reasons well known to himself. To all of them, my grateful thanks.

one

# ESSENTIAL CHARACTERISTICS

In 1535 Ignatius left Paris. His health had suffered considerably and he had been advised to recuperate in his native country. The following year he went from Spain to Italy and, when in Venice, on the sixteenth of November, he wrote a letter to Emmanuel Miona, his confessor both in Alcalá and in Paris. Ignatius, still a layman, urged this learned and saintly priest most earnestly to make the Spiritual Exercises, appealing even to the love and cruel death of the Lord. The letter contains the astonishing statement that he, Ignatius, could not conceive of anything better or more profitable for progress in the spiritual life.[1] This bold judgment was based upon his own experience of some fourteen years earlier. Of his ten months' stay at Manresa he was to testify afterwards that God there taught him as a schoolmaster teaches a schoolboy. This schoolboy, who was blind and had as yet no knowledge of spiritual things, added that, if he were to have thought otherwise, he would have offended God.[2] Nadal and Lancisius, when they spoke of this period in their master's life, used the same comparison to describe the wonderful happenings of those months.[3] The essence, then, of the Spiritual Exercises as Ignatius made them consists in this, that God is teaching or, more generally, God is at work. Turning to the text of the *Spiritual Exercises*, we read in the fifteenth annotation that God should be allowed to work directly with His creature. The sixteenth annotation suggests ways and means to ensure that "the Creator and Lord may work with greater certainty in His creature."

God's activity takes on many forms: He enlightens the understanding (2), He enters the soul, moves it, draws it towards loving Him (330), grants it an abundance of fervor, overflowing love, and the intensity of His favors (320), makes it attain intense affection, tears and other spiritual consolation (322), places in the soul that which the exercitant ought to do with regard to his choice of a state of life (180), and brings the soul's desires into order (16). God even communicates Himself to and embraces the exercitant (15).[4] And this list is by no means complete. Ignatius' words and expressions should not be taken lightly. It is a tremendous claim for any man to make, to maintain that, if one accepts his advice and guidance, God will communicate Himself. Ignatius was aware of it, and so were his first friends and companions. The miracles of conversion that were brought about by the Spiritual Exercises made Ignatius' secretary, Polanco, wonder how they could achieve such impressive results. He knew no other answer than that here God does not work through secondary causes but is Himself directly engaged with the exercitant, and this "liberrimus sed, pro sua natura quae bonitas est, effusissimus" (*Dir.*, 276). This is exactly what caused Ignatius a great deal of trouble. What he thought to be the essence of his Spiritual Exercises savored too much of dangerous trends in the life of the Church at the time, trends associated with the *alombrados* and *dechados*.[5] We will not discuss what reasons the Inquisitors had for suspecting him of false mysticism, quietism, and passivity. It is enough to have stressed the fact that this sort of difficulty could arise. A few years before his death, Ignatius had serious difficulties with some of his own followers who began to display an alarming resemblance to the *alombrados*; the names of Oviedo and Onfroy will not easily be forgotten in this connection.[6]

The suspicion and opposition aroused by this crucial element have had serious consequences for both the reading and the interpretation of the text. Fairly soon after Ignatius' death, far less stress began to be placed on the fifteenth and sixteenth annotations and on the rules for the discernment of spirits, a subject most intimately connected with God's activity in the exercitant.[7] The application and activity of the exercitant together with the role of the director were made more central. A faulty understanding of the word "exercise" made matters worse,[8] and as a result the Spiritual Exercises were turned into an ascetical handbook in no mean measure.

The Spiritual Exercises are essentially a matter of cooperation between the Creator and His creature (16). If God is the main agent, the exercitant will not put any obstacles in the way of God's activity but "will enter upon them with magnanimity and generosity and offer his Creator and Lord his entire will and liberty" (5). Ignatius' greatest anxiety is that the exercitant should be most diligent to cooperate. So he gives many rules and suggestions, advice and guidance concerning external circumstances and behavior as well as the exercitant's inner disposition. With regard to the former, we learn how important it is for the exercitant to withdraw himself from his friends, acquaintances, worldly cares, even from his work and his house "to make the soul more fit to approach and be united with its Creator and Lord" (20). In this twentieth annotation Ignatius uses "apartar" no less than four times in addition to "secretamente" and "se halla sola" (to be by oneself).[9] The exercitant is to banish all thoughts and phantasies that are alien to the subject matter of meditation or contemplation, he should refrain his eyes, do penance in various ways, even deprive himself at times of light and heat. Ignatius insists that the additions, as he calls these rules and regulations, must be faithfully observed. He never fails to bring them to the notice of the exercitant and is careful to point out in what way they have to be changed and adapted to each new phase of the retreat (73-82, 130, 207). He gives detailed instructions about meditation and contemplation, at what time it has to be made, how it should be begun and ended, how long it is to last, how often it is to be repeated, what posture the exercitant should adopt while praying, and so forth, points to which we shall return in the fourth chapter. Such regulations have given rise to the accusation that Ignatius forces his exercitant into a sort of strait jacket; they paralyze free will, seem to make grace a superfluity and thus the Spiritual Exercises become little more than a series of psychological tricks. However, for Ignatius it was a question of God working, God communicating Himself, God even embracing His creature; and face to face with this mystery, nothing must be left to chance, and no liberties must be taken.

As regards the exercitant's inner disposition, more important than any rules and regulations is Ignatius' insistent demand that he must be receptive and sensitive to what God is doing, working, saying. In the second annotation he is warned not to attach too great a value to knowledge, for "it is understanding and savoring or relishing the matter interiorly that fills and satisfies the soul." He should attend to and dwell upon those parts in his exercise "where he experiences greater consolation or desolation or greater spiritual relish" (62, 118) and there must never be any eagerness to move on to other parts until he has been satisfied (76).

Certain dangers are attached to this receptive attitude. When the exercitant is listening to God rather than thinking, when rather than arguing matters out he allows himself to be moved and agitated, when he is more passive than active, there is a real danger of illusions, hallucinations, of motives stirred by subconscious forces or even by Satanic spirits. So, wise director that he is, Ignatius asks the exercitant after every exercise to review what happened to him during the time of prayer (77); he suggests frankness on the part of the exercitant in acquainting the director with his spiritual experiences (6, 17) and he gives no less than twenty-two rules to arrive at a true discernment of spirits (313-336). He even adds a number of rules for thinking with the Church, which seem to have strayed into the *Spiritual Exercises* by accident or perhaps to have been added as a sort of afterthought. In fact, they form an integral part of the book, but this will not be understood unless it is realized how acutely aware Ignatius was of the dangers and possible aberrations which can be, as it were, the price paid for this receptive attitude towards the mystery of God working in and with His creature. For, intense susceptibility and receptivity, even passivity, open the door to an uncritical acceptance of whatever suggests itself to the soul as the true voice of God. This must be counterbalanced by a sober and strict adherence to the mind and doctrine of the Church; obviously, there can be no disagreement between the Spirit that governs and directs the exercitant and the same Spirit that guides and rules the Church (365).

In this connection, two precautions of Ignatius must be mentioned. "Every Christian," he warns us in a preliminary remark, "must be more ready to place a good interpretation on another's statement than to condemn it as false" (22). Without this disposition the cooperation between the exercitant and the director will be hampered. The danger that the former may cling to his own opinions and experiences will be very real, as he will be inclined to consider them as coming directly from God. A second precaution is designed to prevent the exercitant from beginning his prayer with an entirely empty mind or in a state of sheer passive expectancy, of "come what may." Throughout the Exercises, he is told to want, to wish, to desire, which should lead to supplication and petition. "Demandar lo que quiero y deseo," with slight variations, is the backbone of the Exercises as far as the exercitant is concerned.

If the cooperation between the Creator and His creature is the essence of the Spiritual Exercises, the obvious question to ask is what the divine activity seeks to achieve. Indeed, God enlightens the exercitant, moves him, even communicates Himself to him; but does the text contain any more precise information? If God taught Ignatius as if he were a schoolboy, what subjects did He teach him?

The paragraphs twenty-eight to thirty constitute a very important, if not the most important, part of Ignatius' Autobiography. He wrote modestly of special graces received from God. He was granted a deep insight into the mystery of the Trinity and was shown how God created the world. "He seemed to see something white from which rays proceeded" (29). These words recall the text of the contemplation to attain divine love where the exercitant contemplates how all created things on the face of the earth—and these are referred to as God's good things and gifts—descend from above, as the rays of light descend from the sun (236-37). Creation was seen by Ignatius not as an activity of the past but as a continual dynamic presence of God in all things, so much so that it is a sign of perfection "to consider, meditate, and contemplate that God is in every creature by His power, essence and presence" (39). The teaching contained in the visitations and visions, especially that on the Cardoner, appears to have had for its object the cohesion, order, and harmony of the whole of creation as the work of the Trinity. To a certain extent this revelation was in keeping with Ignatius' character. He was a man of order and neatness. In his *Autobiography* he tells us of the way in which, when a wounded soldier at Loyola, he noted down striking sentences about Christ and His Blessed Mother: the words of Christ in red ink and those of our Lady in blue; the paper was glazed and ruled; the letters were well formed, because he was a very good penman (11). It is the order and neatness to be expected of the gentilhombre. Nowhere do we meet Ignatius as a man of order more clearly than in his letters and in the *Constitutions* of the order he founded.[10]

The text of the *Spiritual Exercises* proves that Ignatius is almost obsessed with the question of order and harmony. The title of the book indicates that the purpose of the Exercises is "para ordenar su vida" and it mentions self-conquest as the means to bring this about, as is made abundantly clear when in the notes on doing penance Ignatius states that the end of self-conquest is "that the sensual appetite may obey reason, and all the lower parts be more subject to the higher" (87). According to the sixteenth annotation, the object of the Spiritual Exercises is intimately bound up with God's desire to bring the affections of the exercitant into order (ordenando sus deseos). In a similar way, the exercitant should order his words, his actions, his meals (40, 63, 210). He is never to begin a meditation or contemplation without having asked God that all his intentions, actions, and operations may be ordered purely to His service (puramente ordenadas, 46). He is warned that in any choice or election he must never subordinate the end to the means but on the contrary, order the means to the end (ordenando el medio al fin, 169). Since harmony and order cannot be attained unless discord and disorder have been overcome, it is not surprising that sin is first and foremost disorder (desorden, 63) and that its source is mainly the *affección desordenada* (21, 169, 179). The exercitant is to begin the retreat with great generosity towards his Creator and Lord, "that His Divine Majesty may *dispose of* him and all he possesses according to His most holy will" (5). The autograph text has "ordenar," which Ignatius later changed to "se sirva conformiter." Both the *versio prima* and Roothaan have the translation "disponere," which is also the rendering of the verb "disponer" as used by Ignatius in the first annotation.

"Disponer" is more or less the equivalent of "ordenar." This is evident in the first annotation, where spiritual exercises are said to be any method of preparing and *disposing* the soul to free itself from all *inordinate* affections. In this sense it is found again in the twentieth annotation: solitude is a necessary condition if the exercitant is to dispose himself to receive gifts and favors from the Divine Goodness. The exercitant's vital concern after the meditation on Two Standards will be "how to dispose himself in order to arrive at perfection" (135). The second meaning of "disponer" is: to make use of, to dispose of. It does not occur with this meaning in the Spiritual Exercises, but we believe that the twofold meaning of "disponer" breaks through when Ignatius employs the word "disposición." We return to the first annotation: ". . . we call spiritual exercises every way of preparing and disposing the soul to rid itself of all inordinate attachments, and, after their removal, of seeking and finding the will of God in the disposition of our life (en la disposición de su vida) for the salvation of our soul" (Puhl). What exactly does Ignatius mean?

To answer this question correctly it will greatly help if the first and fifth annotations are considered side by side. We notice the following parallelisms: "to offer God his *entire* will and liberty" of the fifth annotation and "to rid the soul of *all* inordinate attachments" of the first;" (that God may dispose of him) according to His most holy will" (5) and "to seek and find the divine will" (1). It is very likely that the third element, mentioned in these two annotations, shows a similar parallelism: "that God may dispose, or make use, of his person and all he has" (5) and "the will of God in the disposition of his life" (1). The generally accepted translation of the closing phrase of the first annotation, namely, seeking and finding the will of God in the disposition, or regulation, of his life, does not bring out sufficiently what Ignatius meant to convey. The parallelisms between the first and fifth annotations show that the subject that goes with the noun "disposición" is God, and not the exercitant; moreover, there is a very strong suggestion that the twofold meaning of the verb "disponer" asserts itself in the use of the noun. Any true translation should make clear that the exercitant is seeking the will of God concerning the way in which *He* both disposes, that is, orders, and disposes of, that is, makes use of his life. This confirms what was previously seen, that God is the principal agent in the Spiritual Exercises and that His main activity is to order, to restore order in the exercitant.[11] At the same time it recalls how the Spiritual Exercises are a question of cooperation, for the *disposición* as the work of God goes hand in hand with the exercitant's preparing and disposing himself to get rid of attachments, to receive gifts and favors, and so on.

Closely associated with disposition must be composition. The prepositions attached to the common verb indicate how "to *dis*pose" must be followed by "to *com*pose" so that there can be unity and order. It is to be expected that composition will be one of the exercitant's main contributions to a successful retreat. We shall have to say a great deal about it throughout this study.[12]

At Manresa, God taught Ignatius as a schoolmaster teaches a child. The very process of teaching implies that step by step the pupil is made familiar with the subject taught. Where Ignatius is taught order and harmony, these are *gradually* unfolded, placed before him, and put into practice. So much is abundantly clear from what he tells us about his days of penance and prayer in the cave; his stay at Manresa was not merely, not even mainly, a period of sudden illustrations and visions (19-32). A similar sort of gradual unfolding of truth and order lies at the heart of the Spiritual Exercises. The four-weeks division makes this at once evident. Ignatius mentions this order in the second and twentieth annotations, insisting that it should be observed. Elsewhere he warns the director not to disturb the gradual way in which order should be unfolded (11, 127).

The verb "to teach" must not be misunderstood in this context. When God teaches the exercitant He does not give him intellectual knowledge. The Spiritual Exercises do not aim at imparting information about order and harmony of life. Essentially, to make the Exercises is "to understand and savor the matter interiorly" (sentir y gustar de las cosas internamente, 2). The very word "exercise" is sufficient proof that in a retreat right order is not only gradually unfolded but at the same time realized and experienced. This should prevent both director and exercitant from making the mistake of moving about in an abstract sort of order. God works in and with *this* exercitant, that is, with this priest, or this religious, or this layman, and with each at a particular stage of his life. Hence, order can never be achieved unless this individual exercitant tries to find the will of God concerning the way in which God wants to order *his* life, here and now, and very much with a view to his own future. The possessive pronoun in the closing phrase of the first annotation should then be stressed (en la disposición de *su* vida). As the director cannot possibly know in any detail what order means for the exercitant, he must not interfere in this matter, but "as a balance at equilibrium he should allow the Creator to work directly with His creature" (15).

If the gradual unfolding and living of order is the object of the cooperation between God and exercitant, a new light is shed upon those many rules and regulations mentioned above. They are safeguards to make sure that the exercises will be effective. Their function is seen in a better light when we remember that the Spiritual Exercises are not a matter of theory but of practice and that it was only natural for Ignatius to provide an external framework of good order within which right order is being gradually unfolded and realized. Since to find order in the midst of disorder is too difficult a task, the numerous suggestions concerning the order of the day, the order of the meditations and contemplations, the order within each exercise, and so forth, in addition to being safeguards, are intended to be a first realization of order and orderliness. Thus, they become a sign and a symbol of that inward order and harmony which the exercitant seeks. It explains once again why Ignatius attaches so much value to their careful observance.

We need not enter the controversy whether an election or a new disposition is the primary end of the Spiritual Exercises. We have already taken sides: "ordenar" means much more than to make an election concerning one's state or way of life.[13] "Ordenar," naturally, may imply that an election will have to be made; we shall return to this point in the eleventh chapter, when we discuss the three times for making an election. But from the twentieth annotation it is abundantly clear that the Spiritual Exercises are for "those who wish to make as much progress as possible," and from the introduction to the meditation on Two Standards it appears that beyond the matter of the election the exercitant must achieve perfection, that is, right order and harmony "in whatever state or way of life God may grant him to choose" (135). Corroboration is given by the life of Ignatius himself. At the end of the ten months at Manresa there had been no election concerning a state of life: the conversion took place some time before it. Leaving Manresa to travel to the Holy Land, a decision taken before he went to Manresa, he was vague about his state of life and had no clear idea of what exactly God wanted him to do; it was to be revealed only very gradually. Again, this view alone will explain why Ignatius allowed Xavier to take his vows on Montmartre on the fifteenth of August, 1534, and yet did not give him the Spiritual Exercises until a month after.

This observation is of importance to understand that the Spiritual Exercises do not form a finished whole, neatly rounded off by the fourth week. If a sound election is taken to be the purpose, the climax is reached at the end of the second week; the two weeks following are intended to confirm this election, and thus the Spiritual Exercises form a logical, compact structure. If, however, the essence is seen to be an ordering of one's life, there can be no end to these exercises; otherwise, a month's retreat would mean the achievement of order, that is, the attainment of perfection and sanctity. Indeed, the Spiritual Exercises lack a proper ending. We do read, it is true, of the first exercise and of the first day of the fourth week, but nowhere do we read of a last day or a last exercise; we shall deal with this matter in the final chapters. God does not confine His activity to the time of the Spiritual Exercises themselves nor does He unfold what is contained in the mystery of the exercitant's existence in all its fullness during that time. Consequently, the exercitant carries on his task of finding the will of God, unfolded more and more completely as time moves on.

This introductory chapter leads to one all-important conclusion: the Bible must stand central in the Spiritual Exercises. If the Spiritual Exercises are in an exceptional way founded upon the mystery of God's Self-communication and Self-revelation, it is unacceptable to hold that this does not primarily take place through the Bible. The Word of God fulfills an essential, in fact, the essential function, in the Exercises, because in it and through it God reveals Himself and takes up contact with man. It is not a question that the subject matter for meditation or contemplation is taken from the Bible, it is not a question of finding suitable material taken from psalms, prophets or gospels that may be deftly adapted to the purpose of the Exercises. One may not find so many proofs of what should be evident as one would like in the text of the *Exercises* itself. We shall return to this point when contemplation is closely examined. For the present it should suffice to remember that at the time when Ignatius put his exercises together, the whole Bible was a relatively rare book: the art of printing was a quite recent invention. The text of the Old Testament did not play any important part in Ignatius' conversion or during his ten months' stay at Manresa, and, in all likelihood, not for many a year after it. All he had and knew was the New Testament, and quite often he had to content himself with the four gospels. It is difficult to see how, in these days, any director or exercitant could be faithful to Ignatius and to his Spiritual Exercises who does not take and keep the Bible in hand. No one understanding the Exercises will substitute thinking about religious truths for listening to God, who reveals Himself and communicates Himself through the Sacraments and *through His Word,* that is, the Bible.

two

# THE CONTENTS OF THE BOOK OF THE *SPIRITUAL EXERCISES*

The book of the *Spiritual Exercises* displays a disconcerting medley of different methods of prayer, of meditations and contemplations, of rules, notes, instructions, advice, and so on, touching upon a great variety of spiritual subjects. One might well ask whether anything less systematic, less "orderly", could be possible. Yet Ignatius was for about a quarter of a century (1522-1548) perfecting his collection of notes. During the last decade of this period he was writing the *Constitutions* of his order, a work which demanded careful concentration on every word he was to use and which constantly forced him to reflect upon the structure of the whole. It is hardly likely that a mind thus occupied could be satisfied with less accuracy in a work which he valued even more highly than these *Constitutions*. It will then be wise to look closely at what is contained in the book of the *Spiritual Exercises* and examine the way in which divers subjects have been strung together. In this chapter a general survey of the contents of the Spiritual Exercises will be given; details will be discussed later.

The preceding chapter showed that the essence of the Spiritual Exercises consists in the cooperation between God and the exercitant. This holds good of all spiritual exercises, but in a very special way of "todos los exercicios" or "los tales exercicios" (4, 15, 18, 20), by which Ignatius means the Spiritual Exercises of thirty days. In the proper sense of the word the Spiritual Exercises stand for the retreat containing the four weeks. Every other form of giving them involves adaptation. For, Ignatius does not exclusively concentrate on the exercitant described in the twentieth annotation—on the person, that is, who wishes to make as much progress as possible and is free to spend thirty days in solitude. There are also those who are of considerable learning and ability, but who are too busy to disengage themselves from their work and surroundings for any length of time, as we read in the nineteenth annotation. Nor does he forget the many who are of little natural capacity and limited understanding and yet long for peace of soul: the exercitant described in the eighteenth annotation. These three groups do not exhaust the many possible kinds of exercitants. Unless one bears in mind that Ignatius caters to those different people, there will always be a danger of over-feeding some and under-feeding others, as is pointed out in the eighteenth annotation.

Consequently, we have to determine what Ignatius intended for the various groups of exercitants. Our starting point is the Exercises proper. The so-called long retreat begins with the first exercise, which is a meditation on the triple sin; it is followed by four other meditations (45-72) with a number of suggestions known as additions (73-89). The consideration usually referred to as the Kingdom is a transitional exercise between the first and second weeks (91-100). The second week contains the contemplations on the life of Christ, together with five meditations on Two Standards and Three Classes of Men (101-62). Then follow the contemplations of the third week (190-209) and those of the fourth week (218-29). The many references to the mysteries of Christ's life, which are placed together later in the book (261-312), are sufficient proof that this section belongs to the four weeks. The reason why this series of mysteries has been placed outside the framework of the four weeks is given by Ignatius himself, when he deals with the matter of shortening or lengthening the various weeks (4, 162, 209, 226) and when he advises the exercitant to continue meditating or contemplating the life of Christ after the retreat (162). In between the fourth week and this series of mysteries Ignatius placed the contemplation to attain the love of God (230-37) and the three methods of prayer (238-60). At the top of the pages in the photographic copy of the text there is no indication that these exercises belong to the fourth week; but in the fourth annotation Ignatius, speaking of the fourth week, mentions in the same breath the Resurrection, the Ascension and the three methods of prayer. Evidently, if the three methods of prayer are made part of the fourth week,[1] *a fortiori* the contemplation to attain divine love must be included: its very position between the contemplation of the risen Christ and the methods of prayer demands this.

There is a clear break in the matter contained in the book of the *Spiritual Exercises* as soon as the mysteries of Christ's life have been given. What follows is a collection of notes and rules, dealing with the life of a Christian in general. There are two series of rules "for understanding to some extent the different movements produced in the soul" (314-27 and 328-36), some notes concerning scruples (345-51), and a set of rules for thinking with the Church (352-70). Rules for the distribution of alms (337-44) seem to have strayed into this company, just as somehow or other the rules regarding food and drink have been with apparent inadvertence left in the third week (210-17). Why did Ignatius not move them? Surely, they would have found a more unobtrusive place alongside the rules for the distribution of alms. Or are they perhaps part and parcel of the four weeks in a way in which the rules for giving alms are not? We shall provide an answer presently.

Leaving out the twenty introductory remarks, called annotations, we observe that the beginning of the first week does not coincide with the first exercise. The photographic copy has "primera semana" written at the top left-hand corner of the page where Ignatius opens with the words "Spiritual Exercises to conquer oneself . . ."; it is immediately followed by the Presupposition (22) and the First Principle and Foundation (23). The paragraphs that follow (24-44) are taken up with the exposition of the general and particular examinations of conscience and a few remarks about confession and Communion. Only then is the first exercise given. But every page so far bears the abbreviation *p.sa.*, that is, *primera semana,* first week. The explanation must be that the exercitant of the twentieth annotation begins the Spiritual Exercises with the *first exercise,* while the other groups of exercitants, those described in the eighteenth and nineteenth annotations, begin somewhere else. This is explicitly stated by Ignatius. Simple souls and unlettered people are to be given the general and particular examinations of conscience and the first method of prayer. Those too busy for the Exercises proper should have the First Principle and Foundation explained to them and should receive instructions on the two ways of examining their consciences, and afterwards they should meditate on sin. Thus, the first week can be made in two different ways, and it is of importance to note that the first week as given to simple people is not a condensation of what Ignatius gives to the exercitant of the twentieth annotation.

The text of the second week contains a set of instructions about ways and means of making a sound election. Is it not possible that, just as a good deal of matter given under the heading "primera semana" is not meant for the exercitant of the Spiritual Exercises in full but is included for the sake of other people whom Ignatius wishes to help, in a similar way these instructions of the second week are intended for others than those described in the twentieth annotation? When deciding what exercises are to be given, Ignatius does not only refer to age, education, and talent, but adds that "there ought to be given to each what is in accordance with that which he wishes to dispose himself for" (18). The use of "disponer" recalls the first annotation, where all spiritual exercises are said to be inspired by the desire to prepare and dispose the soul in order to seek and find the will of God. In other words, Ignatius has his eyes set on all those who seriously want to find out what the will of God really is, and he will try to help them all. When such people cannot for reasons of age, education, talent, or lack of time make the Spiritual Exercises for a whole month, he does not send them away but will give them instructions suitable to their circumstances (18). Some of these instructions he placed within the text of the first week, some within that of the second week. But as the preliminary instructions of the first week (22-44) were not meant for the exercitant of the twentieth annotation, so the instructions dealing with the election are not of necessity intended for him but are primarily given for an altogether different class of exercitants.

For the present the following points would seem to provide evidence enough to make this opinion acceptable. In paragraphs 169-89, to which should be added the introductory notes 164-68 containing nothing less than the famous "three degrees of humility," the exercitant is never once referred to as "the person who makes the Exercises" or "the person who exercises himself, meditates, or contemplates," as happens constantly in the exercises of the four weeks. Rather, the vaguer *hombre* is preferred throughout. The phraseology used by Ignatius shows no trace of the exercises of the second week, or even of the first week. The words chosen remind one strongly of the preliminary stage of the Spiritual Exercises, which is closely associated with the exposition of the First Principle and Foundation. The motives on which the election is based in what is called the third time are mainly taken from reason, so that indifference has replaced poverty and humility. The climate in which the election is to take place according to these instructions is quite alien to that of the second week.

If, then, it is asked why Ignatius placed these instructions within the framework of the second week, the answer will obviously be that the second week cannot by-pass the matter of different states of life. Ignatius explicitly draws attention to it as soon as the exercitant has spent a day contemplating the mysteries of Christ's hidden life in Nazareth and of His staying behind in the Temple when He was twelve years of age (135). Where a state of life has to be chosen, the subject crops up spontaneously. It seems logical, then, that it should be dealt with now, even though the instructions are not necessarily intended for the exercitant of the long retreat.

The third week, too, has its set of instructions, namely, those on food and drink. No mention is made of them in the text of the contemplations or accompanying notes of the third week; this in contrast with the instructions of the second week (135, 163). Yet it would seem that Ignatius meant these rules for the exercitant in the proper sense of the word. In the fourth rule we read of "internas noticias, consolaciones y divinas inspiraciones," which are words very typical of the complete Spiritual Exercises, as will be shown in the fourth chapter. Any reasonable doubt about this is removed by the fifth rule: "While one is eating, let him imagine he sees Christ our Lord and His disciples at table, and consider how He eats and drinks, how He looks, how He speaks . . . ." (214). This surely presupposes the silence and solitude of the twentieth annotation but would be most inappropriate to the exercitant of the eighteenth and nineteenth annotations. So these rules are primarily meant for the exercitant of the long retreat and are to be applied at once with a view to the future (210). But the question will be asked why these rules are inserted in the third week. A likely answer would be that in the first week the exercitant is too much preoccupied with the purgative life (10, 315) and in the second he *may* be too much taken up with the election of a state of life. Another answer may well be that Ignatius' advice to behave in accordance with the mystery contemplated (130) entails sharing Christ's presence at table. A third answer would be that, as the Exercises proceed, prayer is ever heightened and intensified. But, for Ignatius prayer is not an activity of the spirit only. Throughout the Exercises he is careful to point to the harmony there must be between body and soul: it is always the whole man that is praying. In the third week a higher degree of prayer will mean abstinence and recollection during meals. Another reason will be given when we return to these rules in our discussion of the third week.

With the various parts of the book of the Spiritual Exercises thus laid out before us, one question still remains unanswered: why did Ignatius place the two sets of rules for the discernment of spirits outside the framework of the four weeks, and so outside the retreat in the stricter sense, whereas it is widely agreed that "to be moved by various spirits" is almost the heart of the Exercises? Indeed, Ignatius refers to these rules in the eighth, ninth and tenth annotations, and the two groups contain a reference to first and second weeks in their titles (313, 328). But they show no other link with the text of the Exercises, and the expression "el que se exercita" occurs only once (325). Hence, the answer to the question is that these rules are applicable not merely to those making the Spiritual Exercises but to all those who sooner or later are moved by various spirits, and consequently, in different ways to those who move from sin to sin (314) and those who advance from good to better (315) and all sorts of Christians in between these extremes.

In this study we shall confine ourselves to the Spiritual Exercises of the four weeks. We shall write only incidentally of the many rules contained in the second part of Ignatius' book. The paragraphs preceding the first exercise (24-44) will be left almost untouched, and only reluctantly shall we devote some pages to the instructions on making a good election. For good reasons we shall have to discuss the First Principle and Foundation.

three

## "HE WHO GIVES THE EXERCISES"

Because the cooperation between the Creator and His creature is the essence of the Spiritual Exercises, it does not follow that the task of him who gives the Exercises is negligible. Traditionally, it has been considered of the highest importance, and the fact that Ignatius singles out some of his followers as very good at giving them points to the influential part played by the director.[1] His task is by no means easy. On the one hand, he has to deal with the spiritual life and to a certain extent with the conscience of the exercitant; on the other, he is closely drawn into the activity of God Himself. Mistakes likely to be made might be classified under sins of commission and sins of omission. The director may interfere in things which must be left to God or he may omit things that are his special province.

In the second annotation Ignatius exhorts the director to keep himself somewhat aloof. In preparing the exercitant for prayer he should confine himself to a short and summary explanation of the subject of prayer, enough to give the solid groundwork or foundation of the historical facts (2). It implies that he must not unduly influence the exercitant on the intellectual or emotional level. "Preaching a retreat" is a contradiction in terms. Theological expositions are also out of place and there is only room for such instructions as are directly connected with the various rules contained in Ignatius' book. The worst possible mistake a director can make is to lead others along his own spiritual paths.[2] This explains why Ignatius is almost excessively impersonal in his Spiritual Exercises. Here we have a man brimful of brilliant ideas, visions, and insights, yet he scarcely mentions them; where he does refer to them, as for instance in the contemplation to attain divine love, which corresponds to the great vision on the Cardoner, the objectivity and matter-of-factness with which he treats them is rather striking. It also explains why Ignatius insists on the director asking God that his shortcomings and sins may not be an obstacle to what He wants to achieve in and with the exercitant (*Dir.*, 95-96). The director should always bear in mind that God knows the exercitant better than he does, that God is not indifferent to the exercitant's character, health, disposition, and so forth, and so he should leave it to Him to bring the exercitant to what will suit him best in matters of penance, of posture to be adopted during prayer, of the number of exercises to be made each day, and so on (72, 76, 89). Preferably, he does not even hear the exercitant's confession.[3]

The director must not omit things that are his special responsibility. His main task comprises three elements: he is to give what are commonly called the *points* for the meditation or contemplation (2), he is to explain the various rules, especially those for the discernment of spirits (6-10), and he should adapt the Spiritual Exercises to individual circumstances (18). As there will be occasion to speak of the rules for the discernment of spirits in later chapters, it will now suffice to concentrate on the matter of giving points and of adapting the Exercises.

## Giving Points

In the second annotation Ignatius explains what he means by giving points. The director ought faithfully to narrate the history of the meditation or contemplation; he must not explain and develop the meaning of the history. The exercitant must be given a solid foundation of facts, but must be left to seek and find a clearer understanding of those facts through his own reasoning or through the grace of God enlightening his mind. Ignatius ends the annotation by stating that it is not much knowledge that satisfies the soul but an intimate understanding and relish of the truth. This second annotation makes sufficiently clear what "faithfully narrating the history" is *not*; it does not give satisfactory information as to what it *is*.

With the exception of the first day, Ignatius gives one, or at most two, subjects for contemplation and meditation each day. Accordingly, in the second half of the second week, when the exercitant is asked to make five contemplations on Christ's Baptism, on His Stay in the Desert, on the Vocation of the Apostles, and so on (161), points are to be given once only. This makes matters considerably easier for the director than has been the case in the past, when he was usually expected to give points for each exercise, that is, four times a day, there being no special points for the exercise during the night. But it is hardly possible to tell the same story four times in succession to the same exercitant, nor would such a practice seem reasonable. The only alternatives appeared to be either to change the subject of the contemplations or to explain and develop the meaning of a subject at great length. It became common practice to adopt either or both of these expedients.

In the expression "faithfully to narrate the history," *faithfully* need not detain us. Evidently, it corresponds to "the true foundation of facts" (el fundamento verdadero de la historia). What this means is clear from the way in which Ignatius gives the points of the contemplation on the Incarnation, on the Nativity, on the Last Supper and on the Agony in the Garden, and the points given are intended to be examples for the points of the other contemplations (132, 204, 162). These points prove that narrating the history is not the same as giving the historical facts. The history of the Incarnation has its beginnings not in the historical events that take place in Nazareth, but in the Blessed Trinity viewing humanity in its fallenness, deciding to help, electing a certain way of coming to the rescue, choosing the Virgin Mary, sending His angel, and so forth (102). Similarly, the points for the contemplation on the Nativity do not merely contain what is to be seen and heard on the level of human history; they also tell of God-made-Man embracing poverty and a life of suffering "that after many labors, after hunger, thirst, heat and cold, insults and outrages He might die on the cross," and a genuine part of the history is likewise indicated in the phrase "and all this for me" (116).

Due attention must be paid to the verb "to narrate." Its choice was probably influenced by Ignatius' reading of the *Life of Christ* as told by Ludolph of Saxony, when he was recuperating from his wounds (*Autobiography*, 5). There is a great difference between narrating a story and giving information with or without further explications or interpretations. Information appeals mainly to the understanding, and he who gives the information remains to a large extent outsider both to the information itself and to him to whom he gives his information. He who tells a story addresses himself not to a mind but to a person and tries to draw his listener into the story as he tells it; both narrator and listener become very much absorbed in the story, committed and engaged. In a very real sense they share the joys and the sorrows, the successes and the disappointments, of the characters of the story, so much so that distance in time disappears and the present tense is used in narrating the story. We shall see afterwards how intense this participation by the exercitant is in the story of Christ's life and how important in order to understand and practice Ignatian contemplation.

The director should not tell the story of the meditation or contemplation for the sake of the moral teaching it may contain. Neither must he depict history in glowing colors but should confine himself to the groundwork of the principal facts; he must be on his guard against superfluous embellishments. "To see with the eyes of the imagination the road from Nazareth to Bethlehem, considering how long and wide it is, and whether the way be level or through valleys and over hills, likewise to see the cave of the Nativity, how large or small, how low or high, and how it is prepared," (112) all this is done by the exercitant when he is actually praying, that is, cooperating with God, who enlightens, moves and embraces him. The object of the director giving points by faithfully narrating the history is to help the exercitant to pray, to meditate, and to contemplate, "dar a otro modo y orden para meditar o contemplar," as the second annotation says. More will be said about the director's task of giving points when in the fourth chapter the difference between meditation and contemplation will be discussed.

Adapting the Exercises

The verb "adaptar" does not occur in the Spiritual Exercises. Dealing with the question how to adapt the Exercises to certain classes of people who cannot or will not make the long retreat, Ignatius uses the verb "aplicar" at the beginning of the eighteenth annotation. Problems connected with the adaptation of the Exercises to those of limited ability, to those who wish to attain a certain degree of peace of soul (18), do not concern us in this study as we restrict ourselves to the exercitant of the twentieth annotation. Within the Exercises proper adaptation refers to two topics: to the number of exercises to be made and to the choice of subject matter for meditation or contemplation. As regards the former, a note in the second week suggests that a change in the number of exercises might be profitable even though the exercitant is strong enough to make five exercises each day (133). Similar suggestions are found in the other weeks. Shortening or lengthening the weeks also implies a certain adaptation.[4]

As regards the choice of subject matter, Ignatius deals with it in two places. In the seventeenth annotation he writes that in accordance with the progress made by the exercitant the director may give "some exercises suited and adapted to the needs of a soul moved and agitated by divers spirits." In understanding this annotation correctly, "some exercises" must not be identified with meditation and contemplation. As the context speaks of motions and agitations, it is more likely that Ignatius had in mind primarily the examination of conscience, the consideration of various degrees or ways of humility, different methods of prayer, and above all, praying about, and in accordance with, the suggestions contained in the rules for the discernment of spirits.

The second time that Ignatius refers to adaptation by means of a careful selection of topics for meditation and contemplation, he is rather vague. In the sixth addition of the first week he exhorts the exercitant not to think on pleasant subjects, like Paradise, the Resurrection, and so on; he should rather seek to feel sorrow, and for that purpose call to mind death and judgment (78). Strictly speaking, we are not told of adaptation by means of additional exercises on death, judgment, purgatory, venial sin, imperfections and similar subjects, though these have almost gained a place of their own in the first week. Tradition here goes back a long time. Ignatius' secretary, Polanco, used to give meditations on death and judgment, and so did Cordeses; González Dávila judges that these meditations should be omitted "hardly ever," while the official *Directory* of 1599 holds that by means of these meditations tediousness is removed and the matter is more profoundly investigated.[5] This is a somewhat startling remark if it is realized that additional meditations on death, judgment, and similar subjects are inserted at the expense of repetitions. More will be said about this subject presently.

The question of adaptation as it bears both upon giving points and upon inserting additional exercises must now be examined briefly from a different angle altogether. The exercitant of the first half of the sixteenth century did not have books, probably not even the Bible, at his disposal in the way in which the exercitant these days usually has them at hand. Hence it may be asked whether Ignatius would have given points if the exercitant could continually fall back upon excellent commentaries, expositions, spiritual treatises, and so on. The answer to this question appears to be that from this point of view the situation has not really changed. For although Ignatius presupposes that the exercitant has at least the Four Gospels before him, even so the director is told to narrate the history. Having the text is, therefore, not enough, not even with the best of commentaries alongside it. The exercitant is to be guided into the story by the director, and this is not done by providing commentary on the text. Or, to put it in another way: the director is to teach and help the exercitant to pray, and the best way to accomplish this is to narrate the history faithfully.

Regarding the adaptation achieved by adding exercises, conditions since the time of Ignatius have changed considerably. No one will deny that the exercitant of four hundred years ago was not the same person and Christian as the exercitant today. It is a fact that has to be taken into account by the director. Some few examples will show how great is his responsibility in this matter. The first example concerns the degree of faith which the good Christian in the sixteenth century could be presumed to possess. "Creator, creation, creature" stood for a reality upon which his Christian life was firmly based: his dependence upon God was very much part of his spiritual life. This is not true in the same measure these days. Modern man has made so much "progress" in almost every department of life that a certain amount of disbelief has crept into this fundamental belief of being as a creature utterly and always dependent upon the Creator. Consequently, some deep reflection and meditation upon what is propounded in the First Principle and Foundation are indispensable, even for the exercitant of the twentieth annotation, though Ignatius thinks this rather superfluous.

The second example is taken from the first exercise. Ignatius asks his exercitant to see and taste himself as a piece of wreckage: a soul imprisoned in a body, cast out among wild beasts. He does not prove the truth of this pitiable spectacle; the supposition is that the exercitant is in complete agreement with this "composition" (47). Man's fallenness was an everyday reality and experience. But since Ignatius' time, the situation has changed noticeably. Man is far less the victim of possible calamities of nature, of epidemics, of starvation due to crop failure than he used to be. One need only compare infant-mortality and the expected duration of life then and now to realize how much more man was subject to destructive forces of nature in days gone by than at present. He is proportionately less aware of his fallen condition. The director will make his exercitant reflect upon it more intensely than is suggested in the preludes to the meditations of the first week and will possibly insert suitable considerations.

The third example is taken from the meditation on hell. Ignatius could start from the unshaken belief all around him in the existence of an eternal hell. There was no need to prove it. He needed only to prevent people from thinking that hell was not so bad as the Church proclaimed it to be; hence the peculiar form of his meditation on eternal punishment. Today the situation is quite different. If the existence of hell has not to be established, at least the director will have to see to it that the acceptance of its existence is not merely notional. This entails a different sort of meditation on hell from the one given by Ignatius. The same holds good of the subject of death and judgment. The Church and the Christian of the later Middle Ages, even up to the beginning of modern times, lived in closer familiarity with these truths than we do today. Modern man has pushed them almost beyond his horizon. The stress laid these days on eschatology and parousia is proof enough of serious shortcomings in this respect within the Church. Where Ignatius could be satisfied with mentioning these subjects almost in passing, the exercitant today needs more than a mere reminder. True adaptation seems to call for additional meditations on death and similar subjects.

The examples so far given all belong to the first week. There has also been a profound change where the matter of the three other weeks is in question. Man's faith in God-made-Man is not the same today as it was in Ignatius' time. We need only read the *Life of Christ* by Ludolph of Saxony and compare it with the books of meditations of the seventeenth and later centuries to see the difference. The fact that meditation has practically ousted contemplation these last three centuries proves that the simple but very clear-sighted belief in Christ living among men has considerably weakened. Further proof is given in the text of the Spiritual Exercises itself: modern man does not easily understand how Ignatius could ask the exercitant to make himself a poor little unworthy slave, serving Mary and Joseph in their needs (114) and even kissing the place where they sit or stand (125), just as he finds it difficult to be broken with Christ broken (206). Adaptation is here necessary, but it should never eliminate essential features of the Exercises; adaptation should here take the form of a gradual preparation by which the exercitant might arrive at true contemplation.

Not only man's faith in God-made-Man has changed, his vision of Christ has undergone important alterations. The consideration on Christ as King and the meditation on Two Standards as traditionally interpreted evidently demand a certain adaptation, and so do the contemplations of the third and fourth weeks, although it is surprising to discover how far ahead of his own times Ignatius was, and perhaps even of ours: points that will become clear when the second, third and fourth weeks are dealt with.

The few examples we have given are sufficient to show that the adaptation of the Spiritual Exercises involves a serious reflection on the part of the director upon the needs and wants of the exercitant of these days. He should never lose sight, however, of the unshakable fact that more important than his adaptation of the Spiritual Exercises is his intense concern that God should be able to work freely in and with the exercitant.

The chapter bears the title "he who gives the Exercises." Throughout this chapter, however, the word "director" has been used. The early directories do not know this or a similar word. It is fairly late, and then only gradually, that we come across "instructor," "director," and "retreat-master." In the same way, "he who makes the Exercises" and "he who exercises himself" only slowly make place for "exercitant."[6] Ignatius' faithful adherence to "he who gives the Exercises" confirms what we have said in this chapter; whether he gives points or explains various rules, the director is always the one who *gives* the Exercises and, consequently, makes his exercitant *do* them. And so the exercitant is he "who receives the Exercises" or "takes the Exercises" or "exercises himself."[7] For convenience' sake "director" and "exercitant" will be used in this study, though neither is an improvement upon the expressions employed by Ignatius.

four

# MEDITATION AND CONTEMPLATION

"By the term 'Spiritual Exercises' is meant every method of examination of conscience, of meditation, of contemplation, of vocal and mental prayer, and of other spiritual activities that will be mentioned later" (1). Among these exercises none are more frequently used and more important than meditation and contemplation. In fact, for many people an Ignatian retreat is simply a series of meditations and contemplations. These two forms of prayer will be studied in this chapter.

## Preparation

"As soon as I recall that it is time for the exercise in which I ought to engage, before proceeding to it, I will call to mind, where I am going, before whom I am to appear, and briefly sum up the exercise. Then after observing the third Additional Direction, I shall enter upon the exercise." Thus reads the translation by Puhl of the fifth note added to the second week. Correctly to understand this note, it must be remembered that the exercise is not immediately preceded by an introduction or "points," given by the director, for the supposition is that this has been done the previous evening. The note does not apply to the exercise to be made at midnight or in the early morning, because rising means rising to pray; hence, the exercitant in the second addition is not to admit other thoughts but to turn his mind at once to what he is going to contemplate (74, 130, 206, 229). Neither does it apply to the meditations of the first week, in which Ignatius gives five exercises, apparently for one day only, and each exercise is introduced by the director.[1] Accordingly, it is logical that the note is given in the second week.

Ignatius calls this fifth note the equivalent of the second addition, which was cited just now. The idea of concentrating on the subject matter of meditation and contemplation is evidently common to both the note and the addition. If the text is read carefully, another fact emerges. In the fifth note movement is suggested five times: twice by the verbal forms "vaya" and "voy," by the adverb and preposition of place "adónde" and "delante," and by the verb "entrar"; this is well brought out by Puhl's translation, with which this section opened. The idea of movement is maintained by Ignatius not only in his preference for the expression "to enter upon" (entrar en el exercicio) but also by "to proceed," "to roam about", and finally "to rest and stand."[2] It is not merely a question of an obvious image or a useful comparison; the choice of these and similar words is very deliberate and most meaningful, as will become clear in the pages that follow.

The third addition, like all additions a piece of good advice to help the exercitant "to make the exercises better and find more readily what he desires," (73) suggests that the exercitant should stand for a short while a step or two before the place where he is to pray, there to raise his mind on high and to consider that the Lord God beholds him, then to make an act of reverence or humility (75). From this translation it would appear that little else is meant but an act of faith in the presence of God. Justice is only done to the original "considerando cómo Dios nuestro Señor me mira, etc." when Rickaby's translation is adopted: "to consider how God is looking at me." It is not a question of considering *that* God beholds the exercitant, but *how* (cómo) He beholds him. But "to behold" does not give the exact meaning of "mirar." It is a word often used in the Exercises.[3] Its true shade of meaning may be discovered where Ignatius speaks of the commander of an army who *explores* the defenses and fortifications of a stronghold, in Puhl's translation, or in that of Morris, *inspects* the strength and condition of some citadel; Rickaby here employs "to reconnoitre": "mirar" is evidently not synonymous with "to see" or "to behold" (327).

The third addition does not say that the exercitant should place himself in the presence of God. It is a consideration, the purpose of which is that he realizes *that* God looks at him, and *the way* in which He watches him. He is occupied with God's thoughts about him and he tries to see himself as he is seen by God. But not only *seen* or *watched:* unexpectedly, Ignatius adds "etc." Now "mirar" is usually followed by a decision or a reaction. In the above instance, an attack is decided upon. When in the contemplation on the Incarnation the exercitant considers how the Three Divine Persons "look down upon" (mirar) the whole expanse and surface of the earth and how They "view" (mirar) all nations (102, 105), he next considers how the Trinity decides to redeem mankind. In the second exercise of the first week "mirar" is used no less than seven times: it is followed by a strong reaction in the form of a "cry of wonder with a flood of emotion" (60). In this third addition "etc." apparently indicates that God does not only pay careful attention to the exercitant but reacts to his condition, the reaction being that He will help him by enlightening him, disposing him, communicating Himself to him, even by embracing him (15).

If the exercitant knows himself as he is known to God and at the same time knows himself to be in His presence, he must acknowledge the true relationship that exists between his Creator and himself; accordingly, he makes an act of reverence or humility (75). It is a matter of living the truth, of right order humbly accepted.

The preparatory character of the second and third additions, together with the fifth note of the second week, is underlined by the opening words of the fourth addition: "I will enter upon the contemplation" (76). The verb "to enter" forms a link with the third addition, which is made "a step or two before the place where the exercitant is to make the exercise." As preparatory acts, they are of short duration: the resumption of the fifth note must be brief (un poco), and the third addition should not last much longer than an Our Father. Short as they are, they are important enough for Ignatius to draw attention to them at the beginning of each week and to point out what slight changes are to be made in them (130, 206, 229).

Next the exercitant makes the preparatory prayer, asking for the grace that all his intentions, actions, and operations may be ordered purely to the service and praise of His Divine Majesty (46). The prayer is mentioned at the beginning of each exercise, it is said over and over again, and the wording is never changed throughout the four weeks. By its choice of terms and expressions it reminds one of the First Principle and Foundation; the foundation of the whole of the Spiritual Exercises is evidently the foundation of each individual exercise. Contents and importance of this prayer are better discussed in our next chapter on the First Principle and Foundation.

## Structure of the Exercise

"This meditation contains, after the preparatory prayer and two preludes, three main points and a colloquy" (45, 55, 65), or with a slight variation: "this contemplation contains the preparatory prayer, three preludes and three points and a colloquy" (101, 190). Preludes and points must be closely examined as they are of vital importance not only to understand meditation and contemplation but also to discover what truth there is in the charge not infrequently made against the supposed methodical prayer of Ignatius.

"Prelude" is the accepted translation of "preâmbulo." The word is used by Ignatius in other contexts. Thus, the introduction to the consideration of states of life, which precedes the meditation on Two Standards, is called "preâmbulo" (135); its meaning must be very close to "introduction" as "introducción" is found in the same paragraph. In like manner, a *preâmbulo* precedes the elections (169), and here, too, "introduction" appears to be the obvious translation. Where the word is employed in connection with meditation and contemplation, "introduction" is acceptable as a translation, provided we do not lose sight of the original meaning of "entering" or "making one enter." The exercitant who is going to meditate or contemplate enters a new reality, and he is *introduced* into it by means of the preludes.[4] In this study, "prelude" is preferred to "preamble" or "introduction," solely for the reason that this translation is generally accepted and almost traditional.

What Ignatius calls "punctos," the "points" of the exercise, are the parts of which it consists. Thus, in the first meditation the three points are the consideration of the sin of the angels, the consideration of the sin of our first parents, and the consideration of what is called the third sin (50-52). Similarly, the three points which are found in the majority of the exercises given after the four weeks (262-312) are three parts of one mystery, and these parts follow each other chronologically. If, however, the points of the mystery of the Incarnation as given in this section are compared with the points of the same mystery as found at the beginning of the second week, "points" appears to be used in two different meanings. For, the contemplation on the Incarnation as the first exercise of the second week is certainly not made up of three successive parts; "points" here evidently refers to three different activities of the exercitant, namely, to see, hear, and to consider (ver, oir, and mirar, 106-08). Each time, the object is the mystery in its entirety and all the persons acting in this mystery, but each time mystery and persons are approached from a different angle. The same use of the word "points" is found in the contemplation on the Nativity (114-16), on the Last Supper (194-97), and on the Agony in the Garden (204). In this sense "points" is found for the first time when Ignatius gives his instructions about the examination of conscience, the five points or activities being: to give thanks, to ask for grace, to review, to ask pardon, and to resolve to amend one's life (43). Another clear example is given in the instruction on how to make a sound election in the so-called third time; the six "points" are: to place before the mind the object of the choice, to keep as an aim the end for which man is created, to beg God for grace, to weigh the matter, to come to a decision, and to turn to prayer (178-83). So it is not surprising that the meditation on Three Classes of Men has no points: it is an exercise with one activity only, namely, to meditate (149, 153-55). The exercise on the Kingdom contains two "parts," and each part has three "points" or three different activities, namely, to place before the mind, to inspect (mirar), and to consider (92-97). Both the second exercise of the first week and the meditation on hell have five points, both exercises being made up of five different activities.

"Points" as used in the title of almost all the exercises clearly implies *parts*. This is the result of the inability of any man to perform a number of different activities at the same time: succession strongly suggests parts. Hence it is that Ignatius can write of resting in *the point* where the exercitant finds what he desires (reposar en el puncto, 76) but also of the more important *parts* in which he has experienced consolation (notando algunas partes . . ., 118, 227), without much difference of meaning.[5] Students of the Spiritual Exercises will do well to bear in mind that "points" does not primarily refer to a number of consecutive parts of a mystery that is being contemplated but to various activities of the exercitant.

"Points" in this sense presupposes the presence of something that is the object of the activities concerned; if the points of an exercise are to see, hear, and to inspect or consider, there must be something to see, to hear, and to inspect. Hence, *points* are only possible once the exercitant has been brought face to face with a reality that is the object of these activities. He must first find himself in new surroundings in which there is something to see, hear, and inspect. This is the link between preludes and points; the latter are simply impossible without the former. The exercitant must have been *introduced* into a new reality before he can devote himself to seeing and hearing what takes place. Similarly, there is no sense in making the preludes if they are not followed by the points: what is the use of moving into another reality without opening oneself to what this reality contains?

A true understanding of "points" is of direct influence on the matter of "giving points," an expression, as we saw in the preceding chapter, not used by Ignatius. The traditional way of giving points, both in books and in retreats, in the form of three successive parts of an incident in the life of Christ is not in accordance with the text of the contemplations on the Incarnation, the Nativity, the Last Supper and the Agony. Neither can it be brought into agreement with the practice of Ignatius where he gives three points in the series of mysteries later in his book. The three points given there stand for three different parts of one mystery, each part to consist of the three *points* mentioned in the text of the second week (to see, to hear, to inspect) or of the six *points* of the contemplations of the third week. The probable reason why Ignatius consistently gives three points as three successive parts in this series of contemplations is that he has in mind the exercitant of the nineteenth annotation, who will spend three days over each mystery, spending one hour in prayer each day.

History

This prelude is first given in the contemplation on the Incarnation. It is mentioned again in the contemplations on the Nativity, the Last Supper, the Agony in the Garden, and Christ's risen life (102, 111, 191, 201, 219). It precedes all contemplations on the life of Christ and the meditations on Two Standards and Three Classes of Men.

It is commonly taken to stand for calling to mind the main outlines of the exercitant's subject of prayer. If this were correct, it would be very difficult to see any difference between this prelude and the resumption of the fifth note, which we have just discussed. Nor would it then be easy, or even possible, to explain why this prelude is left out in the exercises of the first week and in the consideration on the Kingdom.

A faulty translation of Ignatius' text has confused matters considerably. Translations as "to bring to mind," "to recall to mind" are inspired by Roothaan's rendering "adducere in mentem." But Ignatius does not write "traer *en memoria*"; he simply uses "traer la historia" (102, 191), and he even omits the verb (111, 137, 150, 201). For "calling to mind", or any act of the memory, Ignatius uses expressions such as "traer la memoria sobre," "traer a la memoria," and "traer en memoria" (50-53, 130). The first prelude, then, is not an act of the memory. "Traer la historia" must be taken to be on a par with phrases such as "traer pensamientos alegres" (206), "traer razones aparentes" (329, 351) and "traer astucias a la ânima" (326), where "traer" means "to make present." In the first prelude the history of what the exercitant is going to contemplate is made present to him, just as the thoughts and frauds of the devil are made present to him.

The first prelude is not successfully made by means of a lively phantasy which easily conjures up the main characteristics of past events. It is more in the nature of an act of the intellect enlightened by faith. This becomes clear as soon as "history" is seen not to be a question of recalling facts and events but to have for its object their *why* and their *how*. The first word of this prelude is always "cômo," that is, "how," and sometimes we find it repeated. To take one example: in the contemplation on the Incarnation the history is "*how* the Three Divine Persons looked down upon the whole expanse of all the earth . . . and *how* seeing that all men go to hell, They decided that the Second Person shall become Man, . . ." (102). So, "traer la historia" is not the same as placing before the exercitant an historical situation which is made up of a number of events; it is not recalling a set of incidents in Christ's life. History in Ignatius' sense refers primarily to God being moved by man's sad plight, deciding to save him, and giving substance to this decision in the Incarnation of His Son and in all the events following after. Hence, the incidents, visible, audible and tangible, are not the essence of this first prelude. They are only the outward form of the mystery of God wanting to redeem mankind. History, then, does not concern the past; it is very much a thing of the present, just as God wanting to help the human family is very much of the present. This history has been given shape in the incidents that took place in the past. To separate these incidents or events from their ultimate *why* and *wherefore* is to reduce a divine mystery to human happenings, and it is to reduce the act of faith and clear vision of the first prelude to a trick of the memory.

It will be instructive to find the answer to the obvious question why the meditations of the first week lack this prelude. It is an utter impossibility to apply "traer la historia" to the sins of the angels or of our first parents. How could the exercitant be ever present at those past events? Or how could these events of long ago be brought into the present in any real sense of the word? Moreover, there is no need for this first prelude, because the subject matter of the meditation is the exercitant himself as a sinful man, who has deserved severe punishment, and, surely, he is present to himself. The exercise on the Kingdom has no history because it is neither meditation nor contemplation. As regards the history in the meditation on Two Standards, it should be observed that here Ignatius used the present tense, which points to the fact that both mystery and the shape or form of the mystery are very much of today. The subject matter is not so much the mystery of God acting "en su eternidad" as the circumstance that the exercitant is here and now involved in a clash between Christ and Satan. This also explains the history of the meditation on Three Classes of Men, By the time that the exercitant makes the contemplation to attain divine love, there is no further need for the first prelude: his present existence has reached such a close union with God that "to be" is "to be present to God." The various ways of making this first prelude will be examined when the different exercises are being discussed.[6]

Events in Christ's life have, of course, their significance and consequently they play their part in this first prelude. Their significance is, however, not situated in these events by themselves, but lies in their being an outward projection of God's decisions and plans. They are an indication of how God works in human history. This outward shape is not something purely accidental or incidental or, even less, purely arbitrary. God has in fact chosen *this* shape and pattern, and as soon as the exercitant has brought himself face to face with the God of history, he turns his attention at once to the pattern in which God reveals Himself: he even considers the house of Nazareth, the road to Bethlehem, and so forth. Readers will here recognize the second prelude.

In the title of the exercises of the first week, the preparatory prayer and the preludes are placed outside the meditation proper, the formula being "this exercise contains, *after* the preparatory prayer and two preludes, three points . . . ." (45, 55, 65). As soon as the second week begins, the preparatory prayer and the three preludes belong to the contemplation, the formula now being "the contemplation contains the preparatory prayer, three preludes and three points . . . ." (101, 190). The first prelude of these weeks, that is the history, is consequently contemplation, and so we are less surprised at Ignatius introducing it by "cómo." Through this first prelude, one might say, the exercitant witnesses how God is setting the stage for the execution of His decisions. But before watching what is going to take place on the stage, he is first going to have a good look at the stage itself; it is Ignatius' second prelude, commonly called the composition of place.

Composition

The second prelude, which is the first prelude in the first week, is a complicated affair. The obvious starting point to understand it properly is to examine the meaning of the word "composition" (composición). It does not have a special spiritual meaning in the ascetical and mystical literature before or in Ignatius' time. Cisneros' *Ejercitatorio de la Vida Espiritual*, with which Ignatius was acquainted, uses it only once; he writes of "la composición y ordenamiento del hombre exterior," which should be a reflection of interior devotion and sanctity.[7] In this sense the word is used by González de Cámara, who testified that Ignatius attached great value to "modestia e composicão do homem exterior," and also by Ignatius himself, when in his directory, dictated to Vitoria, he expressed the wish that the exercitant is to set a good example "con la humildad y composición de su persona." Ignatius used the verb when he wrote to King Philip of Spain and told him that a soul, chosen, visited, and enlightened by the Creator, "compone y dispone de sus potencias interiores," and this with great ease.[8] The original meaning of putting things together, of ordering and harmonizing them, is almost impossible to miss.

In the Spiritual Exercises Ignatius does not explain what he means by "composition"; he only gives various ways of making it (47). The impression given is that in his opinion the word chosen needs no explanation; it should be taken in its obvious sense. The result of putting things together, of com-posing, is a composite being, a whole, a thing which is composed, united, and ordered. This is mentioned twice when the exercitant is asked to consider that his soul is in a corruptible body and that his "whole composite being" (todo el compósito) is like an exile here on earth cast out to live among brute beasts; he then adds emphatically: "I say, my whole composite being of body and soul." This example shows that composition not only means that man makes himself one whole being but also makes himself one with the surrounding reality. Composition implies inner unity and harmony as well as harmony with external circumstances.

There are two ways to make this prelude, and the two methods are widely different. In general, if the exercitant is going to contemplate or meditate upon something visible, as for instance, the life of Christ, composition is brought about by seeing the places where Christ lived; if he turns his attention to something invisible, as for instance, the fact of sin, composition takes the form of a short consideration. The two ways will be dealt with successively, but first it must be pointed out that the expression "composition of place" is misleading. It nowhere occurs in the text of the *Spiritual Exercises*. Ignatius speaks of "composición viendo el lugar," that is, "seeing" or "by seeing" the place. Moreover, "lugar" is not used when there is no question of an actual locality, as for instance, in the meditation on hell and that on the Three Classes of Men.[9] The opinion, therefore, that this prelude is an act of the imagination whereby the wandering mind is held on the matter of meditation or contemplation, is untenable. A lively phantasy has nothing to do with this prelude, any more than it has to do with the first prelude. The second prelude is not a composition *of place*, but a composition *of oneself,* and this, surely, is not a matter of the imagination or phantasy. If it were, it would be incomprehensible why in the first exercise Ignatius did not ask the exercitant to make his composition by seeing the place, that is, by seeing Paradise, and in it Eve handing the fruit to Adam, instead of talking about the soul being in the dungeon of the body.

In the first week the compositions of the first and second exercises are the same: with imaginative vision (con la vista imaginativa) the exercitant will see and consider that his soul is imprisoned in his corruptible body and that his whole self is in this valley as cast out among brute beasts; "I say, his whole self composed of body and soul" (47). Four points should be noted. There is first of all the twofold use of "compósito," which has been referred to above. Second, the verb "imaginar" has been avoided, although it occurs elsewhere in the text.[10] Third, the use of the expression "con la vista imaginativa" seems to be strange, as Ignatius is expressly dealing with something invisible. The strangeness is not removed by pointing out that Ignatius does not write "ver con la vista de la imaginación," which he employed with reference to contemplation or meditation on visible matters only a few lines above in the same paragraph; for there does not seem to be any difference between these two expressions.[11] It is enough here to remember that the object of acts of the imagination in the Ignatian sense of the word is not merely something that is perceptible to the five senses. He speaks, for instance, of tasting sadness (69), of smelling the infinite fragrance, and savoring the infinite sweetness of the Divinity (124). Fourth, due attention must be paid to the verb "to consider," which has been inserted after the verb "to see." The translation "to see my soul imprisoned in the body, and my whole self in this valley" is unacceptable. The exercitant is asked to see and consider that his soul is imprisoned in this body and that his whole compound self is in this vale of tears. Through this composition he is to realize that he is a fallen man, that original innocence has gone and corruption has taken its place, that he no longer lives in Paradise but is in exile.

As regards the composition in the meditation on hell (65), the exercitant knows that hell exists and that it is not a reality with which he has nothing whatever to do. If that were the case, a composition would be needless or useless. But through the first and second exercises he is aware of the undeniable fact that, if it were not for the grace of God, he would be in hell at this very moment. Moreover, he knows that hell still remains a possibility, and that "up till now (61)

God's mercy has saved him from falling into it. So, the fact that there is a hell is not at all something outside the exercitant's life; he must compose himself with it, or, to use modern terminology, integration must be effected. He will achieve this by making himself present to the reality of hell, so much so that he sees how long and how deep it is. It is of slight importance which dimensions are actually assigned to hell, or even whether dimensions are assigned at all; the important thing is that the exercitant realize that hell is, and that it very much concerns him.

It will now be easier to understand what is meant by "composition (by) seeing the place."[12] This way of composing oneself is common to the second, third and fourth weeks, when the subject matter of the contemplation is a mystery in the life of Christ. The first prelude, the history, precedes the composition. So, the exercitant has placed himself in that historic dimension which is inseparable from the mystery of God deciding to save mankind. A certain degree of composition or integration has already taken place, but the shape of any mystery in human history is a matter of time and place or local circumstances and conditions. Further integration will be brought about by the exercitant now composing himself, making himself one, with the actual shape or pattern that God's decision to send His Son into this world has assumed. It takes place by seeing the place with the eyes of the imagination.

The prelude is not Ignatius' discovery or invention. It is most human. The two preludes taken together show a marked resemblance with what happens in any good story well told or written down. A good narrator or novelist will give details of time and at the same time the local background. Without these a story gets caught in a certain vagueness, which makes it difficult for the listener or reader to become involved in and even committed to the story. As a rule, the setting in time and place is given in close succession, sometimes they are interwoven. It is then logical that the composition by seeing the place is not confined to seeing one place. As events happen in different places, the composition will not be limited to only one place. In the contemplation on the Incarnation the exercitant is to see the whole world, which corresponds to that part of the history where he is to make himself present to the mystery of God looking down upon the whole expanse of the earth. He is also to see Galilee, Nazareth and the house in Nazareth, which correspond to the second part of the history as narrated in the first chapter of St. Luke's Gospel. In all "compositions by seeing the place" not once a single place is mentioned: it is the road and the cave in the contemplation on the Nativity, it is the road and the room in the contemplation on the Last Supper (192), the road and the garden in that on the Agony (202) and finally, the tomb and the Virgin's house in the contemplation on the risen life (220).

Although composition by seeing the place is indispensable, it seems to ask for less concentration and effort in these days than it did in the time of Ignatius. When today we recall the historical events that took place in Jerusalem, Bethlehem, or Nazareth, at the lake-side or on the mountain, we surely *see* things more readily than was the case when picture books of the holy places were rare and rather primitive, when there were no atlases of the Bible and similar books. Besides, it is well to recall that both the history and the composition form part of the contemplation, as was pointed out above. They are both part of and a form of prayer. But prayer in the Exercises is not just an act of devotion or piety performed by the exercitant; it is primarily a divine action, for it is God who enlightens, moves and stirs, communicates and embraces. It is, consequently, a thing only to be expected that Ignatius wants the exercitant to turn to the New Testament as soon as he begins the preludes. The history, which, as we have seen, is interwoven with the composition, is a matter of God telling us about His Son and the mystery of His being sent into this world. If Ignatius only mentions the New Testament, it should be remembered that in his days the Old Testament was not merely very hard to come by but also rather difficult to carry about from one place to another. He certainly could not rely on having a copy of the Old Testament at hand for the exercitant in the monastery or house where he was going to make the Spiritual Exercises. The exercitant's share in cooperating with God is not to strain after vividness of representation or archaeological accuracy. These might even prove to be a drawback, as they could easily obscure the *mystery* by overstressing its *shape* with all its visible, audible, and tangible details. Hence, the director is not to make the composition by giving the exercitant precise information concerning the outward circumstances of the Incarnation, Nativity, and so on. He who exercises himself should always make his own composition by seeing the place, "considering the way from Nazareth to Bethlehem, its length, its breadth, whether level, or through valleys, or over hills; similarly, he should see the place or cave, how big, how small, how high, how low, and how arranged" (112).

Such a composition cannot be made in a few moments. The exercitant should take his time over the composition in conjunction with the history, if this prelude is to be made. The preludes are not short preparatory acts. In fact, there is room for meditation in the first prelude (111), as there must be room for consideration in the second, the words "considerar" and "mirar" having been frequently used by Ignatius when he was advising his exercitant about the composition (47, 112, 192, 208; 122, 220). The *points*, standing, as we have shown, for various activities of the exercitant, presuppose his being present at the mystery contemplated. The points are a heightening and intensifying of the spiritual experience which is the heart of the history and the composition. Having been placed in the new dimension or reality of God working in history, the exercitant *desires* nothing more than to become familiar with his new surroundings. He *wants* to see, hear, touch, taste and understand things interiorly (2). A seriously and well made history and composition are indispensable to the points of the contemplation. But in between them, Ignatius inserts his third prelude, which just now was indicated by the verbs "to desire" and "to want."

Petition

Meditation and contemplation are preceded, accompanied, and followed by petition and supplication. On rising in the first week, the exercitant seeks shame and contrition, which implies petition (74). In the second week, he arouses within himself the desire to know his Lord better, and such a desire is wordless petition (130). In the third week, "striving to grieve and sorrow over the great grief and suffering of Christ" (206) appears to be impossible without humble supplication. The short resumption of the contemplation to be made when the hour of prayer has come is called by Ignatius the equivalent of the second addition and, consequently, the exercitant does not merely briefly recall the matter of contemplation but should also desire and ask to know the Lord better (131). As the exercitant approaches God, his first need is to make an act of reverence or humility (75), which is immediately followed by the petition for grace that all his intentions, actions, and operations may be purely ordered towards the service of God (46). It is only to be expected that, when he experiences a new and very close nearness to God working in human history, he feels a great desire to ask and pray for help. This trend continues when the intimacy between Creator and creature reaches its climax in the colloquy.

If the exercitant's spontaneous reaction at this stage of his meditation or contemplation is to address God in petition, there seems to be little point in reminding him to do so. Yet Ignatius does this without fail.[13] It proves that for Ignatius the important thing is not that the exercitant asks and begs but what he asks and begs for. He makes him pray for "that which I wish" or "that which I wish and desire," adding that "the petition must be according to the subject matter" (48).[14] The way in which Ignatius keeps on repeating "to ask for what I wish" suggests that at times this might not be in harmony with the natural man and may involve toil, a word used in the eleventh annotation. "What I wish" gives a hint of a possible flight on the part of the exercitant away from the contemplation and meditation to be made here and now; so, Ignatius warns the exercitant against curiosity concerning what lies ahead (11) and against reading about any other mystery but the one he is contemplating now, "lest the consideration of one mystery disturb the consideration of the other" (127). The exercitant must not put obstacles in the way of his cooperation with God through a lack of concentration or by deviating from the path shown to him by God in the Spiritual Exercises: this is Ignatius' great anxiety at the back of this prelude with his insistent "to beg for what I wish." The third prelude should, then, not be reduced to a simple prayer for some tangible result or fruit. If this were its purpose, the meditation or contemplation itself, that is, the body of the exercise contained in the three or more points that follow, would be the means to come by this fruit or good result. What the exercitant in fact asks is that he may pray well, that he may completely become his own true self in the new reality re-created for him in the first and second preludes. He begs that in this exercise he may live the truth of his own being and realize—in the twofold sense of this word—the dimensions that have been placed before him in the history and the composition. The very first instance of this prelude makes this clear. In the opening exercise of the first week, the exercitant, through the composition, knows himself to be a fallen man. He can now either adopt a matter-of-fact attitude and accept this truth, or he may want to understand interiorly, to taste and relish (2), that is, to live this reality. In the second case, he wants shame and confusion, and he knows himself well enough to be aware that these must be given to him by God. Therefore, he prays for them. When the exercitant is going to meditate on eternal punishment, he knows that but for the grace of God he should be in hell, and so he can never only be a more or less interested spectator. To be his true self involves an acute awareness of what he has been saved from so far and, consequently, he wants to feel an interior sense of the pains of hell, and that is what he asks for (65). When in the second week "what I wish" is to know the Lord better in order to love Him more intensely and follow Him more faithfully, the exercitant really prays for the grace not to be a mere outsider or spectator, not to be deaf and blind, not to deceive himself. This is the same as asking for the grace to be true to his own self, here and now being present at the mystery of the Incarnation, Nativity, Baptism, and so forth.

In conclusion, we stress that the preludes form a firmly constructed whole, and are much more than two or three brief preparatory acts. Their great significance will be further brought out in the section that now follows.

### Points

Because of the vast majority of contemplations, we confine ourselves to this form of mental prayer, although with slight adaptations the main ideas hold good for meditations as well. The points of the contemplation, as has been pointed out before, do not stand for successive parts of the exercise, but rather for various activities, usually to see the persons, to hear what they say, and to watch what they do. The preludes have made the exercitant present at the mystery to be contemplated, the three points aim at greater integration with this new reality. The fact of being present consequently receives a new impetus and a more profound intensity, so much so that the exercitant will now worship the Word who has *just now* become Man (nuevamente encarnado, 109), he will even attend Mary and Joseph in their necessities *as if he were present*, making himself a poor little unworthy slave (114). The points are a further development of the preludes, and the contents of the preludes are intensified in the points, so that contemplation may be said to take place on two levels. The first level is that of history, composition, and petition, the second, that of the points and, parallel with the petition, of the colloquy. Before pursuing the subject of the colloquy, we should observe that the contemplation moves on to a third, and even to a fourth level. On the first level, the exercitant makes himself present to the mystery; on the second, he makes himself familiar with its contents in all its aspects; on the third, he gives in to a clear invitation contained in the points to continue living the new reality of the mystery and to keep on watching because it is inexhaustible. It is the level of the repetitions. The result is a deep familiarity, so much so that all the details of the mystery become meaningful; the life of the senses is irresistibly drawn into the contemplation. It is the level of what Ignatius calls "contemplating by applying the senses." Contemplations at these various levels finally fascinate the exercitant in such a way that the contemplation flows over into the external pattern of the day so that he will behave in accordance with the mystery that is being contemplated and, hence, darken his room or admit light, do penance or omit it, and so on (130).

These four levels, or stages, may be characterized by key words. Regarding the first level, evidently "traer la historia" and "composición" are most typical. As for the second level, "to see, hear, and watch (mirar)" bring out the main characteristics. On the fourth level, "application of the *senses*" indicates its essential feature. Of great importance and very relevant are the key words of the third level of contemplation: "discurrir, pausar, hablar," "to roam about, to rest, and to talk."

## Repetitions

The first key word of contemplation on the third level, that is, of the repetitions, is "discurrir." It is used for the first time when the resumption is explained: the intellect will without distractions *turn over* assiduously the remembrance of the matter contemplated in the preceding exercises (64). Other translations are "think over," "recall and review," and "range over." With the exception of Rickaby's "range over," the other translations do not bring out the meaning of "discurrir," which should be rendered by "to wander about." In this meaning it was used by Ludolph of Saxony, who wrote in his prologue to the *Vita Christi*, "discurrentes per loca singula in spiritu vehementi osculantur terram, amplectantur terram in quibus dulcem Jesum vel stetisse vel sedisse vel egisse aliquid audierunt." It should not be forgotten that Ignatius owed his conversion to a large extent to this *Life of Christ*. In the Spiritual Exercises, the word is found in this meaning when the exercitant is asked to *go through* all the creatures, wondering how they have suffered him to live (60), when he *goes through* the advantages and disadvantages connected with a certain election (180-82), and when he *moves* from hour to hour in his examination of conscience (25). It might be objected that in these examples "discurrir" means "to discuss, to think over, to weigh." This does not seem to be quite true, for in this meaning "discurrir" is at times followed by another verb meaning "to think over, to reason" (2, 182), or the word "entendimiento" is added to it, which surely is completely superfluous if "discurrir" has entirely lost its original meaning "to wander about" (3, 50, 51, 52, 180). Further evidence is given in the colloquy of the first exercise where the verb is followed by the preposition *por* (discurrir por lo que se offresciere, 53).

The verb occurs no less than four times in the first exercise of the retreat: how, then, can it be said to be a key word of the repetitions? The answer is that three out of those four times it is joined to "con el entendimiento," where consequently the translation "to discuss" appears more appropriate. Besides, in the explanation of the resumption "discurrir" is used in close proximity to "sin divagar"; the common translation "without distraction" does away with the very strong suggestion of movement contained in the expression. The two verbs taken together can only mean "to wander about without straying." Movement is closely related to rest, and hence "discurrir" is found side by side with "hacer pausa" and "reposar"; they are of the essence of repetition and resumption. For, the exercitant must pay attention to and dwell upon those points in which he experienced consolation or desolation (62), and he will always rest where he finds what he desires without being anxious to proceed further (pasar adelante: notice this expression of movement) until he has satisfied himself (76). There is here a clear echo of the closing words of the second annotation: it is not to know much, but to understand and savor the matter interiorly, that fills and satisfies the soul. It is interesting to observe that in this addition the exercitant is advised "to wander about and reason" (discurriendo y raciocinando).

One cannot very well mention "hacer pausa" and "reposar," followed by "satisfaction", without recalling at once "peace, tranquillity, and quiet," which is a sure sign of the Good Spirit being at work in those who are progressing to greater perfection (333). The action of this Good Spirit is delicate, light and sweet, as a drop of water falling on a sponge (335). Repetitions and resumptions consequently are closely associated with consolation, which leads us to speak of the third key word, "hablar."

This verb does not occupy a conspicuous place in the exercises on the third level. It is used by Ignatius in his explanation of the colloquy (54). It is, however, rather remarkable that when he indicates the form of the colloquy, "hablar" is no longer used: is "to talk" too common, too familiar for the first week, or perhaps for meditation? For in none of the colloquies of the first week is the verb used. He does use it as soon as he writes about the first colloquy of the second week, which is attached to the first proper contemplation (109). Thus, the combination contemplation—"hablar" seems to establish itself.

The colloquy does not always imply that the exercitant begins to address God. Ignatius writes: "El coloquio se hace propriamente hablando así como un amigo habla a otro" (54). The insertion of "propriamente" is significant. A simple paraphrase would be: The colloquy in the proper sense of the word takes place when one talks with another just as friends do. There appears to be a clear suggestion that the colloquy does not always or easily reach this point of perfection; the text of the colloquies corroborates this. In the first week the exercitant inspects (53), gives thanks and resolves to amend his life (61), prays and begs (63) and recalls those who have gone to hell (71). He does not move beyond "razonar," which has been inaccurately translated by Roothaan with "ratiocinari." It is not synonymous with "to reason," and it lacks the intimacy of "hablar."[15]

In the second week, in the contemplations therefore, the exercitant ponders what to say (hablar) to God, to the Incarnate Son, to His Mother (109). In the third week, the word "hablar" disappears, and Ignatius resorts once again to "razonar" (199), just as he does not employ the expression "persona que contempla" but falls back upon "persona que se exercita": there is too much toil and effort for pure consolation in the third week. The conclusion appears to be that "hablar" does not only presuppose contemplation but also a fairly intense degree of consolation. For this reason it should be joined to "discurrir" and "hacer pausa" as a key word typical of the third level of contemplation or contemplative prayer. This leads to the conclusion that the colloquy, based as it is upon *hablar,* occurs in its most proper sense in the repetitions. *Discurrir* will make the exercitant come to rest sooner or later (hacer pausa, reposar), but in its turn this will lead to the almost unbelievable reality of conversing with God, the Incarnate Word, and His Mother.[16]

## Meditation and Contemplation

Even a cursory reading of the text of the Spiritual Exercises shows that Ignatius is careful in the use of the words "meditation" and "contemplation." Thus, he will never refer to the contemplations of the second, third and fourth weeks as meditations. When he is speaking of the exercises of the four weeks in general, he will speak of meditations and contemplations. Evidence will be adduced in the course of this section. Relevant is this incident: early drafts of the *Examen Generale* and the *Constitutions* were sent by Ignatius to a number of his companions, asking for their comments and corrections. Salmerón pointed out that the phrase "meditando y contemplando sus pecados, los passos de la vida y passión" might be amended to read "meditando sus pecados, y contemplando los passos y misterios"; the correction was accepted by Ignatius.[17]

There can be no doubt that meditation takes a minor position in the Spiritual Exercises, although in the tradition of the Society of Jesus and, in fact, of the whole Western Church contemplation has been almost completely superseded by meditation. The first traces of this tradition can be discerned soon after the first approbation of the Exercises.[18]

To determine what exactly is the difference between meditation and contemplation, the two exercises should be placed side by side. There are only five meditations, namely, in the first week, the first two exercises and the meditation on hell; in the second week, the exercises on Two Standards and Three Classes of Men. There is neither a meditation nor a contemplation on the First Principle and Foundation. The exercise "del Rey" is no more than a consideration, as will be discussed in a later chapter. All the other exercises belonging to the thirty days' retreat are contemplations. The subject matter of the contemplations, with the exception of the repetition and resumption in the first week, are mysteries of Christ's life: mysteries, not events. The subject matter of the meditations is facts or truths, and those which directly concern the exercitant himself. In the meditation on Two Standards it is the simple fact of knowing oneself to be involved in a struggle between good and evil, between Christ and Satan. In the meditations of the first week it is the fact of the exercitant's own sinfulness and fallen condition, while in the meditation on hell it is the fact of hell, "saved from which up till now." Mainly through the use of his natural faculties the exercitant tries to understand these truths and facts: memory, intellect, and will are mentioned in the first exercise; the second requires the exercitant to recall, to ponder, and to consider; in the meditation on hell he looks and listens, tastes and touches; "to consider" dominates the meditation on Two Standards, while in that on Three Classes of Men the exercitant takes notice of the fact that there are three classes of men.

"Contemplar" is frequently used by Cisneros. Ignatius must have been quite familiar with Cisneros' opinion that contemplation is intimately connected with the unitive way. He distinguishes three ways of contemplating, which are really three stages. They are: to be present, to meet the Father in the Person of Christ, and to become united with Christ Himself.[19] Evidently, Ignatius with his "the Word, newly become incarnate" and "making myself a poor little unworthy slave helping as if I were present" and with his frequent mentioning of sharing Christ's sufferings and sorrow, had a similar conception of contemplation. Contemplation can never be a question of merely being present and watching indifferently. One cannot be really present at a mystery without being moved, as is clear from the phrases quoted just now. So, contemplation is essentially and closely linked with consolation, for consolation is any interior movement in the soul by which it is inflamed with love or stirred by sorrow or joy, in greater faith, hope, and charity (316). The link is so close that as soon as there is true consolation, meditation turns into contemplation, even though the subject matter remains the same. A clear instance is found in the first week. The fourth exercise is a resumption of the third, but the third is a repetition in which the exercitant will pause at those points where he experienced greater consolation or spiritual relish (62).[20] When in the resumption the exercitant is asked to wander about (discurrir) "las cosas contempladas," it can only mean that he should dwell upon those parts where meditation developed into contemplation on account of many interior movements. Another example is given in the second week. When speaking of the repetitions of the meditation on Two Standards, Ignatius uses the word "exercise" (148). It is not a mistake, or a lapse, when at the end of the meditation on Three Classes of Men he calls this repetition a contemplation (156). When the exercitant or, in general, any Christian experiences desolation, he should insist more, so one reads in the sixth rule for the discernment of spirits, upon meditation and much examination of conscience (319); the omission of contemplation is as striking as it is accurate. In the thirteenth annotation Ignatius writes that for one in consolation it is easy to continue for a whole hour in contemplation; but in time of desolation the exercitant must overcome the temptation and remain a little more than the full hour in the exercise: notice, exercise, not contemplation. Similarly, in the sixteenth annotation the exercitant is described as fighting against inordinate attachments and, logically, he is told to give himself perseveringly to prayer and other spiritual exercises. But when in the second annotation Ignatius speaks about interior understanding and spiritual relish, it is "he who contemplates" that he has in mind. In the second addition of the first week the exercitant is advised to turn his thoughts on rising to what he is going *to contemplate,* whereas the exercise he is going to make is a meditation (74). How accurately it is used is clear from what follows: he will arouse himself to shame and confusion; interior movements are once again associated with contemplation.

Ignatius uses both "meditation" and "contemplation," or the comprehensive term "exercise," when he deals with the Exercises in general. Thus, the preparatory prayer is to be made before contemplations and meditations (49); the exercitant will stand a step or two before the place where he is going to meditate or contemplate (75); after the exercise he will consider how he has succeeded in the contemplation or meditation (77). The director will explain the method of meditating or contemplating and narrate the facts of the contemplation or meditation (2). But in the nineteenth annotation only "meditation" is found, which indeed is very relevant if one recalls the type of exercitant described there. Hence, we cannot afford to overlook the fact that in the fourth addition—wedged in between the third and the fifth, where both "meditation" and "contemplation" are given—the exercitant is told to enter upon the contemplation now kneeling, now prostrate, now lying face upwards, now seated, now standing (76); "contemplation" should be stressed, the implication being that Ignatius does not care so much which posture the exercitant adopts when he is meditating. The reason for giving instructions on this topic to him who contemplates is revealing: If he finds what he desires, the exercitant shall not change his posture, just as he must be in no hurry to move on to other parts of his contemplation till he has been satisfied. It is a question again of interior movements and consolation, and hence "contemplation" is the only word that fits this situation.[21]

## Close of the Exercise

As regularly as "the preparatory prayer will be the same" is found at the beginning of each exercise, "close with an Our Father" is found at the end. Every exercise has a clear beginning and a well-marked end. Ignatius undoubtedly wants the hour of prayer rounded off. Not only must there be no shortening of the hour because the exercitant feels desolate and finds it hard to spend the full hour in prayer (12), in like manner there must be no continuation beyond the proper time because he is in consolation and great fervor. In other words, the duration of the meditation or contemplation is dependent neither upon desolation nor upon consolation. In either case, at the end of the hour, or exceptionally a little later in the case of desolation (12), the exercitant will say the Our Father. This will be a prayer of trust and faith when he has tasted desolation, it will be a prayer of great gratitude and of praise when he has indulged in the unearthly sweetness of the colloquy and its "hablar."

When the exercise is over, the exercitant "either sitting or walking, will consider for the space of a quarter of an hour how he succeeded in the meditation or contemplation. If poorly, he will seek the cause of the failure . . ., if he has succeeded well, he will give thanks" (77). The practice here recommended in the fifth addition is known as the review. Its purpose and the way in which it is to be made demand a brief examination.

The verb "mirar" is used three times, and no other verb of similar meaning is found. It is a time, therefore, of looking carefully and closely at the exercise just ended. The translation "how I succeeded," which is general, is probably derived from the *versio vulgata*. It was adopted by Roothaan, and reads: "quomodo mihi successerit." The autograph text reads: "mirar cómo me ha ido,"—"how things went with me," which is more meaningful. It does not refer to the way in which the exercitant said the preparatory prayer, made the various preludes, and in general applied himself to the exercise; surely, in this case Ignatius would have used a verb in the active voice. Nor does it mean that the review is a brief repetition of the main points of the preceding exercise. In either case it would be rather difficult to explain why a quarter of an hour is needed for a simple examination of the exercise. The expression refers to what *happened* to the exercitant during the hour of meditation or contemplation, to the way in which he has been moved and agitated, experienced consolation or desolation, received spiritual insights and greater clarity, to the way in which God worked and he cooperated. He is not only to recall these various interior movements; he has to examine whence they came, because it is by no means certain that they were all caused by God. The review is the time in which he applies the various rules for the discernment of spirits as they have been explained to him by the director (7-10). This can only mean that Ignatius does not want the exercitant to occupy himself with the source of spiritual movements while they actually take place. The reason is that such a reflection upon their origin during the hour of prayer would be the end of that receptivity and susceptibility, mentioned in the first chapter, which are indispensable if there is to be cooperation between God and His creature (15, 16). Ignatius, and with him the exercitant, can afford to banish self-examination and self-reflection from meditation and contemplation, if the exercise is followed by a time in which the various movements experienced are, so to speak, sorted out. At the same time, the exercitant will inquire into the cause why possibly there have been no agitations, and if this is to be attributed to his own fault (6, 77), he will ask pardon. In like manner, if he has been moved, if he has received spiritual insights, or in general, if he has been in consolation, he will give thanks and next time set about the exercise in the same way, a piece of advice that recalls the preceding addition about his posture when praying, and resting there where he has found what he sought.

Normally, the review is followed in the course of the day by the repetition or resumption. The special feature of this exercise is that the exercitant wanders about those parts of the exercise where, as we have seen, meditation became contemplation (64), or where contemplative prayer became heightened and intensified, which is associated with the words "discurrir, pausar, hablar." These points of intensified prayer have to be recalled: "discurrir por *la reminiscencia* de las cosas contempladas (64). But this reminiscencia takes place in the review, whose purpose is to recall and examine what happened to the exercitant in the way of spiritual experiences. Hence, it certainly looks as if the review is also an indirect preparation of the next repetition or resumption of the exercise.

Although there is room for prayer in the review, for contrition as well as for thanksgiving, it must not be made into a time for formal prayer. Therefore, it must be made by the exercitant sitting or walking; kneeling is excluded. Hence, in no case must the review be turned into an additional quarter of an hour's meditation or contemplation. This would undermine its true purpose. For the review also means getting away from the exercise proper; it is placing oneself at a distance from it and looking at it from the outside. Probably, Ignatius had another good reason for it. The exercise, be it meditation or contemplation, be the exercitant in consolation or desolation, is always an intense spiritual experience. The transition from this experience to the usual duties of the day might well prove too sudden if there were no opportunity to adapt oneself gradually to what is normal life. If a rather colloquial expression be permitted, the exercitant must be given the opportunity to cool down somewhat, or to find his feet again. The review is thus seen to be very wise advice, and a quarter of an hour does not seem to be too long to achieve the result for which it is meant. If, then, the review is properly made, another noteworthy advantage can be discerned. The danger of being rather absorbed by the divine experiences of meditation and even more so of contemplation (10, 15) is that the time of prayer carries with it something so extraordinary that it becomes unnatural or somewhat abnormal: just now we spoke of a return to normal life and the duties of the day. Thus a gap between prayer and life may be opened, which surely is the last thing Ignatius wants to happen; it would do away with composition altogether. The review, as it were, brings the divine experiences of the hour of prayer into everyday life. They are now seen as belonging to the exercitant's life. Thus the review serves the very useful purpose of facilitating the integration of the supernatural into what is natural, of prayer into the duties of normal life. Again, a quarter of an hour does not seem to be too long.

In this chapter the main outlines of meditation and contemplation have been presented. Details will be filled in when the exercises are examined as they are made in the various weeks.

five

# FIRST PRINCIPLE AND FOUNDATION

In the opinion of Ignatius, a relatively small number of people were suitable to make the Spiritual Exercises in full.[1] The reason is not that any special qualities of endurance and fortitude, found in few men, are needed; it is a question of spiritual ripeness. The exercitant should be able to enter the Exercises with magnanimity and generosity, offering his Creator and Lord his entire will and liberty so that the Divine Majesty may dispose of him and all he possesses as He thinks good (5). He is expected to wish to make as much progress as possible, and he is supposed to give his whole attention to one single interest, namely, the service and praise of his Creator and Lord and union with Him (20). He is referred to in the fifteenth annotation as "ánima devota," an expression found in the description of the first time of making a good choice, when God so moves and attracts man's will that he follows, without hesitation or the possibility of hesitation, what has been manifested to him (175), or again in the second set of rules for the discernment of spirits, where Ignatius deals with the subtleties employed by Satan as an angel of light to deceive man, who is here also called "ánima justa" (332). The expression stands for the devout, dedicated person, bent on finding the will of God, to whom God wishes to communicate Himself and His very special graces. We will return to its use in a later chapter. The exercitant's maturity also implies that he can begin the first exercise with the prayer that *all* his intentions, actions, and operations may be *purely* ordered to the service and praise of the Divine Majesty (46). There are not many who have this spiritual maturity, and Ignatius took his time to prepare suitable candidates. Now and again, as for instance with Francis Xavier, the preparation lasted a considerable time.[2]

There is an unmistakable affinity between the description of the exercitant on the threshold of the Spiritual Exercises, as found in the first, fifth, fifteenth and twentieth annotations, and a kind of preliminary note, called First Principle and Foundation (23). It is not only that they have themes of dependence, indifference, and order in common; they are also marked by a similar choice of words: Creator, Lord, Divine Majesty, will of God, service, praise, and so forth. The resemblance is so conspicuous that further proof is superfluous.

Starting Point of the Spiritual Exercises

The opening exercise for the exercitant of the twentieth annotation is the meditation on the triple sin (45). The First Principle and Foundation precedes it, but is nowhere called a meditation or even an exercise. It lies outside the Exercises, and that is why it was referred to just now as a preliminary note. If it is objected that Ignatius mentions this note more than once in the text of the Exercises, two points should be carefully noted: first, he only speaks of explaining it (19),[3] of considering it, and keeping it before one (169, 177, 179); second, when he mentions it, he is not dealing with the exercitant in the proper sense of the word. He has in mind a Christian, well educated and talented, engaged in public affairs and necessary business, so that he cannot spend thirty days in solitude and yet might need to make an election or otherwise come to a reformation of life (19).

Well educated and talented: this suggests that the explanation of this preliminary remark is not an easy thing. It is the reason why it is not given to those less talented, to the untutored and illiterate, and so in the eighteenth annotation the First Principle and Foundation is not mentioned at all. Engaged in public affairs or necessary business: the autograph text uses "embarazado," which might be rendered as "taken up with" or "absorbed by." Such persons tend to lose sight of end and means, and are prone to forget what is the true spiritual foundation of life. If they are going to be helped to make a good choice or to reform their lives, the why and wherefore of creation must be clearly placed before them (169, 189). Thus the explanation is given why this preliminary note sounds as dry as it is logical. It is a question of common sense and close argumentation rather than of reverence and humility. And it is with an act of reverence and humility that the Exercises open (75).

If the First Principle and Foundation is intended for the exercitant of the nineteenth annotation, it does not follow that the person who makes the long retreat can leave it untouched and act as if it does not concern him. For, as has been said, even the wording of the initial disposition of the exercitant, as given in various annotations, shows close affinity with that of the First Principle and Foundation. The exercitant's first prayer will be that all his intentions, actions, and operations will be purely ordered toward the praise and service of God: it is a prayer brimful of echoes of the text of the First Principle and Foundation. It may happen that the would-be exercitant is not, or not yet, so well disposed that he can say this prayer; evidently, some days of preparation are then desirable to help him toward the required disposition. It matters little whether such days of preparation are actually made part of the Exercises and take place in an atmosphere of silence, solitude, and prayer. What must be stressed is that these days of preparation aim at bringing about in the exercitant the disposition demanded by the annotations mentioned above and by the preparatory prayer. It is very difficult to see how exercises on the First Principle and Foundation, such as are often found in commentaries and have become common since Roothaan gave them a place in his edition of the *Exercises*, have a legitimate place within the retreat. It is dangerous and confusing to ask the exercitant on the very first day *to meditate* upon the *text* of this preliminary note, as it will force him to reflect upon subjects that are just now beyond him, which lie outside the initial disposition and which come up as subject matter of contemplation and meditation in different perspectives later in the Exercises. To give one rather notorious example: perfect indifference, described in the preliminary note, does not stand at the beginning of the Exercises. It is *resignation* that the exercitant longs for, and in the course of the retreat this will develop toward spiritual poverty.[4]

It is generally agreed that nowadays a few days of preparation are needed in every long retreat. One of the reasons for this is that psychologically the transition between normal everyday life and the tremendous spiritual experience of God wanting to cooperate with this exercitant must not be too sudden but gradual. It may then be wise to recall the First Principle and Foundation, but unwise to begin coolly reasoning about it. The exercitant does not want theory; he accepts the truth of the preliminary remark. If he did not, he would be far removed from the desire for a thirty days' retreat. But the fundamental truth of his existence has probably become too much a question of notions. These are never brought to life by adding theory or abstract thinking. He is in no need of being reminded that "man was created": he wants *to taste* the truth of his being God's creature. He does not want to think about his Creator and Lord, he wants to approach Him, meet Him, be united with Him (20). From the first beginnings this Creator and Lord is Father, Son, and Holy Spirit, as is irrefutably proved by the colloquy of the first exercise (55). He is a God of majesty but also of goodness (53, 59, 61), He is a God who wishes to communicate Himself, wants even to embrace the exercitant (15) and put all his desires in order (16). God is very much concerned about the exercitant. It is contrary to both the text and the spirit of the Spiritual Exercises to place before the exercitant, when he begins the retreat, the Divine Being who made him and upon whom he is dependent.

The first day of the retreat is steeped in wonder and amazement. In three of the five exercises the exercitant is occupied with comparing

God's wisdom and his own ignorance, God's power and his own weakness, God's justice and his own iniquity, and above all, God's goodness and his own wickedness (59). He has no words when he discovers how he has been served and helped by the whole of creation, from the angels down to the fruits of the earth (60). This wonder and amazement are not the result of the meditations of the first day; they are part, at least implicitly, of his initial disposition. They should be made more explicit if the need is there. As we have suggested, the need will normally be there because of the sudden transition which the Spiritual Exercises make inevitable. So it seems obvious that the days of preparation should be a period marked by adoration. For adoration is both the way to wonder and its expression. Yet, not of adoration only, for the true relationship between God and the exercitant also demands that the latter acknowledges God to be his Creator and Lord, and this implies reverence and humility.

To conclude this section: the Spiritual Exercises never begin with an explanation, they begin with a prayer: "that all my intentions, and so forth". Days of preparation do not aim at conviction but, once again, at prayer, and the prayer is one of reverence, humility, and adoration.[5] Incidentally, the conclusion may be pointed out that from the first beginning the retreat is a time of consolation, peace, and joy. We find this mentioned by early commentators,[6] but what else does one expect when God is about to communicate Himself, to embrace the exercitant, to work with and in him? There is a delightful warmth about the Exercises, which contrasts sharply with the chilliness of many a traditional start of the Ignatian retreat.

## Main Points

Although the various elements of the First Principle and Foundation will only show their true colors later in the Exercises, some more important words and phrases must be studied now.

All the things on the face of the earth—an enumeration of them is given in the second exercise of the first week (60) and they are mentioned in the contemplation to attain the love of God (236)—are created for man to help him. This is Puhl's translation of the second part of the opening phrase. It is not accurate enough. Ignatius uses "para" three times in succession: "para el hombre, y para que le ayuden en la prosecución del fin para que es criado." This preposition and conjunction is frequently used by Ignatius, especially in the paragraphs dealing with man's destination (169, 189). Its underlying meaning is finality, a being directed toward. "Para el hombre" is not the same as "por el hombre." All things were created with a view to man; they are as many proofs of God's esteem and care for him.

The phrase is immediately followed by "para que le ayuden." In between these two phrases we find the conjunction *y*, which is preceded by a comma, as is proved by the autograph text. It disappeared in both the *versio prima* and *versio vulgata;* it was restored by Roothaan.

That one letter is of importance. If it were omitted, the translation would be, that all things have been made for man to help him, the implication being that man would be helpless without them. But the second phrase does not contain a specification of "para el hombre," which, in fact, would amount to a limitation.[7] If anything, it is a further extension. Because all the other things on the face of the earth have been created *para el hombre*, their function is to help him, to be of (some) help to him. But man's initial sovereignty given in "para el hombre" is never diminished by man's dependence on creatures. "Para que le ayuden" might be translated as "that they should *serve* man" or "be of service to him." This interpretation finds an affirmation in the fifth point of the second exercise of the first week, where the exercitant stands very much amazed that creation should have continued to acknowledge him as its lord by serving him (60). It is further borne out by the use of the verb "quitarse" in the second part of the First Principle and Foundation.

Ignatius draws a conclusion from the opening sentence; man must *make use of* creatures insofar as they help him, and he ought *to withdraw himself* from them, or *rid himself of* them, insofar as they prove a hindrance. The words in italics are the translations of "usar" and "quitarse" respectively. Now, "quitarse" is not exactly the equivalent of "not to use," or of "to rid oneself of," or "to withdraw oneself from." From its frequent use elsewhere in the Exercises, the verb does not indicate a mere negative attitude; it denotes something rather positive.[8] An accurate paraphrase would be that man does not want to have anything to do with a certain matter, that he keeps away from it with a strong suggestion of having no wish to acknowledge his need for help from any particular thing. It reminds one of not needing and not wanting things. This fits in admirably with the meaning of "para el hombre," and together with it, it brings out the sovereignty of man over the whole of creation. But is it then not surprising that Ignatius falls back upon "indifference" to describe this superior attitude toward all created things?

Indifference

The text reads: it is therefore necessary to make ourselves indifferent. "Therefore" (por lo qual) indicates a transition from theory to reality. Up to this point the First Principle and Foundation has confined itself to the relationship between God and man, and between man and all created things; now a practical conclusion is drawn from it. But a practical conclusion concerns *this* man; hence, Ignatius switches from "hombre" to "nos." However, we are fallen men and are by no means able to handle *usar* and *quitarse* as regards created things. This fact is not proved by Ignatius, he accepts it, and concludes that we have *to make* ourselves indifferent to all created things in order that we might arrive at an attitude of "balanza" and "equilibrio," as we read in the directory dictated to Father Vitoria (*Dir.*,

90). For to fallen man whatever has been made and has been given to him constitutes a potential danger, even good things like health, riches, honor, and a long life. Ignatius significantly adds "de nuestra parte," that is, "as far as we are concerned, as far as we have any say in the matter." This restriction shows that fallen man must not practice indifference in a blind, unlimited sort of way. Indifference is not an end in itself. Because fallen man often lacks that superiority or sovereignty over created things which should be his in virtue of the "para el hombre," he needs indifference to establish right order, to restore perfect balance.

A first condition to attain this indifference is to regard his own nature and the end for which he was made, or, in the words of Ignatius, the wish and the desire to choose what God wants him to choose (23, 180, 183). So, indifference by itself is never the last word, because indifference never makes it plain what the will of God for this man involves. Thus we can easily understand why Ignatius appears to favor *resignation,* as soon as he has to deal with this exercitant. For resignation does not designate the relationship between man and things, as indifference does, but between man and God who gives or does not give, who decides and makes this man choose one way or the other. Resignation tempers indifference, mellows it, makes it more human and personal, and thus paves the way for humility and spiritual poverty that will soon dominate the Spiritual Exercises.[9]

*Magis*

Another objection has to be faced. Words like resignation and balance, to mellow and to temper, are difficult to bring into line with the radical demand and the strident tone of the closing phrase with its very rigid *solamente* and *más:* only desiring and choosing what is *more* conducive for the end for which we have been created (solamente deseando y eligiendo lo que más nos conduce para el fin que somos criados). Some, more modern, translations will be given in a note.[10]

One may well ask whether this translation is correct and whether the underlying interpretation of the text can be maintained. From the First Principle and Foundation it cannot follow that man has to choose the more perfect thing and that he even has to set his desires on what is more perfect, on what is more conducive to the end for which he has been made. There can be no doubt that in the text indifference is given a further explication; the phrase in question is introduced by "en tal manera que," which in both *prima versio* and *vulgata versio* is translated by "ita ut," while Roothaan preferred "adeo ut." But the phrase dominated by "solamente" and "más" apparently does away with all indifference and with all "balanza y equilibrio."

To arrive at the logical conclusion and interpretation, no one can afford to overlook how Ignatius himself inserts the expression "de nuestra parte," which, it would seem, should be stressed. Quoting once again the autograph text, we read: "Por lo qual es menester hacernos indiferentes a todas las cosas criados, en todo lo que es concedido a la libertad de nuestro libre albedrío . . ., en tal manera que de nuestra parte no queramos más salud que enfermedad . . . ." ("It is therefore necessary to make ourselves indifferent to all created things insofar as it is permitted to the liberty of our free will to do so . . . in such a sort that we do not for our part wish for health more than sickness . . ."). It should be remembered, as was pointed out before, that the First Principle and Foundation shows a clear transition from principle, or theory, to foundation, or general practice, the transition being indicated by the change from *hombre* to *nos*: we must make ourselves indifferent in order that as fallen men we may recapture our original position as lord of creation and shake off our subjection to and dependence upon creatures. But there is a second transition, that from general practice, incumbent upon all men, to what each individual man has to perform. This transition is marked by "de nuestra parte," already preceded by a very clear reference to the individual man's free will. No man must or is even allowed to make himself indifferent to those creatures that God has meant to be a special help for *him*. So, a warning is sounded by Ignatius, and if "de nuestra parte" were omitted, any suggestion that "de parte de Dios" plays an important role would be completely obliterated, and one would be obliged to strive after unlimited indifference. But individual man, faced by a choice, is not guided by his desire and election of what is more conducive to the end for which he has been made, but by what God has decreed shall be more conducive for *him* as this man in this situation, with this character, with this task to fulfill.

The great stumbling block to making this interpretation acceptable appears to be the use of *más*, which precedes "nos conduce." For the first time the famous or notorious *magis* of Ignatius and Ignatian spirituality confronts the exercitant. It is, however, rather significant that it is omitted in the *versio vulgata*. When Pereyra cites the Spanish text, this crucial little word is not there ("solamente eligiendo lo que nos ayudará para el fin que somos criados," *Dir.*, 149), and Helyar's rather fragmentary copy of the Exercises reads: "manifestum est quod nos debemus esse indifferentes circa ista creata; verbi gratia, ut ego absolute nec secundum quid debeo velle magis prospera quam adversa . . . nisi in quantum iudicavero hoc vel illud esse mihi melius ad laudem Domini . . . ." (*Ex. Sp.*, 624). From these two instances the conclusion must be drawn that *más* is certainly not stressed in the context and that it does not have the meaning of a true comparison. Indeed, *más* is often used as a true comparison, as for instance in the sentence just preceding the closing phrase in question: "no queramos más salud que enfermedad." Neither can it be denied that quite frequently *más* means no more than *rather* or *especially*, as it does in modern Spanish. Thus, the rules for the discernment of spirits "conducen más para la secunda semana," where the translation is that they are more useful for the second week, not at all implying that they are *more* useful for the second than for the first week (328). Similarly, when Ignatius says that "es más concedido" for those who are perfect to swear, the correct translation can only be that "the perfect should be allowed to swear by a creature rather than those who are imperfect" (39); a true comparison would only make nonsense here. A vital instance of the use of *más* in this meaning will be examined in the following chapter.[11]

So, the correct paraphrase of "más nos conduce" and its most logical interpretation is that we should only wish and desire those things which are specially meant for us to lead us to the end for which we have been created. It is, then, logical that the exercitant in the preparatory prayer never asks that all his intentions, actions, and operations may be directed toward the *greater* praise and service of God, which surely should be inevitable if *más* were a true comparative in the First Principle and Foundation. Similarly, when making his election, the exercitant or any other Christian does not ask God "to place in his soul that which he ought to do in regard to the matter proposed, which will be to His *greater* praise and glory"; Ignatius writes "que más su alabanza sea," which is satisfactorily translated by Puhl as "to promote His praise and glory" (180). Again, "to the *greater* glory of God" is avoided in the prayer that is the third prelude of the meditation on Three Classes of Men, where the text has "para eligir lo que más a gloria de su divina majestad" (152). One may well ask whether the drive toward the *greater* glory of God and for ever *more* mortification is typically Ignatian. In our opinion, it is certainly not found in the First Principle and Foundation. This is not the same as saying that it is not found in the Spiritual Exercises. After all, the First Principle and Foundation lies outside the Exercises. The subject will re-enter the discussion in later chapters.

*Maior Dei Gloria*

The end of man's existence is expressed in the three words: to praise, to reverence, and to serve God ("alabar, hacer reverencia, servir a Dios"), and Ignatius adds that this is the way to save his soul ("mediante esto salvar su ánima"). Many a time the question has been asked why no mention is made of the First Commandment, why Ignatius leaves out the love of God. An indirect and partial answer will be given in the closing paragraphs of this chapter, a more complete answer will be found in the gradual exposition of the Spiritual Exercises. Another question that should be asked is whether Ignatius chose the words just quoted carefully and arranged them just as carefully, or whether he put them down as they occurred to him. This question leads to another: when in the course of the Exercises words like salvation, service, praise, glory, reverence, and so on, are found, are they used in a haphazard way, or is there a certain system in their usage? This investigation will be linked up with a similar examination of the use of the words God, Lord, Creator, Divine Majesty and Divine Goodness. Such investigations may not be of overwhelming importance in order to understand the book of Ignatius. If, however, it can be shown that Ignatius is in fact systematic and accurate in the choice of these words, it follows that the text of the Exercises must be read word by word, and that close scrutiny of every term and expression is not only fully justified but is a duty from which no director can escape.

Taking the use of "divina majestad" as our starting point, we discover that the expression only occurs within the framework of the four weeks and in the annotations which in a very special way refer to the exercitant of the long retreat (5, 16, 20). The sections that are not primarily meant for this retreatment (sections 21-45, 164-189) do not contain the expression. Thus, in the section dealing with the elections and the reformation of life, the words God, Lord and Creator, or a combination of them, are used more than fifteen times; there are only two exceptions, namely, in the description of the third degree of humility (which is understandable, because it is an anticipation of the third week) and in the closing prayer of the first method for making a good choice: an exception which will be discussed afterward. The expression is not used in the rules for the discernment of spirits, for distributing alms, for scruples, or for thinking with the Church, except in two cases which, as we shall later see, are not so much exceptions to a systematic use as confirmations. All this seems to indicate that where there is meditation and contemplation or where there is a more personal approach to God, "Divine Majesty" will be preferred; where a more formal relationship is in effect, other words appear to be obvious choices.

Next we discover that God is spoken of as "Divine Goodness" when—if the expression be permitted—the situation looks pretty grim for the exercitant, as in the note following the meditation on Three Classes of Men, where he asks God to choose him for actual poverty, if this is more pleasing to the *Divine Goodness* (159, 151). When the possibility of actual poverty is directly envisaged for the first time, the exercitant will appear before the *Divine Goodness*, although one would spontaneously expect the expression "Divine Majesty" (98). That "Divine Goodness" is used when God is the Giver of graces and favors will cause no surprise (20).

In the note following the meditation on Three Classes of Men, "Divine Goodness" is found just as it had its place in the composition of this meditation (151). In the body of the exercise, "God" or "God our Lord" is used when the first two classes are briefly described; "Divine Majesty" is added when the third class is the subject of meditation. Those who belong to this third class show a striking affinity with the exercitant: a comparison between the wording and contents of the third point of the meditation and those of the sixteenth annotation proves this clearly. "Divine Majesty" is employed in direct connection with the will of God as revealed to the exercitant ("God placed in his will . . . ." 155). The combination "Divine Majesty—divine will" is also found in the meditation on Two Standards when God is spoken of as choosing or electing the exercitant and as being served by this choice (146, 147). It occurs again in the third kind of humility and the note following it, where "service" plays an important part (167, 168). The introduction to the meditation on Two Standards also combines "Divine Majesty" and "divine will" (135).

The will of God implies that God wants to make use of the exercitant. Hence, when the exercitant offers his Creator and Lord all his liberty and his desires "in order that His Divine Majesty may make use of his person . . .," the change from "Creator and Lord" to "Divine Majesty" is significant (5). It corresponds with what we read in the introduction to the meditation on Two Standards: we begin to investigate and ask in what kind or state of life His Divine Majesty wishes to make use of us (135). We have already pointed out how this idea also occurs in the note following the three kinds of humility and in the third point and colloquy of the meditation on Two Standards (168, 146, 147). The impression is thus given that Ignatius speaks of God as Divine Majesty as soon as God as Sovereign Lord enters the life of the exercitant who has declared himself willing to serve and to obey and to be used by God. This is confirmed in the sixteenth annotation, where the exercitant approaches *God* in a rather objective mood and makes his own decisions; as soon as he begins to pray, he begs that the *Divine Majesty* will bring his desires into order, because the one thing he wants is the *service* and honor of the *Divine Majesty*. The apparent exception found in the instructions to make a good choice now becomes very relevant. The person making an election is told to pray to *God*, and he prays for the grace that *His Divine Majesty* may be pleased to accept and confirm the choice made. The change from "Dios nuestro Señor" to "divina majestad" is very appropriate ("ir a la oración delante de Dios nuestro Señor y offrescerle la tal elección para que su divina majestad la quiera rescibir y confirmar, siendo su mayor servicio y alabanza," 183).

It must not be thought that words like Dios, Criador, Señor lack warmth and color, are rather impersonal and businesslike, and take a somewhat pitiable place beside "Divine Goodness" and "Divine Majesty." There is, however, a difference, and it may be summed up in this way: where the initiative is with the exercitant and the movement is consequently from man to God, Ignatius uses "Dios, Criador, Señor"; where God's initiative and activity are stressed and God wants to make use of man, where consequently the movement is from God to man, Ignatius prefers "Divine Goodness" and "Divine Majesty."[12]

If Ignatius is careful in using words and expressions referring to God, the next question to be investigated is whether he is as accurate when he speaks of service, praise, honor, glory, salvation, and perfection.

A suitable starting point is given by the explanation of three kinds of humility. In the first kind, the salvation of one's soul is mentioned. In the second, which is more perfect humility, salvation and the service of God play their part. In the third, which is the most perfect humility, salvation and service have disappeared, and Ignatius now speaks of praise and glory (alabanza y gloria). At the same time, "Dios nuestro Señor," found in the description of the first and second kinds of humility, has made way for "divina majestad." Mere obedience to the will of God is not the same as true service, as is clear from the description of the first kind of humility. Doing one's duty, which is the theme of the second kind, is indeed service, but the motive of salvation plays a conspicuous part. Moreover, the true service which implies willingness to be used by God does not come to the fore. It is only when, because inspired, service is accompanied by praise that perfect service is given to the *Divine Majesty*. So, the triplet—praise - service - Divine Majesty—comes natural to Ignatius. It describes the disposition of the third class of men (167) with a significant change from "Divine Majesty" to "Divine Goodness" in the note following, as has been pointed out before. It is found in the preparatory prayer, where the exercitant prays that all his intentions and actions may be directed toward "the service and praise of His Divine Majesty" (46). It sums up the final disposition of the person who made an election (183).

In the twentieth annotation the exercitant is asked to disengage himself from ill-ordered concerns in order to "serve and praise God our Lord"; in the line following, the appellation "God our Lord" is changed to "Divine Majesty."

Contrary to the order given in the triplet above, "service" is usually placed first. In the First Principle and Foundation, however, it follows "praise," and "reverence" as well. The reason for this change appears to be the movement from theory to practice, or in general, from disposition to action. Thus, in the fifteenth annotation, God will embrace the exercitant "to love and praise Him" (en su amor y alabanza), but will then dispose him for that way of life in which he will better *serve* Him in the future. Similarly, in the introduction to making a good election, the praise of God is mentioned first, but as soon as means are chosen to attain this end, "service" and "to serve" dominate the text (169). In the explanation of the third time, praise of God and one's own salvation are mentioned in connection with the end of life, service and salvation when the means are discussed (177). Speaking of what the third class of men *do*, Ignatius logically has the combination service-praise and indeed confines himself to service when the force behind it is mentioned (155). The combination praise-salvation is found at the beginning of Ignatius' remarks on the matter of election (169) and on the third time (177), and it occurs again in the second and in the fourth points of the first method of making a good choice (179, 181); each time it is found in close proximity to a phrase expressing the purpose for which man is created.

The three kinds of humility give as motives for being humble, respectively: obedience joined to a great anxiety to save one's soul (primera manera . . . es necessaria para la salud), salvation together with the service of God (siendo igual servicio de Dios nuestro Señor y salud de mi ánima), and the praise and glory of the Divine Majesty (siendo igual alabanza y gloria de la divina majestad); in the note following the third kind of humility "service and praise of the Divine Majesty" is used (165-68). Special attention should be paid to "gloria." It occurs elsewhere. Its meaning and function are well illustrated in the second way to make an election in the third time. The motives of the love of God (184) and of perfection (185) have been introduced, and so it is mainly the *disposition* of the person who has to make a choice that is in question. Against the background of the motives of love and perfection Ignatius speaks only of "gloria de Dios nuestro Señor," in fact, he speaks of the "*mayor* gloria" and the "*mayor* perfección" (185). This close association of God's glory with love of God and perfection shows itself again when the exercitant asks God for the grace to choose that which *promotes* the glory of the Divine Majesty (152), where it should be remembered that this prayer, the third prelude of the meditation on Three Classes of Men, is inspired by the exercitant's desire to discover and want that which is *more* pleasing to the Divine Goodness. There is no need to prove that in trying to find out what is more *pleasing* to the Divine Goodness, the motive of love is very strong. So, "gloria" appears to occur where love, perfection and generosity are at work. Hence its accurate, perhaps even obvious, use in the third kind of humility, and hence its place in the closing phrase of the sixteenth annotation, following upon "sólo servicio y honra." Accordingly, where "más" is found, "gloria" is never far away, as in the paragraph dealing with the reformation of life (mayor alabanza y gloria de Dios nuestro Señor, 189), in the first method for making a good choice in the third time (más en gloria y alabanza de Dios nuestro Señor, que más su alabanza y gloria sea, 179, 180) and in the second rule for distributing alms (para mayor gloria de Dios nuestro Señor y mayor perfección, 339). For its occurrence in the *Constitutions* of the order which Ignatius founded, we refer the reader to a note.[13]

As was the case with the use of the expression "Divine Majesty," there is a suggestion of intimacy and warmth when Ignatius uses "gloria." It is more personal than any other similar word, and hence it is not surprising that in the opening phrase of the exposition called the First Principle and Foundation we look for it in vain. Perhaps we should say that we should not look: love is not found in a first principle, nor for that matter in a foundation.

We have not dealt with the words in question in any exhaustive way. Contrary to the opinion of Nonell,[14] we hold that Ignatius did not use them at random. If the subject is not pursued any further, it is because one has to be careful not to urge the matter too much, for this reason, that the book of the *Spiritual Exercises* is composed of rather divergent materials, corresponding to various classes of exercitants. As in this study we confine ourselves to the exercitant of the twentieth annotation, a detailed examination of all places where these words occur might be confusing.

In the second annotation Ignatius stresses the importance of relishing and tasting the matter interiorly; both the director and the exercitant should learn to relish and taste also the words which Ignatius chose with such great care.

six

# THE FIRST WEEK

The essence of the Spiritual Exercises is that God is at work in and with the exercitant who wants to know interiorly, taste, relish, and live the truth of his own being and existence. This truth is gradually unfolded to him. The starting point is the encounter between the creature and his Creator, the former offering all his desires and liberty to God in his wish to make as much progress as possible (5, 20), and God being eager to help him, to enlighten him, to communicate Himself to him, and even embrace him (15, 16). The first step forward consists in this that the exercitant turns his eyes upon himself: he is a servant and one who has been unfaithful, and therefore he seeks to arouse himself to shame and confusion (74). Difficulties and questions at once assail the exercitant, the director, and the student of the Spiritual Exercises. To mention three: First, he who makes the Exercises considers himself a very wicked sinner, worthy of hell not once but many times, without as yet having given a thought to his sins (48, 50, 52). Second, he asks for shame and confusion before attending to their motive and source, and even before considering the wickedness of his evil deeds. Should shame and confusion not be the result of the meditations? Why beg for apples when one is immediately afterward to climb the tree? Third, why does the exercitant at the end of the third and fourth exercises, which are the repetition and resumption of the first and second, pray for a deep knowledge of his sins after having meditated upon them in the second exercise and having been conscious from the very first moment of the retreat of having grievously offended his Lord, from whom he has received many gifts and favors (74)? This difficulty cannot be set aside by making a distinction between a qualitative and a quantitative estimate of sin; in the second exercise, or for that matter, in the first, the exercitant does not only face the question how numerous his sins have been, but how wicked as well.

These fairly obvious difficulties make the beginning of the first week seem hardly logical; they may even give the impression of carelessness. Moreover, Ignatius does not mention the number of days the first week is even approximately to last. Where the exercitant at the first beginning of a strenuous undertaking of thirty days is entitled to precision and clarity, Ignatius is vague, giving no more than five exercises, all of them meant for the one and apparently only day. Indeed, he speaks of the possibility of lengthening and shortening the four weeks of the retreat (4), and he returns to this subject in the second, third and fourth weeks, telling the exercitant how to set about it; but where the need of more information is the greatest, which undoubtedly is the case in the first week, the text does not contain any hint of an explanation.[1]

To give a convincing reply to these questions, one should not lose sight of the thorough preparation that is supposed to precede the exercises, of the spiritual maturity that marks the true exercitant, and of the high degree of prayer that he has reached. The "cómo Dios me mira, etc." of the third addition (75) points to a certain familiarity with the prayer of faith. To ask the exercitant to spend at least five hours in mental prayer on the first day of the retreat indicates that the exercitant is well versed in mental prayer; to presuppose that he can turn his thoughts from the moment of rising not only to God but to himself as a disloyal knight who wants to be thoroughly ashamed of himself (74) proves that he is not just a beginner in the spiritual life. The exercitant does by no means start from some absolute zero. On the contrary, how could he do so, when his first prayer is to ask God for nothing less than the grace that *all* his intentions, actions, and operations may be *purely* directed to the service and praise of God (46)? This prayer seems to suggest that the exercitant is aware that he has failed in the past. It is at this point that the immediate preparation for the first meditation begins, and careful attention must be devoted to the first prelude, which is the composition.

First Exercise

"The composition will be to see with the eyes of the imagination and to consider that my soul is imprisoned in this corruptible body and my whole composite being is in this vale, as it were, in exile among brute beasts; I say, this whole composite being, of soul and body" (47). This rather literal translation of the first prelude brings out the important fact that the composition consists in a consideration, and that the object of this consideration is that man's soul is imprisoned in the body and that man himself is in exile. This can only mean that in the composition the exercitant is to see and consider himself as a fallen man, cast out from Paradise. Possibly, the images used by Ignatius, although found in Scripture,[2] do not appeal to the exercitant, but the purpose of this composition should not escape him: he must realize that he is a fallen man. He is warned not to accept the sad situation in which he finds himself, subject to corruption and death, as a sort of primary and natural fact. This would at once prove disorder and disharmony; for what is highly abnormal (man's fallen state) would then be considered and taken as normal, as willed by God from the beginning. The exercitant has to realize by means of and in this prelude that he was made "little less than the angels" and that he was meant to be the lord of all the things on the face of the earth, without a trace of corruption and with the most perfect harmony between body and soul, with Paradise as his true country, but that little is evidently left of this original situation.

The second prelude appears to be somewhat illogical. The exercitant will ask for shame and confusion; that is, surely, strange if he cannot help being a fallen man. He is not at fault himself, he is only the victim of his first parents' miserable failure. To this objection there is a double answer. Original sin has given every man what might be called a very unpleasant character. It matters little whence this unpleasantness comes, it is always something to feel ashamed of; if he does not feel shame, he should ask for it, because it is part of what true order involves. The second answer goes further. Not only is the exercitant a fallen man; he has done little to mitigate or improve his sorry plight. He has made matters worse, because he has sinned. Ignatius does not prove this; he accepts it, and the exercitant has to accept it, and he does accept it if the time of preparation has yielded the results for which it was meant. It is logical, then, that he should pray for shame and confusion. If he does not experience the need for them, there is no harmony, and the composition has been left incomplete.

In the fourth chapter, the *points* of the exercise were shown to be a further development of the two or three preludes. Consequently, it can hardly come as a surprise to discover how the meditation that follows the two preludes can only be a deepening and expanding of the composition, of one's experience as a fallen human being, who has every reason to be ashamed of himself. The text makes this quite clear. True, one might initially get the impression that the sin of the angels, of our first parents, and of any sinful man are the subject matter of the meditation. The title seems even to suggest this. But the three points, dealing with these three sins, each time lead up to the conviction that the exercitant is a very sinful man, worthy of damnation. They only serve to make clear what it actually means to be a sinful man, unbearably proud, a creature no longer of grace but of malice (50), to be full of corruption (51), to be most ungrateful (52) and, consequently, only too deserving of eternal punishment (48, 50, 52). The three points, be it noted, are wedged in between the second prelude, which is a prayer for shame and confusion, and the colloquy, in which the exercitant turns to the "Creator on the cross." The three points must not be given a sort of independent existence as dealing with three different sins. The three sins only fulfill a subsidiary function and are only intended to drive home the full implications of the two preludes; they intensify the exercitant's composition. Accordingly, this exercise has no prelude called the history; in fact, it cannot have one. The subject matter of the meditation is the exercitant himself as a fallen man, *here and now*, in this *present* situation. The history, in the sense of "traer historia" of the angels or of our first parents, would cut away the solid basis of the *here and now*, and instead of forcing the exercitant *to be himself* would only invite him *to think about others*.

It is generally found rather difficult to follow and be in sympathy with Ignatius where he stresses the eternal damnation that the exercitant has deserved, especially as he has not so far been asked to consider how often and how grievously he has sinned, which will take place in the second exercise. Either Ignatius is not quite honest here, sacrificing truth and honesty to piety, or he is a gloomy pessimist who can only see evil, or he simply exaggerates as a kind of ascetical expedient. Now in the first place, Ignatius nowhere actually says that the exercitant deserves to be condemned because he has committed many or any *mortal sins*, not even where this is apparently strongly suggested in the second prelude containing the contrast between "un solo pecado mortal" of the angels and "por mis tantos peccados" (48). In the second place, through the preceding composition the exercitant knows himself to be a fallen man who has cherished his fallen condition by his own sins. In so doing he has accepted, even underlined, his outcast condition, which is the same as deserving to be condemned forever. Ignatius avoids making the distinction between mortal and venial sins, between serious and less serious transgressions of God's law. He fastens upon the essence of all sin, which is a matter of acting against the Divine Goodness (52). It is a certain disposition of heart and mind that makes man into a great sinner, deserving of hell.

In maintaining that the opening exercise has for subject matter not the first, second and third sins but the sinful exercitant himself, a seemingly formidable objection must be faced: it is the title of the exercise. The usual translation runs: "The first exercise is a meditation *by means of* the three powers of the soul upon the first, the second, and the third sin." The autograph text may or may not read: "meditación con las tres potencias"; it is by no means clear. What is perfectly clear is that Ignatius writes three times "*de* las potencias" at the top of the page.[3] Now, the subject matter of meditation is always preceded by the preposition *de*. Thus, the second meditation is entitled "de los pecados" and the fifth "del infierno" (55, 65). In the second week, the meditations are "de dos banderas" and "de tres binarios de hombres" (136, 149, 156). In the nineteenth annotation, the preposition *de* is used three times in quick succession following the word "meditación," and the same is found in Ignatius' explanation of the composition (47). In other words, nowhere in the Exercises is "meditación" followed by the preposition "sobre." Consequently, the correct translation of the title is: meditation on the three powers of the soul as regards, or in their relation to, the first, the second, and the third sin. Hence, Ignatius could not possibly place a comma between "potencias" and "sobre," as has been misleadingly done by the editors of the text in the *Monumenta Ignatiana* edition. The first meditation, then, is a meditation on the exercitant's reactions to the three sins. The subject matter is his thoughts about, his response to, and his attitude toward his own sinfulness. This takes the form of *traer las tres potencias sobre* the sins of angels and men. The expression runs parallel with "traer los cinco sentidos sobre."[4] What the exercitant sees, hears, tastes, and touches is the essence of the application of the senses; what he thinks and holds and the way in which he reacts is the essence of this meditation, which consists in "traer las potencias." Logically Ignatius advises the exercitant to ask for the grace to be ashamed of himself (not: of his sins), and he is told to reflect upon himself (not: upon his sins, 48, 53). It looks as if Ignatius were somewhat concerned lest the exercitant by restricting his attention upon various sins should lose sight of himself as a sinful man. But he will not allow his exercitant to be an outsider or an observer to his own sinfulness. He takes hold of him, as it were, by means of an "I say," which remarkably enough is found in each of the three points and nowhere else in the meditations and contemplations to come.[5]

In this first exercise the exercitant is very much thrown back upon himself, in shame, but also in confusion (48, 50, 74). Confusion means that one cannot grasp what has happened or what is happening. The exercitant tries to realize where he ought to have been at this very moment, and he looks for an explanation why he has not been condemned and why he is still alive. An explanation must be found, and so he poses a number of embarrassing questions and seeks and finds the answer to them in his Creator on the cross (55). There Ignatius leaves him, "that he might wander about what now presents itself to his mind" (53).

One more important aspect of this meditation must be considered. Any composition made by a creature cannot leave out the Creator; composition is not the same as a kind of self-occupation. But the composition made by any sinful man can never leave out God against whom man has sinned. Now, in making the first exercise there is not merely the danger that the attention is shifted from the exercitant to other beings who have sinned, in this case, angels, first parents, and any man, but there is also the temptation to concentrate so much on the action of the sinner that its Victim is completely forgotten. Ignatius, however, wants the exercitant to realize how in the end any sin is acting against God's infinite goodness (52) and any sin involves throwing away grace (50) and Paradise (51). He forces the exercitant to reflect upon what the Creator did for him, and being placed on the cross, how He became the Victim of sin. All this reinforces the conviction that the three sins of this meditation are really of minor importance; to occupy oneself with them is no more than a means by which one tries to arrive at a more perfect composition of oneself as a fallen, sinful man in relation to a God of infinite goodness.

Second Exercise

Ignatius begins the second exercise by pointing out that the composition is the same as in the first, but this is only partly true. Indeed, the text will be the same, but the contents have changed. The exercitant is once again this fallen man, in exile, but this time he is very much aware of being in the presence of God, who is both the Infinite Majesty and a God of goodness and patience (53). Thus the composition leads not only to shame and confusion but also to grief and sorrow. The exercitant will ask for them in the second prelude (55). Grief and sorrow are associated with contrition in the fourth annotation.

Contrition essentially involves the past; it does not recall so much past sins, as the past itself. It is of the utmost importance to be aware of this fact if we wish to understand the second exercise correctly. The reason is that after the first exercise sin cannot be seen as a mere transgression of the law of God. Sin implies that the sinner has been greatly favored by God, has experienced His infinite goodness, even to His having come down from eternal life to temporal death to save mankind (52, 53, 74). The composition of this exercise is, therefore, gradually extended to include the whole past, still very much carried along by the exercitant as part of his existence now. In the first point he is asked to consider the places where he has lived, the persons with whom he has lived and conversed, the offices he has held. This reconstruction of the past is meant to aid him in calling to mind his many sins (56). But calling to mind sin is of little use and, in fact, impossible, unless at the same time the exercitant recalls God's continued goodness. Ignatius makes explicit mention of this in the fourth point of this meditation, and the fifth and final point contains an exclamation of wonder, because notwithstanding his sinfulness the exercitant has always been faithfully helped and served by angels, men, and the whole of creation. The point must be stressed, because Ignatius has been accused of seeing and being interested in sin only. But for him to be alive was identical to being the recipient of gifts and favors (74), to be a creature was identical to being looked after and favored by God's infinite goodness; to be alive was to be loved by God (65). Existence itself points to "tanta piedad y misericordia hasta agora siempre" (71).

This should be borne in mind when at the beginning of the second exercise the exercitant is asked to recall "all the sins of his life." It looks as if he is required to concentrate not on his past, but on the sins he has committed. This is unlike Ignatius, because it would reduce the exercise to a minute examination of conscience, which is rather purposeless for one who already knows himself to be a great sinner, many times worthy of damnation. If it is answered that Ignatius had in mind a general confession, it must be pointed out that the text makes no mention of it anywhere in the first week as given to the exercitant of the twentieth annotation.[6] Besides, how long is such an examination of *all* the sins of one's life going to take? After all, *el processo de los pecados*[7] is only the first point of the exercise, to be followed by four more and a colloquy. We shall soon see how Ignatius wants the exercitant to compose himself with the whole of his past.

To understand the first point, it is necessary to pay careful attention to what Ignatius prescribes in the second point. There we read: "The second point is to weigh the sins, looking at the loathsomeness and the malice which every mortal sin committed contains in itself, even supposing that it were not forbidden" ("Ponderar los pecados mirando la fealdad y la malicia que cada pecado mortal cometido tiene en sí, dado que no fuese vedado" 57). The closing phrase sounds very strange, as if there could ever be a mortal sin which was not forbidden. The past participle "cometido" seems entirely superfluous; surely, there is no need to recall mortal sins that have not been committed. Above all, "mortal sin" is almost incomprehensible. It suggests that the exercitant should concentrate on the malice of every *mortal* sin and should pay no heed to venial sins, as they are of less importance. And what is the use of concentrating on the malice of *every* mortal sin, as the essential wickedness of any mortal sin is always the same?

All these objections disappear as soon as "pecado mortal" is translated by "capital sin." In a lengthy note the meaning of "pecado mortal" will be discussed.[8] But there can be no reasonable doubt that in this second point Ignatius asks the exercitant to examine how loathsome and how wicked every capital sin is of which he is guilty (cometido), even though it may only be a question of faults and it might be possible to think that God would overlook them.[9]

In accordance with this translation and interpretation of the second point, there can be little doubt that "todos los pecados" in the first point stands for capital sins. Now, capital sin stresses the evil disposition, not the evil action. Hence, the subject matter of the first two points of this second exercise is the disposition of the exercitant in the past. This disposition, however, cannot be recalled without the exercitant regarding God as a God of majesty and goodness. In the first exercise, the exercitant is not occupied with the sins of others, not even with his own sins, but with himself as a sinful man who owes his continued existence to a Creator on the cross. Similarly in the second exercise, the exercitant is not occupied with his sinful actions of the past but with himself as a person who has received many favors and graces (74) from a God of infinite goodness (52) and as a person who has behaved in a manifoldly shameful way. ("Manifold" refers to the evil dispositions from which his many sinful actions have proceeded.) The third point can now be better understood. Ignatius is driving home how shameful the exercitant's attitude toward God has been, and he ends his observation by asking the exercitant to see himself as *an ulcer and an abscess.* The image used by Ignatius may not appeal to us. Perhaps we prefer to use terms like "disease" or "sickness"; there is no objection, provided we remember that the disease or sickness is of our own making.

A first reading of the text of this exercise, in the light of the traditional explanation, hardly leaves room for the good that the exercitant may have done in the past: the past is only a question of sin. While it cannot be denied that he is directly confronted with the lost dimension of his own sinful state and sinful history—a dimension which every man is only too inclined and too anxious to forget—, nevertheless, he cannot lose sight of the many gifts and favors he has received from God, who never ceased loving him (74, 65) and even of the good things he has done in the past. In the colloquy of the first exercise he examines (mirar) what he has done for Christ. There is no proof that this is a rhetorical question and that the answer is a foregone conclusion: nothing at all. Much as he may have given in to evil inclinations, there has also been love, as is clear from the way in which the love of God is, perhaps unexpectedly, mentioned in the meditation on hell (65). This meditation on hell contains a strong suggestion, to say the least, that faith and good works have not been absent in the exercitant's past (71).

How little the exercitant is really occupied with the *sins* of his past and how much Ignatius wants him to be himself with the whole of this past very much part of the present, is further clarified in the fourth and fifth points. It is not merely that sinful actions are no longer referred to, not even indirectly. What happened in the past has to yield place to the situation of the present moment. For, the exercitant shall now consider who God is, against whom he has sinned, by comparing his ignorance with God's wisdom, his weakness with God's power, his iniquity with God's justice and, finally, his own wickedness with God's goodness (59). In the end he is amazed at the discrepancy between the past and the present. The only solution for any reconciliation between the two is to see the past in a different light: it has been a time of angels guarding him, of saints praying for him, of the whole of creation not only suffering him but actually helping and serving him (60).

In the course of this second meditation the composition becomes intensified, compact. At the end of the exercise there is greater oneness and integration with the past, with a God of power, justice, wisdom, and goodness, and with the whole of creation, now no longer a vale of brute beasts and a place of exile but filled with creatures patiently serving a human being still looked after by his God. The composition has taken almost unmanageable proportions. The exercitant experiences his existence as a great mystery. It prompts him to ask questions. The colloquy of the first exercise contained four questions, and the final point of the second exercise again has four questions, each of them introduced by "cómo," and all of them inspired by amazement that cannot be properly channelled into logical statements. In the colloquy the exercitant talks things over (razonar), trying to discover why God his Lord has given him life up to this moment (61).[10]

Repetition and Triple Colloquy

The third and fourth exercises are respectively a repetition and a resumption. There does not seem to be any great difference between the two; in the other weeks the place of the resumption is taken by a second repetition. In the repetition, the exercitant will dwell on the points in which he has felt greater consolation or desolation or greater spiritual relish (62); in the resumption, the understanding will wander about the things that have been contemplated in the preceding exercises (64). Ignatius speaks of *cosas contempladas*. The verb and the noun "contemplación" have not been used in the first three exercises. But the third exercise has been described in terms which are typical of contemplative prayer: to dwell on consolation, desolation, spiritual relish. From what we have said, the development of meditation toward contemplation must seem to be unavoidable.

Where meditation becomes contemplative prayer, it is expected that the ensuing colloquy will lead to more intimate and more spontaneous *hablar*. It is understandable that Ignatius allows the exercitant to explore (discurrir) what presents itself to his mind (por lo que se offresciere, 53). But why does he strike a kind of warning note in the resumption where he tells the exercitant to be on his guard against *straying* (sin divagar), and why does he evidently restrict the *wandering about* to a certain selection of points (cosas contempladas)? Why does he not leave him as free as at the end of the first exercise? Why not wander about what presents itself to the exercitant's mind? A second question, closely connected with this, is why the exercitant finds himself tied down to a rather schematic colloquy immediately following upon his first experience of consolation, desolation, and spiritual relish, and why the colloquy has to be repeated after the resumption (63, 64). For the exercitant is left no choice regarding both form and contents of the so-called triple colloquy. He shall ask for various favors, and for these he shall turn first to the Blessed Virgin, next to her Son, and finally to the Father. There seems to be little left of what a true colloquy should be: where is the spontaneity of an intimate *hablar*?

Now it is not quite accurate to maintain that the colloquy is merely petition. "Pedir" is used only once, namely, when the exercitant begs for knowledge of the world. Indeed, the colloquy is certainly inspired by the hope that the Blessed Virgin may obtain for the exercitant a deep knowledge of his sins and understanding of the disorder of his actions. But as no word such as "pedir" or "demandar" is used, the inference is that these gifts are the matter of conversation: the colloquy is a question of *hablar*, and it is these favors that the exercitant talks about. It is an important point. The colloquy must on no account be turned into a prayer of petition.

Regarding the favors that are hoped for, these point to what the exercitant or at least Ignatius considers as serious deficiencies. Ignatius is always occupied with the development of order, of composition, and he is quick to spot possible lacunae which might very well escape the exercitant when he indulges in a high degree of contemplative prayer. To know oneself as a great sinner does not necessarily imply that "he feels an interior knowledge of his sins" (sienta interno conoscimiento de mis peccados), nor does it imply that he has a clear idea of the element of disorder or deordination in his daily actions (sienta el dessorden de mis operaciones). The word "sienta" should be duly stressed. An abstract sort of knowledge is of no use; unless knowledge of one's sins and the disorder in one's actions, however noble they may look to us, penetrates the very marrow of our existence, there is no true composition. Ignatius is evidently afraid that the exercitant will be satisfied with shame and contrition, even tears: it is not enough.

The most important word in the colloquy has not been mentioned yet. It occurs three times, once as a noun, twice as a verb. "Aborrescimiento" means detestation; its object is one's sins, the element of disorder in one's actions, and the world. In the directory dictated to Vitoria, Ignatius said that the second exercise is not an examination of conscience with a view to confession but should induce *horror* (*Dir.*, 104), and according to Pereyra the purpose of the first week is *un aborrescimiento grande del peccado . . ., un aborrescimiento de sí mismo* (*ibid.*, 147). Shame, confusion, contrition, tears: it does not mean that love of the evil done has been completely banished. Sin gave enjoyment, and part of the exercitant's still imperfect composition is that there are traces of the attachment to or affection for the evil he has committed. It is too much to suppose that because he is sorry for his sinful actions, their source and inspiration, namely, the inordinate attachment, has disappeared for good. Ignatius now cuts at the roots of the exercitant's sinfulness. He must not be satisfied with, and merely rely on, shame and contrition: there must be detestation both of the sins committed and of every element of disorder in all his actions which betray some inordinate attachment. It is a hard thing to achieve. It is even a hard thing to ask and pray for this detestation. So, Ignatius tells him to talk about it "in order that the Blessed Virgin may obtain this grace for him." We believe that we have also discovered the reason why Ignatius gently but firmly leads the exercitant into making *this* colloquy. There is a real danger that he might turn away from inescapable conclusions; in other words, he must face the future.

Detestation looks to the future, and so does the decision "to amend and order one's life." The dimension of the future is added to the exercitant's composition. It has indeed never been entirely absent;

no dimension is ever completely lacking. It may have become blurred or neglected, but as long as man is a creature and a Christian, all the dimensions are there. The Spiritual Exercises purport to restore order, that is, to bring to fullness of life all the dimensions of man's life. In the first colloquy of the first week, the exercitant was asking himself questions about his future: What must I do for Christ? (53). The "up till now" of God's patience in the colloquy of the second exercise implies that the exercitant is occupied with, possibly even worried about, the future. This is made abundantly clear by what immediately follows: he will resolve to amend his life for the future (para adelante, 61). In this exercise, the dimension of the future is made much more explicit; consequently, and for this reason, Ignatius wants the exercitant to approach the *Eternal* Father. In the following exercise, which is on hell, it is the love of the *Eternal* Lord that he is thinking about (65), and in the final exercise of this first week, he turns his thoughts to the *Eternal* King (91, 95, 97). This dimension of the future naturally leads us to speak of the exercises on death, judgment, and hell.

## Exercises on Death, Judgment, and Hell

Ignatius is not only vague, as we have shown above, concerning the way in which the five exercises of the first week have to be distributed when the week is prolonged, he is equally vague regarding information about any meditations outside the five mentioned in the text. He does say that at times the exercitant will do well to call to mind death and judgment (78). He does not say that formal meditations should be made on these subjects. From the directories it is clear that to provide meditations on death and judgment has been common practice from early times.

This poses another question: should these meditations precede the fifth meditation of the Exercises, which is an exercise on hell, or should they follow it? May the sequence given by Ignatius be interrupted? The obvious answer appears to be that additional meditations should follow the meditation on hell, for the exercitant should first find out whether the five exercises given by Ignatius are sufficient to move him to shame, sorrow, tears, and contrition. If these five, supplemented if necessary by repetitions, are enough, there is no reason to go on to other subjects. This is in accordance with the rule that it is not more matter that satisfies the soul, but to relish and savor things interiorly (2). On the other hand, it may seem illogical to begin with a meditation on hell and then go on or should we say return to those on death and judgment.

The solution to the problem is once again given by reflecting upon the part played by the composition. It has been pointed out that the triple colloquy reveals how the dimension of the future is explicitly brought to the exercitant's attention. This dimension implies eternity. It also implies the possibility of hell, as will be shown presently, and it implies death and judgment. As these last two precede eternal punishment, the logical order would be to insert meditations on death and judgment before that on hell. It should be stressed that these meditations are added only when the reality of death and judgment has become too vague, when the suggestion of Ignatius to turn one's thoughts in the course of the day to these two subjects has proved to be impracticable or insufficient (78). When the decision is taken to add meditations on death and judgment, the reason and motive must never be to scare the exercitant into not committing sin any more. Their purpose is always the restoration of what is involved in order and harmony. It is the truth of one's composition that inspires and gives shape to the decision, as it inspires and shapes the meditation on hell.

The fact of eternity and immortality together with a call to amend one's life is fundamental in the exercise on hell. "For always" (para siempre) has been before the exercitant's mind from the second prelude of the first exercise onward (48), and the expression was used again in its third point (52) and in the exclamation of the fifth point of the second exercise (60). If on the one hand the exercitant admits that he has deserved to be eternally condemned (48, 50, 52), and on the other he knows himself to have been saved "up till now" (61), the concern about the future is there at once: "up till now" must be followed by "henceforward" (adelante, 61). Gratitude is accompanied by what is almost worry about the future. He knows himself too well not to be aware of possible ingratitude and of the temptation to forget all about the love of God (65). Thus, his attention is irresistibly drawn to the possibility of hell, and this possibility now becomes part of his composition. The fifth exercise is not a meditation on the punishment that is hell. As was true of the other exercises of this first week, the subject matter of the last exercise is the exercitant himself, this time with the new dimension of the possibility of hell added to the composition. This is clearly brought out by the various parts of the exercise.

Regarding the first prelude, which is the composition, the exercitant will see the length, breadth, and depth of hell. The fact that hell exists is not made part of his composition: he has been aware of it from the second prelude of the first exercise onward. It is its nearness that is now driven home, a singularly apt expression in connection with any composition. Hell is so near that he can see it. The word "place" (lugar) is not used; hell is not a place for Ignatius, it is a reality that, as it were, surrounds him. As for the second prelude, the possibility is joined to this nearness. But this possibility is not a question of serious sin, it is closely connected with faults, which make the exercitant blind and deaf to the love of the Eternal Lord (65).

Regarding the five points, they can only be a further intensifying of the preludes. Nearness implies that one can actually see, hear, smell, taste, and touch the reality at which one is present. The whole life of the senses is drawn into it. Here the question, so often asked, must be faced: why does Ignatius not mention the pain of loss? The answer appears to be that the exercise is not a meditation on the painfulness of hell, but on the nearness and possibility of hell. This only calls forth a second question: why did he concentrate on the pain of the senses? The answer is that he does not. The nearness of hell is driven home—to use the expression again—by stressing the sense of being present as a human being, body and soul; as nearness is based primarily upon what is perceptible to the senses, and only secondarily upon further reflection, the exercitant will see, hear, smell, taste, and touch. A third question is, whether this form of making the exercise appeals to man today. The answer is that in all probability it does not appeal to him at all, and that it is even, perhaps, a total impossibility. The reason is not that his faith in the existence of an eternal hell has considerably weakened. In this case, he has to make a different kind of meditation on hell, as was pointed out in the third chapter. The real reason is that modern man has become too much body and soul. We shall soon see how Ignatius could not think in terms of two component parts of which man is made up; he attacked the idea indirectly when explaining what composition means. As a direct consequence, the life of man is not the life of the body and the senses and then, on another level, that of the soul. It is the whole man who perceives through his senses and it is the whole man who thinks. Modern man has not achieved the integration of the life of the senses, of the body, and of the faculties of his soul in the way in which it came almost naturally to Ignatius and many of his contemporaries.

Finally, regarding the colloquy, it fits in logically with the preludes and the points, but there is a very neat and significant shift with reference to the focal point of the meditation. The exercitant is fully aware of the nearness and the possibility of hell, from which he has been saved up till now. In other words, hell is not merely a possibility; it is always a hell which he has deserved many a time. He cannot afford to lose sight of it. Once again, it must be made part of his composition. For this purpose he will divide all those who are in hell into six groups, then he will discover that as yet he does not belong to any of them. The reason is not that in contrast to those in hell he himself has believed and has acted according to God's Commandments, but because "Christ our Lord has shown such great pity and mercy, always, up till now" (hasta agora siempre . . . tanta piedad y misericordia, 71).

## Closing Remarks

There is very little in the text of the first week to support the view that at the beginning of the Spiritual Exercises the exercitant is occupied with what are called the eternal truths and that, consequently, the meditations of the first few days do not constitute more than a sort of prefix to the Exercises proper. The opinion is untenable. The first week shows a gradual building up of the exercitant's composition, but at the end of it he is not a self-centered person. His composition moves him outward to his God and Creator, and even more, to his God hanging on the cross. It cannot be stressed strongly enough how at the end of the first week the exercitant can only explain the mystery of his still being alive, which is mentioned no less than three times (60, 61, 71), by referring to Calvary. The cross is not an anachronism that has strayed into the first week but really belongs to the third week. Without Calvary and the cross there is no true composition at all, and the first week becomes like a thing suspended in mid-air. The exercitant has the experience of being a man saved and redeemed, but how can he be saved and redeemed without an act of salvation and redemption? The roots of his continued existence are in this historical fact of Calvary. It is not quite accurate; it is not Calvary and the cross with which he is linked up so intimately, but with God Himself coming down from eternal life to death here in time (53). Even this is not quite accurate. The coming of the Lord should not be reduced to what might be called a profitable event in history; it must be accepted or rejected, and on this decision depends damnation and hell. The exercitant's life is inescapably connected with faith in and acceptance of the Incarnate God, as was the life of the various groups of people mentioned in the final colloquy of this first week.

The first week is, then, not to be separated from the weeks that follow. The exercitant is not going to contemplate a sort of abstract God with whom he has little to do except that He happens to be his Creator. He is forced to turn his attention to Him who is the only explanation of his continued existence. A redeemed man, better, a man "redeemed up till now," must turn to his Redeemer. The other weeks can never be a time during which the exercitant reflects upon certain important religious truths or certain devotional practices. It is a time spent with his Redeemer. This implies that throughout the three weeks to come the exercitant will always be aware, so to speak, of his own identity. The composition of the first week is never set aside but ever complemented, so that "made Man for me" or "for my sins" (por mí, por mis peccados) will be found again and again.

The great importance of the exercitant's composition will make itself felt in the outward shape of his daily life. Composition demands harmony between on the one hand, his own feelings and convictions, and on the other, his outward actions and his behavior. Thus, he will deprive himself of light, close the shutters and doors of his room, and bring such matters as sleep and food in line with his composition. Ignatius deals with these points in the rules concerning penance (82-89). The word "penance" must not be taken in the negative sense often attributed to it, so that it comes to stand for unpleasant practices performed for the sake of their unpleasantness. In the Exercises, acts of penance are a matter of harmony between body and soul, achieved or seriously sought after. It is *man* who is praying, "digo todo el compósito de ánima y cuerpo" (47), and the body shares the experiences of the soul.

We do not think that exercises on venial sin, on tepidity, on conversion, and similar subjects fit in with the first week, nor do we think that they further the true composition of the exercitant. The inherent risk of meditations on these topics is that they deflect the concentration of the exercitant from the truth about his own being to a set of truths which, however valuable in themselves, have, in fact, no bearing upon what he is really to seek and find in the first week. He does not want to know about things connected with contrition, sin, conversion, and so forth: he wants to know himself, and this implies his desire to know God, a Creator on the cross. It must be remembered that "to know" in this context only feebly expresses what Ignatius wants the exercitant to experience. Groping after the right expression, he does not succeed beyond "to understand interiorly, to taste and relish": and we have to be satisfied with it.

seven

# THE EXERCISE "DEL REY"

The exercise which so far we have called the Kingdom and which is commonly known as such is one of the most difficult for any director to give, and it is probably the most difficult to understand. At the end of the first week the exercitant feels the need to pray for grace in order that henceforth he might amend and order his life; this is understandable. What is difficult to grasp is that within an hour of asking for the grace not to turn a deaf ear to God, he should be so much changed as to make an offering of himself, even to the extent of imitating Christ in suffering wrongs, abuse, and poverty (91, 98).

The exceptional character of this exercise is obvious as soon as careful attention is paid to the details of the text. It has no colloquy.[1] It is the only exercise in the book which does not end with an Our Father.[2] It is neither meditation nor contemplation; the word "exercise" is used, and none other (95, 99). Neither do the verbs "to meditate" and "to contemplate" occur, so that the exercise apparently shows no development toward either meditation or contemplation. The verb used is "to consider"; only once is it replaced by "mirar" (93). Not unreasonably the exercise may be called a consideration. Further, it has only one repetition, to be made before dinner or supper (99). It does not belong to the second week, because the first exercise of the second week is the contemplation on the Incarnation (101). Neither does it form part of the first week: the autograph text carries the inscription "second week" in the top left-hand corner.

The preludes of this exercise include a "composition by seeing the place" and a petition but no "history." In this respect it seems to belong to the first week. Moreover, the exercise is characterized by a certain vagueness, by something impersonal. Collective nouns, such as Christian princes and people, all subjects, whosoever and everybody, all those who have common sense and all those who wish to be moved by love, abound (92-97). The text contains a single use of the first person plural (95), and it is only in the prayer of the second prelude that something more personal is detected (91).

All this points in one direction: the exercise is the transition from the first to the second week. It takes place on what is nowadays called a day of repose, on which only two exercises are made. The exercise is a consideration, and in a consideration the exercitant is not much involved: he is a spectator, even an outsider.[3] The exercise looks forward to the second week. It is expressly stated that it is meant to be a help to contemplate the life of Christ (91), with the suggestion that, if it is no help, it may be omitted. This is in blatant contradiction with the opinion that the exercise "del Rey" is one of the key meditations, a kind of cornerstone of the edifice of the Spiritual Exercises.[4]

It is not surprising, then, that the exercitant is not being called by the King. In the second prelude the petition is for grace not to be deaf to the King's call, presumably, "when the call comes." When the exercitant applies the parable to Christ, there is no trace of anything even approaching the conviction "and in a similar way I am called by Christ." The exercitant only *considers* that it is *worthy of consideration* to look at Christ, the Eternal King (95), and this is what he is going to do in the second week. Consequently, there is no colloquy, for at the end of the exercise there is nothing to talk about. Very emphatically, the oblation is not a colloquy (98) nor is it made by the exercitant. He considers possible reactions to a call made by a good king, and, a fortiori, by the Eternal King. He observes that there are those who follow their sound judgment and common sense, and decide to join in the adventure since victory is assured (94, 95). He also notes that there are those to whom the Person of the King appeals more strongly than His cause. They are moved by love more than by reason and judgment, and their dedication goes further. All this is observed, noted, and considered by the exercitant as an outsider.

Preludes

The transitional character of this exercise is further brought out by a more detailed examination of its structure and its purpose. As usual, the first prelude, which is the composition, contains the key to a right understanding of the exercise. At the end of the first week the composition of the exercitant was clearly marked by his awareness of being a creature saved *so far* (hasta agora) and of being somewhat worried about what is to come (para adelante). His continued existence he cannot explain without the Creator on the cross, or more accurately, without God coming down from eternal life to death here in time (53). He cannot be fully himself without this essential link with Christ. His composition entails the history of Christ's life ending in His death on Calvary. But although his composition contains an essential connection with the life and death of Christ, there is as yet no question of the exercitant being drawn into the story of Christ's life. At present he is a beneficiary, not a participant. It is not the life of Christ that is made present to him. This remains at this stage a thing of the past, whose good results, however, are evident in the fact that he is still alive (61, 71). Hence, the exercise has no history as first prelude. But the composition "by seeing the place" indicates a shift from the good results to their source. The link with the life and death of Christ is now made much more explicit.

Two points ask for attention. First, Ignatius uses the past tense of the verb (predicaba); its accuracy is very striking. There was really no other choice once the first prelude, the history, had to be discarded. Elsewhere, Ignatius uses the present tense as he did in his explanation of the composition (47), although as a rule he is satisfied with merely mentioning the places.[5] Second, the exercitant will see the synagogues, towns, and villages where Christ our Lord preached (91). Ignatius does not write "where Christ lived and suffered." Again, this is to be expected when we remember that in the fifth and closing meditation of the first week, hell is said to be the result of neglecting Christ either by refusing to believe in His coming or, though believing, refusing to accept His teaching (71).

After this composition and in harmony with it, the exercitant asks for the grace which he desires. It will be here to ask of our Lord the grace that he may not be deaf to His call, but prompt and diligent to accomplish His most holy will (será aquí pedir gracia a Nuestro Señor, para que no sea sordo a su llamamiento, mas presto y diligente para cumplir su sanctíssima voluntad, 91). In this sentence the meaning of "llamamiento" must be rightly assessed. Noun and verb are used five times when the exercitant contemplates the vocation of the apostles, but "vocación" is used almost in the same breath (275). Similarly, in this exercise we find "vocación" and even "petición" (95, 94), both nouns referring to Christ's *llamamiento*. The call proceeds from the preaching which is mentioned in the first prelude: it would be impossible to listen to the preaching of Christ and to remain deaf to the call which it is meant to convey. This explains the expression which may sound as an anticlimax: to be prompt and diligent to accomplish His most holy will. Why did Ignatius not write something like: but prompt and generous to accept the call whatever it may entail? The answer is that the exercitant, knowing himself well at the end of the first week, is anxious to receive the grace of discerning the call that proceeds from the teaching and preaching of Christ. This is a call to fulfill the will of God in the first place; it is a call to acknowledge Christ as *Lord*.

The Marietti edition of the text of the *Spiritual Exercises* places at the top of the page "Del Reino de Cristo." The autograph text nowhere speaks of the Kingdom of Christ. It calls the exercise "del Rey." We even have to be careful with this expression. It is not very important. When the exercitant makes this exercise, he reads "Rey" twice in the title (91). The word is not new to him, because throughout the first week, every morning on rising, he compared himself to a knight about to appear before his king (74). In the parable the word occurs four times. But in the two preludes the word "Señor" is used. In the application of the parable to Christ "Rey eterno" is found twice (95, 97); each time it is accompanied by "Señor." The oblation is made to the *Señor eterno* (98), which accords with the advice to apply the example of the temporal *king* to Christ our *Lord* (95). After this exercise the word "Rey" does not occur any more.

The two preludes follow immediately upon the meditation on hell. In this exercise the exercitant prayed to the Eternal *Lord* (65), and talked matters over with Christ our *Lord* (71). Evidently, Christ remains the Lord when and if the exercitant makes the exercise "del Rey." There may not be much to choose between "Señor" and "Rey": they are not very divergent in meaning. The fact itself that Ignatius limits the use of "Rey" to this exercise and makes only moderate use of it, surely has its significance.

Parable and Application

The main part of the exercise completes the composition, and it is easy to guess in what direction this will take place. Knowing that he owes his continued existence to the Lord's patience, mercy, and goodness (71), the exercitant will turn from the benefit to the Benefactor. It is not the call in the sense of a very special appeal, exceptionally made to him, that dominates the exercise "del Rey." It is not a very special task for which he is chosen and called that lies at its heart. It harps on one string, namely, the goodness of the Lord. The key words of the parable and of the application are "Rey tan liberal y tan humano," which will echo in the expression "hermoso y gracioso" of the meditation on Two Standards (144). The text of the exercise does not primarily deal with the task set before the king nor with the way in which he is going to achieve success nor with the conditions of following and helping him. It deals with the king's utter unselfishness and total dedication to God, and this is in the end the main motive for going with him. In the parable the king does not explain how noble his undertaking is. He does not speak of results and does not urge his subjects to be generous because his cause deserves the greatest generosity. He states what he intends to do, and in his address it is the appeal of *tal rey* that should move and stir good subjects.

There can be one application only of this parable: it is to be convinced that it is worth while to look at Christ and before Him the whole world which He calls (95). Ignatius is somewhat illogical. True parallelism between the parable and its application requires this: if we consider the call to his subjects of the temporal king, we shall now consider the call of the Eternal King, or perhaps: how much more worthy of consideration it is to consider the call of the Eternal King. Ignatius shifts the emphasis from the call to the person who calls, and from the king to Christ the *Lord*. In the parable the call is marked by warmth and intimacy as the king talks with all his own (*habla* a todos los *suyos*). In the application there appears to be distance and aloofness: the King calls the whole world and each in particular, and says (llama y dice). The exercitant is impatient to contemplate the life, not the call, of the Eternal Lord. All his attention will be focused on the Person of Christ. Each day, early in the morning on rising and at the beginning and at the end of every exercise, he will beg that he may know the Lord better (130, 103, 109).

The exercise is not made obligatory by Ignatius. He is satisfied with a vague indication that the exercise is meant to be a help. If it is not, let it be omitted (91). If the exercitant dwells upon the *tanta piedad y misericordia* of God (71) during the five or six days that the first week may last, he will not require any elaboration of "Rey tan liberal y humano," and he cannot possibly fail to hear the appeal made to him by this King who is the Creator on the cross of the first exercise of the first week. Nor is he in need of any special admonition to cease being a *perverso cabellero* (94). He has been praying for help to amend his life from the moment that he asked what he would do for Christ (53). The exercise "del Rey" does not add much, if anything, to this disposition of the exercitant. For if he makes the exercise, he only considers what good subjects *will* do. It is significant that Ignatius drops the auxiliary verb "ought to" (deben), which he used in the parable, and substitutes for it the future tense (96, 97).

If the exercise be omitted, would the exercitant not be deprived of a very pronounced apostolic turn that is given to his life by the consideration of the parable and its application? There can be no doubt that tradition has used this exercise to make the exercitant aware of a vocation to the apostolate. But we have already pointed out how the call has to make way for the appeal made by the Person of the Eternal Lord and King. Besides, the exercise does not ask the exercitant to commit himself in any way to a task in furthering the interests of the kingdom. The oblation, as was said before, is not made by the exercitant. It will be made by those who are moved by love at a time that God thinks good. And when the oblation is made, apostolicity puts in a very modest appearance. An oblation "to imitate Christ in bearing insults" has little to do with conquering the world for God.

For another reason we have to be careful to understand this exercise correctly on this point. In the address made by Christ, Ignatius writes that it is Christ's will to conquer the whole world and all enemies (todo el mundo y todos los enemigos, 95). This word is spoken to the whole world and to each one in particular (todo el universo mundo, al qual y cada uno en particular llama y dice). "Todo el mundo" is used twice, once with reference to those who are asked to help the King, once with reference to those who have to be conquered. The whole world is invited to help the Lord in conquering this same world, no one excepted. Every man has to be conquered, and at the same time is called upon to conquer. To move away from the terminology of the parable and its application, the exercitant is asked to realize that he must be saved and at the same time is invited to save others; he is to be redeemed and at the same time is called to be co-redeemer with Christ. At the end of the first week, the exercitant is clearly aware of being in need of salvation. So much is proved by "up till now," to which we have referred a good number of times. The new element which comes to the fore in the exercise "del Rey" is that of co-redemption. But this is not to be isolated nor over-stressed, as we believe has been done in the past. His need of salvation will force the exercitant to contemplate his Saviour in order that greater knowledge might bring him to greater love, which is the proof of continued salvation. Greater love will lead him on to faithful service, and that is where he will share Christ's task of saving the human family.

After what has been said, it does not seem necessary to examine this exercise in further detail, and there does not seem to be any need to enlarge upon expressions in the text that have been made into catch phrases. In their Latin form they have become part of the spiritual outfit of many religious: "agere contra, magis affici, insignes se exhibere, oblatio maioris momenti, imitari Te in omni vituperio et omni paupertate tam actuali quam spirituali." They have often been given an interpretation which is incompatible with a correct reading of the text. Quite frequently they have been taken from their context, so that, for instance, "agere contra" has become rather distorted.[6] In general, they have not been related to what precedes in the first week and even less to what follows in the weeks to come. Yet all that is contained in the exercise "del Rey" will be found in the other weeks, but with its proper meaning, because in its proper setting. Thus, the wish to be moved by love (97) will become intense love, "to signalize oneself in every kind of service" will take on the shape of resemblance to Christ suffering, the King addressing His subjects will show Himself as the Lord sending His apostles and disciples to spread His sacred doctrine, to conquer the world will prove to be the same as helping everybody, and so on.

When the director decides that the exercise had better be omitted, it is not only the text, the structure, and the purpose that should be motives for doing so. The impact of the exercise is very much less nowadays than it was in the days of Ignatius. The reason for this is that, on the one hand, the Kingship of Christ has less appeal in our day and, on the other hand, the element of surprise in being called to be an apostle has gone, thanks to Catholic Action, the lay apostolate, and similar movements. We will return to this presently.

### "Magis Affici"

One expression must be singled out for special examination. The autograph text reads: "los que más se querrán affectar y señalar en todo servicio de su rey eterno y señor universal" (97). The *versio prima* reads: "qui magis desiderabunt insignes fieri" the *versio vulgata*: "ii, qui se obsequiis illius prorsus duxerint mancipandos," while Roothaan's translation is "ii qui magis affici volent," and to make the meaning clear he adds: "qui majori affectu esse volent." It is Roothaan's translation that has left its stamp on various modern translations, as for instance, that of Morris: "those who wish to show greater affection," or Puhl's: "those who wish to give greater proof of their love," or Mottola's: "those who wish to show the greatest affection." The French translation of Courel reads: "ceux qui voudront aimer davantage"; the German translation of Raitz von Frentz: "Jene, die eine grŏszere Hingabe üben," while Urs von Balthasar writes: "Jene, die sich mehr ergreifen lassen." In these translations "mâs" has been joined to "affectar," and it has been given the main stress. Thus an element of quite exceptional dedication has been introduced, which, to say the least, is not quite in keeping with the prayer to be said in all probability by the exercitant some three weeks later, where he does not go further than a very humble "give me Your love and Your grace" (234).

The true translation is given, as is often the case, by Rickaby: "they who shall be more desirous to show affection and signalize themselves in entire service of their King." This rendering brings out the point that "affectar" and "señalar" are on a par and that both are dependent upon "mâs querrân." Even more important is the fact that Rickaby did not overlook the contrast between "all those who have judgment and reason" (95) and the group mentioned in the paragraph under discussion. The opposition is certainly not between subjects of the Lord who are moved by love and those who wish to be moved by greater love. The contrast is between common sense as motive and love as motive. Consequently, the first group has before its mind the cause, and possibly the success promised together with a rich reward ("he will likewise follow Me in glory"), the second is more desirous to fix all attention on the Person of the King, and wishes to be guided by love more than by anything else. And so, once again, it is not dedication and apostolate that lie at the base of this exercise, but the need and the wish to love the Lord.

When we leave "mâs" where Ignatius put it and do not confuse it with a comparative, the true reading suggests itself at once. Almost instinctively the verbs "affectar" and "señalar" will now be stressed, and there will not be any great danger of forgetting the future tense of the auxiliary verb "querrân," written, incidentally, in the third person plural. The exercitant considers the various attitudes that can be adopted to a royal invitation; spontaneously he will be drawn to those "who rather wish to be moved by love."

At the beginning of the following chapter we will show what new very wide dimensions are to be added to the exercitant's composition. In order to prepare the exercitant for this extension of his composition Ignatius inserts this transitional exercise. The exercitant accustoms himself to the fact that his life is caught up in that of the whole human family all over the world, that Almighty God is very much concerned not merely about saving him, the exercitant, but saving everybody, that God's designs are opposed by enemies, and so on. Where the exercitant today appears to be much more aware of these wide dimensions and these startling facts (the whole world has been thrown open to him through modern technique, and the civilization in which he lives is no longer Christian in the sense in which it was so at the end of the Middle Ages and the beginning of modern times), the need for this transitional exercise seems to be proportionately less. Moreover, the parable of king and conquest, of knights and soldiers following him, does not have the same appeal today. This is not so much because kings and knights belong to another epoch altogether, but much more because the underlying reality of conquest, namely apostolate, is nothing new to this generation, whereas it was very new to the Christians in the days of Ignatius. The exercise is meant to be a help, and, consequently, when it does not help, it would be better to omit it. No harm will be done, provided the final meditations of the first week and the first contemplations of the second week are understood and given correctly.

We are well aware of having deviated considerably from the traditional interpretation of this exercise. In our opinion it is not solidly founded upon the text. It can hardly be absolved from the charge that in essential points it violates the freedom of the exercitant; and the fifteenth and seventeenth annotations stress how much this must be safeguarded by the director. There has been in the past too much pressure, too much insistence upon an oblation to be made now, at this stage of the Exercises, irrespective of whether the exercitant is ready for it or not. There has been too much stressing of "agere contra," and the exercise, by the manner in which it was presented, has given the impression that no loophole was to be left to the exercitant: he was to be forced into the army of Christ, or otherwise he would be considered a useless Christian, a *perverso caballero*. Overemphasis of these and similar points went hand in hand with a rather serious distortion of the image of Christ and of the Father, who sent Him. It has fixed upon the spirituality of the Spiritual Exercises the stamp of the military, and it has been responsible for an overestimation of the ascetical at the expense of the mystical.

eight

# THE SECOND WEEK: THE FIRST HALF

There is no break between the first and the second week. The first week is not introductory or preparatory. It is not true that the retreat only starts properly with the second week. It continues smoothly and evenly. Yet when the second week begins, wholly new dimensions are placed before the exercitant. Some of them may have largely disappeared, some of them may have become blurred, some may have lost their importance for the exercitant. Whatever the case may be, the exercitant must now be made fully aware of them and integrate them into his composition. These new dimensions are obvious as soon as the text is taken in hand.

First: the exercitant is brought face to face with the Blessed Trinity. This mystery played its part in the first week, but almost incidentally, as when in the colloquy of the repetition and resumption the exercitant addressed the Blessed Virgin, then the Son, and finally the Father; there is no explicit mention of the Trinity, and the Holy Spirit is not named at all. In the second week, the primary object of all contemplations is the mystery of the Trinity.

Second: the exercitant now knows himself to be surrounded by the whole human family, of all times and of all places, of every race, of every form of civilization, and so on. Indeed, in the first week the exercitant came to realize that angels and saints prayed and protected him and he discovered that the heavens, sun, moon and stars, fruits, birds, fishes, and other animals had been at his service (60). But, enumerating these creatures, man himself seemed almost purposely omitted. In a certain sense, the exercitant might almost have been a sole survivor of an extinguished race. Now, however, he knows himself to be in this world full of men (102), with so many divers races (103), such a variety of persons in all sorts of circumstances and conditions (106), scattered over the whole extent and surface of the earth (103). He knows that he belongs to this family, that he is one of its members.

Third, he realizes that he is drawn into the relationship that exists between the Trinity and mankind. He is caught up with the human family acting in a certain manner by thought, word, and deed, and thereby moving forward to its own destruction. At the same time he shares mankind's relationship with one God in three Persons. The exercitant reacts to this knowledge and thus works out his decisions. Ignatius allows at least three days for him to grow accustomed to these new dimensions.

Preludes

In the first prelude, which is the history, Ignatius refers to the surface and circuit of the earth, filled with human beings. He returns to it five times, which is remarkable for a man of few words as he was. He is not satisfied with the expression which he used in the First Principle and Foundation; "haz de la tierra" does occur (106, 107, 108), but now he has recourse to "planicia" (102), "redondez" (102, 103, 106), and "capacidad" (103) to impress upon the exercitant the evidently important part played by *todo el mundo* (102). This is not enough. He draws attention to the human race (102), to all the nations (106), and all the people on this earth (106, 107, 108), and he makes mention of their color, dress, behavior, health, age, and emotions (106). The exercitant is asked to draw a detailed picture of the human family. The varied details concern what is perceptible to the senses. Underneath the rich variety of details there is a certain uniformity. A closer look reveals how the people in this world are all the same, all on their way to death and hell, and consequently all badly in need of salvation (102, 106). The cause of this sad situation is that they have rejected and cast out their Lord and Creator. Indeed, Ignatius does not expressly state this. But among the varied activities of all the people on the face of the whole earth, no mention at all is made of their worshipping and serving God. On the contrary, they are depicted as swearing and blaspheming (107), as wounding and killing each other (108). Ignatius takes this situation for granted, he does not prove that such is the actual situation of fallen mankind. It has been part of the exercitant's composition ever since the first exercise, with its colloquy directed to the Creator on the cross, to the Creator, that is, for whom there is no room in this world.

What has been said so far about this prelude can hardly be "history" in the technical sense which the word has in the first prelude. History in this sense is to make present "how the Three Divine Persons look upon the whole expanse of the earth filled with human beings" (102). Furthermore, it is to make present how They do not remain unmoved and will not leave mankind to its own resources but decide to save the human race; how the decision takes shape and the

Second Person will become Man; how God waits for the fullness of time and then sends Gabriel to a little village called Nazareth. We have used the expression "to make present" before, when we were explaining what Ignatius meant by this first prelude. Here is the place to concentrate on how the exercitant is made present to the mystery which he is to contemplate. Ignatius tells the exercitant to take the New Testament. It is the word of God, telling the exercitant about God's Son. In the second chapter a brief exposition was given of telling and listening to a story well told: how the past is made present and how both narrator and listener share all the joys and sorrows of him or her whose story is being told. The story is never the same as a series of events and incidents: it is the why and wherefore, the way in which these events affect the person, the way in which he reacts, and so forth, that make the story. This is the reason why Ignatius asks the exercitant not to forget about the many things that happened before the angel was sent to Nazareth. This is not just a historical event: it was prompted by a decision and this decision was the result of a certain situation to which God reacted in a certain way.

In other words, one cannot understand the word spoken by God, unless one is acquainted with the background of the story He is going to tell. The exercitant cannot do much with information, if he is to contemplate God's mysteries. The first prelude, consequently, is primarily an activity of God Himself, addressing the exercitant and telling him about Himself and His Son, whom He sent into this world. It is what we read in the fifteenth annotation come true again.

The word of God must not be read, it must be carefully listened to and pondered. As the words counted in numbers are scarce, the exercitant should pay most careful attention to every single word of God. They are all charged with meaning. He should be aware of the fact that the word of God has taken on form in the language of the early Christians, most of them convert Jews, and he should understand it as it was understood by them. It is only then that the story comes to life, and it is only then that he can be made present to the mystery that is being narrated.

The exercitant and the director should here give some thought to the use of the Old Testament as well as the books of the New Testament, outside of the Four Gospels. These are not mentioned in the Spiritual Exercises, and, as we remarked at the end of our first chapter, the text of these parts of the Bible did not play any part in Ignatius' conversion, as far as can be ascertained. It is unlikely that he used them at Manresa. Copies of the whole Bible were relatively rare at that time. We live in happier times from that point of view. If Ignatius makes his exercitant take the New Testament in hand as soon as God is going to tell him all about His Son, there can be no doubt that today he would make him listen to the word of God as spoken in the pages of Old and New Testaments. Both director and exercitant would seem to show a lack of loyalty toward the Spiritual Exercises, if they were to give or make—to illustrate this by means of two examples—the contemplation on Christ's Baptism without reading the fortieth and forty-first chapters of Isaiah, or the meditation on Two Standards without reading the twelfth and thirteenth chapters of the Book of the Apocalypse.

The first prelude runs smoothly into the second, which is the "composition by seeing the place." Simultaneously with the history, the exercitant will see the whole face of the earth inhabited by so many different people, and he will see Mary's house and room in Nazareth (103). In this way the mystery is made present reality to him, and he is fascinated by what he is witnessing. He will feel the need to ask for understanding and insight into the mystery. At the same time there will be the desire to stay where he is and make himself familiar with the mystery in which he finds himself. Hence, he will make the third prelude, in which he will ask that he may know the Lord made Man (104), and then he will move on to what are called the points of the contemplation. We repeat what we gave as our opinion in the fourth chapter: the three preludes take time and probably will take up the greater part of the first exercise.

The Points

The three points are an elaboration of the preludes. The exercitant dwells upon that which has been made present to him. Ignatius uses the verbs "to see, to consider, and to look carefully" (ver, considerar, mirar), and in the contemplation on the Nativity he adds "to contemplate" and "to observe" (contemplar, advertir, 114, 115). Details are now carefully observed. Thus, there is a marked contrast between "las personas divinas" and "las personas sobre la haz de la tierra," which is found at the beginning of each of the three points. To drive home the details, the opposition *unos-otros* occurs no less than six times. But as in the preludes, the exercitant is not asked to direct his attention to two objects, namely, God and the human family. He is present at the interplay, as it were, between God and mankind, and so he dwells upon "*cômo* las tres personas divinas miran toda la haz de la tierra" (106), as he does in the second and third points. Above all, he dwells more explicitly upon God's reaction and decision. The key word deserving every attention is "in so much blindness" (en tanta ceguedad, 106). The word "malicia" might have been the obvious choice where Ignatius deals with the reaction of God, watching mankind on its way to perdition. Ignatius wants the exercitant to realize that God does not see man's malice so much as his blindness. The word carries overtones of an explanation, almost of an excuse. A blind man cannot see, cannot know God. It is then to be expected that God will let the light shine and take away the blindness. He will show what He is really like, He will appear among men as God-made-Man, make Himself understandable in terms of human behavior, human words and actions, and so on. It foreshadows the oft-repeated prayer of the exercitant that he may know Him; it is because he does not know Him that there is little love. There is no way to win back the bride except by God showing what He is like. That is why Christ was sent into the world, that is what God is going to talk about in the contemplations.

The preludes open the door into the mystery; the points that follow are like dwelling there. Gradually the exercitant penetrates the mystery, and as things become clearer, he knows to what great extent he is himself involved. In the prelude Ignatius writes of the Second Person becoming Man (102); at the end of the contemplation he speaks of God *just now* made Man for him. It is true that Ignatius does not actually insert in the colloquy "por mí"; he did so, however, in the third prelude, that is, the prayer. But the colloquy is a matter of thinking over what the exercitant ought to say (pensando lo que debo hablar, 109). The unexpected insertion and choice of "pensar" points to the fact that the exercitant is overwhelmed by the impact of the mystery: it is too much and he really does not know what to say. He has reached the point where he should speak and talk to the Three Divine Persons, to the Incarnate Word, to His Mother, but he cannot find the words. Ignatius is not going to give him much help. "According to what he feels" is rather vague, and Ignatius only adds that he must be practical and keep in mind following and imitating the Lord.

The preludes and the points constitute the contemplation, every contemplation. Two important conclusions should be stressed. First, from now onward, the Spiritual Exercises are explicitly Trinitarian. There can be no contemplation which is not first and foremost a contemplation of the Blessed Trinity. There is no great danger of losing sight of this fact, provided the contemplation on the Incarnation is taken to be an example, as are the contemplation on the Nativity and the first contemplations of the third and fourth weeks. The first note of the second week contains the remark that the preparatory prayer and the preludes should be prefixed to the exercise "as these have all been explained in the contemplations on the Incarnation and the Nativity" (159). As far as the exercises of the third week are concerned, Ignatius says that the form to be observed is the same as that given and explained in the second week (204). From the directory of González Dávila we learn that these contemplations on the Incarnation and the Nativity must be explained in a special way, because all the others follow their pattern (porque a la forma dellas van todas las demas, *Dir.*, 509) and the same advice is given by Cordeses (*ibid.*, 548). Second, all the contemplations to follow will have for their subject matter not incidents in the life of Christ but mysteries. Ignatius is most careful to speak of mysteries whenever he is dealing with events in Christ's life.[1]

The difference between mystery and historical event will have become clear from what we have said in the fourth chapter and in this chapter. The events or incidents are never more than the mystery made perceptible to the senses. The historical facts are the human expression of the mystery that stretches back into the life of God Himself, that is, into all that happens by Him and to Him, beyond this moment and beyond this place. It is only because the *mystery* is made present to the retreatant that in a very real sense he can pray to the Word *recently* made Man (109), that he can move about in the cave of Bethlehem to such an extent that he will give what help he can, making himself a little unworthy slave (114), even kiss the place where Mary and Joseph have stood (125), and that he can smell the infinite fragrance and taste the infinite sweetness of the Divinity (124).

The mystery is far more important than its form in history. The incidents, consequently, play a secondary part only. Ignatius does not give the exercitant a course of contemplations covering the whole life of Christ. There are only two "events" for each of the first three days; these suffice for the whole of Christ's hidden life. The four or five days allotted to the second part of this week have for subject matter one event each day. This means that the public life of Christ is reduced to a handful of events. But not only this: it is of relatively slight importance whether or not an event is contemplated in all its details; there is no question of an exhaustive treatment. More than once the exercitant is told not to move on to another point until he feels satisfied (2, 76, 118). He is even advised to return to the incidents already contemplated (130), and there is no sense in reading or considering any other mystery than the one he is contemplating on this day (127).

It is not easy to be fully aware how real and intense the re-*present*ation of the mystery of the Trinity is according to Ignatius. The exercitant has even to be warned against the danger of becoming completely absorbed by it and lost in it. The warning is given in the third prelude: the exercitant asks for a greater knowledge of God, in order that this knowledge might lead to love, and this love might lead to closer following of the Lord (104). It is for this reason that, somewhat prosaically, Ignatius in the two examples of the contemplations on the Incarnation and the Nativity tells the exercitant "to reflect and to draw fruit" no fewer than six times, and a similar expression is used four times in the final contemplation of the day, called the application of the senses. There is no indication in the text of the *Exercises* that Ignatius wanted the contemplations of the exercitant to be practical or that he desired to give them an apostolic turn. "To draw fruit" (sacar provecho) implies that the exercitant must somehow profit by what he has seen or heard or witnessed. It seems quite clear from the third prelude, which precedes these admonitions, all of them found in the points of the contemplation and the colloquy which follows them, that profit means knowledge that moves to love and imitation.

Two Types of Contemplation

The text shows that the technique, if this word be permitted, of the contemplations on the Incarnation and the Nativity is different. When two examples of contemplating the mystery of Christ's life are given it is unlikely that the second is a duplicate of the first. It is reasonable to suppose that they represent two different ways of making a contemplation.

The contemplation on the Incarnation relies on contrasting certain realities. The exercitant looks at the Three Divine Persons, at the human race, and at the persons directly involved in the event of the Incarnation. He listens to what each of these "parties" says and watches what each does. His gaze shifts repeatedly from the Trinity to the members of the human family, and from mankind to the angel and the Virgin in Nazareth. In doing so he becomes conscious of the contrasts that are involved. What holds his attention is the play, and the scenery where it unfolds. In the second contemplation on the Nativity, these broad dimensions of the Trinity and the world make way for something more homely. The first prelude confines itself to Mary and Joseph as they come down from Nazareth on their way to Bethlehem, where the Child is born and where the angels sing. The composition is in harmony with this history, and the exercitant will see the road, the fields and the cave. The attention is concentrated more directly upon the actors and the acting than upon the play itself.

In the contemplation on the Incarnation, the mystery of salvation and redemption is central. The exercitant contemplates God deciding to redeem mankind, choosing a mother, sending His angel, and so forth. The contemplation on the Nativity stresses the Saviour and the Redeemer. Hence, the first contemplation is more majestic, the second more intimate. There is grandeur and splendor in the former, there is warmth and lowliness in the latter. A detail such as the little donkey in the contemplation on the Nativity would be out of place in that on the Incarnation, in which there is no room for a "como se puede meditar pîamente" (111). The exercitant can be a poor unworthy little slave in the contemplation on the Nativity; he would not feel at home as such in the contemplation on the Incarnation. This explains "todo esto por mî," which contains a strong personal appeal to the exercitant in the former (116).

The shift of emphasis from the play to the actors, from redemption to the Redeemer, is also mirrored in the contemplative activities of the exercitant. We referred to this in a general way above, but a more detailed examination is instructive. In the first contemplation the exercitant is asked to see and consider (106), to hear (107), and to look closely (108). Basically this set of activities is found in the second contemplation, but there are important additions. Thus, in the first point, he will not only see the Virgin and St. Joseph, but he will look attentively, contemplate, and even attend them in their necessities (mirândolos, contemplândolos y serviêndolos en sus necessidades,

114). In the second point, he is not asked to listen, but to consider, observe, and contemplate what is being said (mirar, advertir y contemplar, 115). In the third point, we read "mirar y considerar lo que hacen" (116). Evidently, the exercitant is much more engaged; the impression is given that he is almost a fellow-actor. Rather significant is the slight change in the advice given by Ignatius. In the contemplation on the Incarnation, the exercitant is told "to reflect in order to derive profit" (refletir para sacar provecho). In the first and second points of the contemplation on the Nativity, the advice is "to reflect *upon myself* in order to derive profit" (reflectir en mí mismo, 114, 115). It makes the exercise more personal. The third point does not tell the exercitant to make this act of self-reflection; Ignatius did not feel the need to add this advice now, as "reflitiendo" is immediately preceded by "todo esto por mí."

Of interest it is to note that Ignatius speaks in this case of *spiritual* profit. In the third point, the exercitant occupied himself with the cave, already pointing to the cross, and the toil, the hunger, the thirst, the heat and the cold, the insults and the reproaches that lie in between. There is a temptation for the exercitant to move away from these unpleasant considerations, and so Ignatius stresses the fact that he, the exercitant, must derive some *spiritual* profit.

The two examples provide different methods of making a contemplation, and the exercitant is expected to employ them both. Traditionally, the contemplations on the Incarnation and the Nativity have been considered introductions rather than examples. Consequently, the proper method of contemplating has been derived in a very one-sided way from the contemplation on the Nativity. This one-sided view has eliminated from the Spiritual Exercises not only the mystery of the Trinity as subject matter of all contemplations, but also that wide sweep of mankind that should play its part in every contemplation. The result has been that contemplation has often been reduced to a reflection upon the people encountered in the incident, or more accurately, upon the incident itself.

A faithful following of the Exercises makes use of both types of contemplation on the first three days of the second week. Ignatius does not give any indication which mystery of Christ's life lends itself to the first method, which to the second. Possibly the presentation in the Temple and Christ's obedience to His parents in Nazareth will be mysteries more suitable to be contemplated according to the pattern laid down in the contemplation on the Incarnation. The flight into Egypt and the incidents which took place in the Temple when Christ was twelve years of age require a method similar to that used in the contemplation on the Nativity, if only because the element of suffering and toil is rather conspicuous in these two mysteries.

The two methods must not be kept separate. For, when the exercitant is contemplating the actors, he is present at the play, and there can never be a play without the actors. In the third and fourth contemplations, which are the two repetitions, the exercitant is expected to be occupied with the play, the acting, and the actors. After a few more days, the exercitant will contemplate each mystery in the two different ways explained; there will only be one mystery for each day.

Application of the Senses

Pursuing the useful metaphor of the play and the actors, one might say that the fifth exercise of each day asks the exercitant to have a good look at the stage itself, this in the widest sense of the word, including the costumes worn by the actors. Having spent a day in contemplating the mystery and having been with the persons "as if he were present," he has become very familiar with what takes place in the mystery. He feels at home, and it is not surprising that visible and audible details now become significant. What is perceptible to the senses is to Ignatius not something merely external and material; it is part of the form of the mystery and very much one with it, just as body and soul are one. There is no fullness of mystery except the mystery is clothed in what is very human, namely, all those details that can be perceived by the senses. But it is only when the exercitant understands the mystery that he can understand its external aspects. If the expression used by Ignatius in this exercise, usually known as an application of the senses, is considered carefully, "traer los cinco sentidos" suggests that the exercitant make his senses present to the mystery, or make himself present to the mystery insofar as he is a creature of five senses. In this way the exercise completes the four preceding contemplations.

Well known is the controversy whether or not the application of the senses is a higher form of prayer than contemplation. Ignatius seems to be somewhat hesitant to call this exercise a contemplation. He speaks of "la tertia contemplación" and similarly, "la cuarta contemplación" (118, 120), but this is followed by "la quinta." However, one naturally adds "contemplación." The verb "contemplar" is used in the third point. Of greater importance is the fact that Ignatius does not insist on the application of the senses being made. He does not impose this exercise, which makes it unlikely that it is a very high form of prayer. It is a useful exercise, it may help (121).[2] Moreover, it does not seem probable that the scenery could ever be more important than the play and its actors, and that contemplation of the former would exceed contemplating the latter. Yet, not one of these and similar objections carries conviction. A satisfactory solution will not be found, the reason being that the question itself proceeds from the false idea that the application of the senses is an exercise different from the contemplations that precede it on the same day. In fact, it is contemplation continued, contemplation rounded off. Essentially the application of the senses implies that the exercitant, after long contemplations of the mystery, has become so familiar with it that its every detail grows meaningful, is lit up, as it were, from within. Whatever perfection of prayer may be reached in this fifth exercise of each day does not spring from the application of the senses but from the intensity of the preceding contemplation of the "como si presente me hallase" and of composing oneself and being united with the "Señor ansí nuevamente incarnado." The application of the senses may be compared with gathering the fruits; growing them is surely more important.[3]

## Closing Remarks

The additions of this second week need no discussion, except for two expressions, both occurring in the second addition. Immediately on rising, the exercitant is to place before himself the contemplation he is going to make, desiring to know better the Eternal Word Incarnate (130). It is this desire to know the Lord better with which he is predominantly occupied from the early morning right through the day. Four or five times each day he will pray to know the Lord more intimately, as we read in the third prelude of each exercise. Behind this prayer is an ardent longing for knowledge of the Lord, which makes imperative the stressing of the word "mâs" in the second addition and of "interno" preceding "conoscimiento" in the third prelude.

Regarding the second expression, we notice how the third prelude has the combination "amar—seguir" (para que mâs le ame y le siga). In the second addition Ignatius prefers "servir—seguir" (para mâs le servir y seguir). The change is self-explanatory as soon as it is remembered that in the second addition the exercitant is not yet contemplating; he is on his way to his contemplation, and so the more businesslike and practical "servir" takes the place of the more contemplative and more effective "amar." Interesting and instructive is the change made in the colloquy, where Ignatius uses the combination "seguir—imitar" (para mâs seguir e imitar, 109). The choice of "imitar" sounds rather unfortunate. Somehow, it grates in the context of the contemplations. It does not seem to harmonize very well with the composition of the exercitant, who is concerned with greater knowledge and love of the Lord, and with joining Him, following Him, going with Him, words that echo from the exercise "del Rey" (93, 95). He is not much interested in the exemplarism that is suggested by "imitar." It occurs where, of all places, one would least expect it; the high degree of prayer of the colloquy and its "hablar" look incompatible with the down-to-earth question of imitation. But Ignatius, accurate as he always is, had no other choice. The colloquy always implies that *this* man is conversing and talking things over with God. If the colloquy is the height of prayer, it is only so because it is the height of truth and order. Hence, in every colloquy the exercitant is being very practical in the midst of his intimate conversations with his Lord. There is a continuous line stretching from the first colloquy, in which the exercitant asks what he ought to do (53), through the second, in which he resolves to amend his life for the future (61), and the triple colloquy with its stress on overcoming disorder (63), to the colloquy following the meditation on hell, with its implied warning that faith must be accompanied by good works (71), and hence to the colloquies of the second week. In the colloquies of the third week, the combination of intense contemplation and very practical decisions will assert itself inescapably to the exercitant.

"Imitar" must not be isolated from "seguir," nor must it be thought to be of greater importance. The latter verb denotes the disposition which is the source of good actions. But these good actions are precisely those in and through which the exercitant *imitates* Christ. Hence, in this first half of the second week, "seguir" is used three times (104, 130), whereas "imitar" is found only once (104). Thus, "seguir" is employed by Ignatius when he writes of the apostles being called to follow Christ (175, 275), but as soon as the exercitant of whatever annotation, the eighteenth, nineteenth, or twentieth, is asked to put the following of Christ into practice, "imitar" appears in the text. The meditation on Two Standards has it (139), as do those on Three Classes of Men (147) and the third kind of humility with its subsequent note (167, 168). That it is found in the rules for food and drink (214) and in the examination of conscience, as given in the first method of prayer (247), is expected.

A detailed examination of preludes, points, additions, of single words and combinations of terms, and so forth, must not result in not seeing the wood for the trees or in taking means for the end. Hence, it is well to recall the sixth annotation. The essential activity consists in the exercitant's experience of consolations or desolations, and in his being agitated by divers spirits. If there is little or nothing of this, he must be questioned about the Exercises, whether he makes them at the right times, and how, and also if he observes the additions (6). The annotation shows the importance of the directions given by Ignatius. They are meant to be a help in order that the cooperation between the Creator and His creature might take place the more surely (16).

nine

# TWO STANDARDS AND THREE CLASSES OF MEN

Two contemplations are singled out by Ignatius for special mention. They are the exercises of the third day of the second week. Their subject matter is "how the Child Jesus was obedient to His parents at Nazareth" and "how He remained in the Temple, leaving His adopted father and His natural mother to devote Himself exclusively to the service of His Divine Father" (134, 135). They bring up the matter of the election of a state of life, for Christ's obedience to His parents is an example of the state of life which consists in observing the Commandments, while by staying behind in the Temple, Christ gave an example of the second state of life, which is that of evangelical perfection. These words are written by Ignatius after the contemplations have been made. They are found not when he introduces the third day, but when the fourth day is made the subject of certain instructions. This suggests that he does not want his exercitant to occupy himself with the question of an election till after the two contemplations have been made. He merely points out that no exercitant contemplating the hidden life of Christ can avoid facing the fact that there are two possible ways of Christian life, and so he "will investigate and ask in what kind of life or in what state the Divine Majesty wishes to make use of him" (135). Attention must be paid to the choice of the word "investigar," found in unexpected proximity to "demandar." It proves that finding the will of God always demands cooperation between God and His creature. Neither should it escape attention that Ignatius is once again inspired by, and clearly refers to, the fundamental and very important fifth annotation: it is the Divine Majesty who wishes *to make use of* (se servir) the person of the exercitant.

This investigation does not upset or even change the smooth order of the retreat. The exercitant will continue to contemplate the life of Christ, but also he will turn his attention to the question of various states of life and of making a choice. If a choice has to be made, that is. It is possible that the exercitant has already placed himself in one of the two states of life: he is married or he is a religious. In this case there is no room for further investigation into this matter. But the introduction given by Ignatius to this investigation overleaps its bounds at once, because ultimately it is not a question of making an election or not, but of disposing oneself in order to arrive at perfection in whichever kind of life or state (135). Hence, there must be no restricting the exercises that are to come, to a method for arriving at a sound choice of a state or way of life. The exercitant is asked to attend to his disposition, to that disposition which most surely and safely leads him to perfection. Be it noted that the new element introduced here by Ignatius is not that of perfection: in the twentieth annotation the desire for nothing less than perfection is said to be the foundation of the exercises. It is the road the exercitant has to go to reach perfection that is now of the utmost importance. At this point one might perhaps expect Ignatius to have given a well-composed packet, so to say, of very practical advice: do this, and you are on the right road to perfection. This would have been falling into the trap which he is always very careful to avoid, namely, to direct people according to one fixed pattern, as if the detailed will of God is the same for everybody, as if God does not take into account character, talents, tasks, and so on, of each individual person. Ignatius consequently remains as little practical as ever. He will try to give his exercitant some insight into what life is really about. What has been contemplated so far does not embrace the fullness of reality. Much more is going on than has been unfolded up till now. He wants his exercitant to attend carefully to the intention of Christ his Lord, which by itself is not a very startling suggestion. But it is followed by the admonition to turn his attention also to the intention of "the enemy of human nature." This is something new, and to Ignatius something frightening.

## Two Standards

The exercise on Two Standards is a meditation. This is to be expected since its purpose is to gain insight into what is happening in this world. The first prelude, which is the history, makes it at once clear that there is more to life than merely being saved by God. If history proves anything, it demonstrates how bitterly Satan is opposed to this mission of God's Son. There is a battle being waged for the love and loyalty of man. Christ calls and wants all men under His standard; similarly, Satan tries to gather all men under his. By means of the composition, the exercitant realizes how he belongs to this world. He will see the place, that is, the whole world, now not only "the great extent of the earth, inhabited by so many different peoples" as he saw it in the contemplation on the Incarnation (103). It is now like a battlefield, made up of two regions, one reserved for those who acknowledge Christ as their Leader, one for the enemies whose head is Lucifer. Both the exercitant and the student of the Spiritual Exercises must not permit the somewhat flamboyant imagery of the exercise, although founded upon Scripture, to turn their attention from the essential facts. The whole surface of the earth, which the exercitant scanned and considered in the contemplations of the first three days, is now seen not only to be peopled by men of all races, civilizations, and so forth, but also to be divided between good men and enemies, *buenos* and *enemigos*. This is immediately related to the presence of Satan and his fallen angels, who "overlook no province, no place, no state of life, no individual" (141). Apparently, their presence is easily detected; the rather fearful imagery of smoking thrones of fire suggests that it is impossible to miss the existence and the presence of the evil spirits (140). This may raise a question. If fraud and deceit are the usual weapons used by Satan and if workers of fraud and deceit prefer to pass unnoticed, so that it is an arduous task to discover Satan's presence, as Ignatius is only too anxious to point out in his rules for the discernment of spirits, why, then, the plain of Babylon, the throne of fire and smoke, and Satan's appearance inspiring horror and terror (140)? To answer this question, it is necessary to be well aware that the exercitant is making the preludes to the meditation. The history and the composition unfold to him what life really is, and for the moment he is faced by the fact that Satan is and that he is active; the methods adopted by him as the enemy of human nature do not concern the exercitant yet. That Satan is and that he is active have to be driven home. Not that the exercitant of Ignatius' day did not believe in the existence of Satan: late medieval literature is full of references to Satan's presence. But people tended to see Satan as a figure of fun, hardly to be taken seriously. Ignatius knew that the exercitant's idea of Satan, and consequently his sense of reality, were badly in need of correction. So, Ignatius asks the exercitant to make these preludes and see this world as a battlefield, where Christ is not faced by a figure of fun at all, but by a being still wearing something of almost regal splendor and power. There is no mistaking the implication that he, the exercitant, is no match for this fallen angel. Ignatius has recourse to what we called flamboyant imagery in order to stress a very important aspect of man's life in this world.

By means of the two preludes the exercitant is brought to see a world full of men who are the object of divine compassion and at the same time the object of hatred by Satan, who as the enemy of human nature, hates whatever is human. God not only wants all men to be won back to His love; now He also wants them all under His standard, which means—and here we anticipate the second point of the second part of this meditation (145)—that He wants to send so many persons, apostles, disciples, and so forth, throughout the world in order to spread His sacred doctrine among all men. In other words, it is not merely the dimension of man being attacked by Satan that is added in the preludes but also that of God being in need of help in order that all men may hear His sacred doctrine. We underline this point, because traditionally the aspect of a battle going on has almost completely dominated the aspect of man being called to help God. At the back of the preludes there is a clear reference to the words of Scripture: "As the Father has sent Me, so now do I send you." It would be a bad mistake to restrict this mission to apostles and disciples; significantly, Ignatius adds *etc.* in his enumeration of those who are sent (145).

We have pointed out in a previous chapter that making the preludes is not a matter of a few moments but constitutes by itself the greater part of the first exercise. This is illustrated by the third prelude, the prayer that follows the history and the composition. The exercitant will ask for knowledge of the deceits of the rebel chief as well as for knowledge of the true life exemplified by Christ. This prayer proceeds from the belief in Satan's reality not as a figure of fun but as an enemy of human nature, who works in terms of beauty or friendship, who turns himself into an angel of light, whose deceits are not easy to discern. But this belief is the fruit of the first two preludes, and it takes time to develop and assert itself. It should also be noticed that the exercitant asks for knowledge of what is actually happening. Hence, the meditation is not a question of the director giving information about the ways and methods used by Satan and those used by Christ. True insight is a gift of God, for which the exercitant must pray.

Intention of Satan

The various parts, usually called the points, of any exercise are a further elaboration of the preludes. There can never be any break between preludes and points. The points are the preludes on a higher level of prayer. Hence, the description of the battle itself between Christ and Satan can never be explained in terms of expedience, as inducing the right disposition for making a choice in whatever state or way of life. The doctrine of Christ, for one thing, should be spread throughout the world; it is not given merely because it is useful for anyone faced with an important choice. On no account must the meditation on the intention of Christ and the intention of Satan be reduced to the instrumental function of making a sound election. Nor should it be interpreted as an immediate preparation for some sort of conversion. The intention and the sacred doctrine mentioned in this exercise derive their value from the truth that mankind is involved in a battle, and neither intention nor doctrine is conditioned by the external circumstance that the exercitant has to choose a state of life. There is no room for a utilitarian interpretation. In this case there would be a complete break between the preludes and the exercise proper, and the preludes would be little more than tricks.

If the intention and the doctrine are not drawn up by Ignatius *a posteriori*, in order to fit a certain situation, and if they are not shaped by the wish or urge to move the exercitant to choose what is more pleasing to Almighty God (151), two other interpretations have to be rejected. At the time of the Reformation there was considerable hunger for wealth in both Church and state, and it is not without good reason that Ignatius falls back upon the desire for an office or benefice as an example of inordinate attachments in the sixteenth annotation. But the conclusion is completely unwarranted that in this meditation Ignatius is moralizing against riches as the source of all evils and thus indirectly pleading for poverty as the one remedy. This opinion is very hard to reconcile with Ignatius' own experience during his ten months at Manresa and the time preceding them. There would never have been the many rules for the discernment of spirits if Satan's activity concentrated upon the matter of riches and poverty.

A second interpretation, also to be rejected, holds that Ignatius exploits the intentions of Christ and Satan as a sort of counterblast against the temper of his time. This was marked, as is generally admitted, by a spirit of independence and fostered by great achievements in the field of geographical discoveries, science, technique, the arts, and so forth. In this interpretation, the meditation on Two Standards is inspired by the deep stirrings that are associated with the Renaissance. Ignatius, clear-sighted as he was, was God's chosen instrument to stem the tide, and therefore he insisted on a predilection for dishonor and failure. Indeed, the Spiritual Exercises have undergone the influence of the time in which they were composed, just as Ignatius was undoubtedly and unavoidably a man of his time. It is going too far to maintain that the spirit and temper of the first half of the sixteenth century conditioned "the sacred doctrine" that apostles, disciples, and so forth, were to spread throughout the whole world. There would be something dishonest in having Christ Himself instructing His apostles and disciples with what, in fact, would be Ignatius' own ideas on how to convert the world. At the same time nothing less than Christ's sacred doctrine would be reduced to the category of useful means for combatting evil and Satanic influences. This is unacceptable.

Hence, what Ignatius gives as Christ's intention and doctrine has value that is for all men of all times, of all places, just as the intention of Satan is the same throughout the history of mankind. Only in this way can the essential link between the preludes and the points of the meditation be maintained. Any discussion, therefore, of the nature of the struggle in which the human family and its every member is involved must take its starting point from the fact and mystery that there is indeed a battle raging between God and Satan, and not from special circumstances of time and place. The battle must not be considered to be a useful expedient to illustrate certain ascetical opinions of Ignatius.

After this lengthy introduction, we turn our attention to the first part of the meditation. It deals with the intention or plans of Satan. It does not by any means come as a shock to learn that Satan leads men to great pride, and it seems exaggerated to have the exercitant pray earnestly for knowledge of what the enemy has in mind. If this is granted, with some important qualifications, about which more will be said in the course of this chapter, the legitimate conclusion is that the frauds and deceits, the difficulties and the subtlety of it all, are not bound up with pride but with the road that leads to pride. In short, why should riches and love of honor lead to pride, and, parallel with this, why should poverty and love of insults be the path to humility? Is there no other road both to the one and to the other? Does, in fact, Satan always follow this method? Is what Ignatius writes about Satan's intention indeed of universal application? An accurate reading and right understanding of the text will give the answer to these and similar questions.

The starting point of Satan's temptation is man's desire for riches. Ignatius does not use "deseo," but prefers the much stronger "cobdicia"; it does not occur elsewhere in the Spiritual Exercises. When Ignatius speaks of riches, he does not mean money in the first place. It is not money that makes a man rich. This is abundantly clear from what Ignatius means by spiritual poverty. Any parallelism between the intention of Christ and the intention of Satan would be completely destroyed if riches only or mainly stood for money, because without any doubt poverty certainly does not stand for lack of money. When in the sixteenth annotation Ignatius deals with some inordinate desires, no mention is made of money but of an office and a benefice. Financial advantages go along with these, but the essential element that makes an office and benefice so desirable is the security that they carry with them. Security is closely allied to independence, and it might clarify matters if it is recalled how "of independent means" has become synonymous with "rich."[1]

Taking this intense desire to be rich as his starting point, Satan tries to make man seek the honors of this world (142). The translation is not exact enough. The subtlety of the temptation lies in this that a rich man will the more easily *come to* or *attain* the honors of this world, honors which, according to Ignatius, are vain, worthless.[2] There is no question of *seeking* the honors of the world, but a man who has what he wants will naturally not be slighted nor passed by; there is no room for *menosprecio* (146) in his life. He will be judged a wise and prudent man in this world, according to the words of the third kind of humility (167). Ignatius does not condemn these honors of the world; they come one's way when one is rich and independent. But they are empty; one should not attach any value to them. Moreover, they are dangerous, because they easily lead to pride. It is worthy of note that nowhere does Ignatius maintain that Satan tempts man to pride or *to seek* the honors of the world. It is only stated that Satan takes as starting point of his temptations man's desire to be rich—in the sense explained above—and there is a strong suggestion that all the rest will follow: he will receive his share of the esteem of his fellow-men and he will turn into a proud man.

The remarkable thing about this procedure is that no action whatever is taken against God: He is not even mentioned. That is exactly where the subtlety comes in. Satan encourages the self-satisfied, independent man, who, therefore, thinks he is without need of God. It does not mean that this man is wicked, malicious, an infidel, that he now hates and detests God: nothing of the kind. In fact, he is not even said to be a sinful man. Ignatius adds significantly that only now Satan becomes truly active, "leading man to all other vices." Temptation now gives way to "inducir," and evil dispositions (vicios) put in their appearance, from which sins will sooner or later proceed.[3]

Where a mistake is likely to be made in this matter is when pride is taken to mean open rebellion against God, or even rejection of Him. Pride is very closely connected with self-sufficiency and hence with self-complacency. This is evident from the text of the first exercise of the first week, where falling into pride is said to be the result of refusing to help oneself by means of God's gifts. It is the refusal to acknowledge that one is in need of the help of God's gifts that, according to Ignatius, constitutes pride.

We have used the words self-sufficiency, self-complacency, and independence as intimately bound up with riches and pride. But the subtlety of Satan's intention does not lie in man's occupation with himself. The subtlety is found where this self-occupation gradually obscures and in the end obliterates the acknowledgment of the presence and even the existence of God. Self-occupation slowly but surely induces estrangement between man and God, till in the end God just does not mean a thing to him, as the expression goes. The framework of religious duties and practices may still be there; there is no question of man having turned to sinful actions, or of breaking the Commandments; by any standard he still gives the impression of being a good Christian. But he has become estranged from God. God has become a stranger to him. Such a man thinks he has no need of God, no use for Him.

It is not easy to understand why at this point Ignatius suddenly lashes out, as it were, when he writes of "overweening pride" (crescida soberbia). The word "crescida" is for Ignatius emotionally charged.[4] He is not exaggerating when he uses it in this context: it indicates the firmness of his conviction that what may look harmless and very human harbors in fact the worst disposition of man. Ignatius could never take a flattering view of man. There is no need to repeat what he wrote in the first exercises of the first week. It might be useful, however, to recall how he underlines man's utter dependence upon God, who not only kept him alive but goes on helping him through angels, fellow men, the elements, and so on (60). This man now allows himself to be led to pride, a pride which, in consequence, can only be swollen, unbounded, overweening. It will be difficult to understand the intention of Christ unless "crescida soberbia" is grasped with all its over- and undertones.

### Intention of Christ

The intention of Christ (136) is referred to as sacred doctrine in the second point of the second part of the meditation, and it is contained in the address which Christ makes to all His servants and friends (146). It is introduced by "por el contrario," which is what one expects. The two enemies do not fight in two different parts of the same field. It is a head-on clash, which is stressed by the threefold use of the word "contra" (146). The exercitant has been made familiar with such violent opposition from the beginning of the retreat when he was told in the thirteenth annotation to pray a little longer when being tempted or when in desolation, so as to accustom himself not only to resist the enemy but to overthrow him. When the rules for scruples are explained to him, he is advised to follow the same tactics. The expression now used is "hacer per diametrum contra la tentación" (351).[5] There is, then, no reason to be surprised that Christ will lead those under His standard to humility. Two questions require an answer: what exactly is humility according to Ignatius, and why are spiritual poverty and the desire for insults and contempt the road to humility?

The answer to the first question is given when Ignatius deals with three ways of being humble (164-67). Briefly, from what he says of the first way it appears that man's humility is obedience to God as his Lord and Master (165). From his description of the second way it is clear that humility eliminates man's own wish and desire as finally decisive where a choice is to be made (166). From the third we learn that the highest humility implies the desire to be like Christ, who is poor, despised, and deemed foolish (167). The factor common to these three kinds of humility is the rejection of self-occupation, self-sufficiency, self-complacency, in short, the elimination of self before God who is Lord yet died for man. It is exactly the opposite of pride.

The first step leading to this humility is spiritual poverty (142, 146). It is described in the sixteenth annotation, where it might be said to be the equivalent of right order. By means of examples its true nature is illustrated in the second and third classes of the meditation on Three Classes of Men. Here the direct opposite of spiritual poverty is expressed in the phrase, "God comes to what man desires" (de manera que allí venga Dios donde él quiere, 154), its true essence is stated in the phrase, "according as God our Lord shall give him to wish" (según que Dios le pondrá en voluntad, 155). That this spiritual poverty places man on the road to humility needs no proof.

One of the gravest difficulties in the Spiritual Exercises is the desire for *opprobrios y menosprecios*, twice mentioned in succession

(146) as the second step that leads to humility. It is an essential element of Christ's intention and sacred doctrine, and while spiritual poverty and humility have been commonplace terms in the ascetical and mystical literature of all ages, the desire for insults has hardly played a part.

One must not isolate this desire for insults and contempt. This not only because it is wedged in between spiritual poverty and humility, without which it will never be properly understood, but also because Ignatius is dealing with contrasts. The honor and esteem of the world, toward which the rich man is gradually and often almost imperceptibly guided by the evil spirits, strike Ignatius as false, because man is such a pitiable creature, what with his fallen condition, his utter dependence upon God and upon creatures, and his existence by the sheer grace of God. (Cfr. once again "tanta piedad y misericordia siempre hasta agora," 71). Therefore, so Ignatius appears to argue, man ought to long for the opposite of worldly honor as a simple matter of right order and truth.

This reply is not satisfactory. There remains an obstacle to any sincere, spontaneous acceptance, and this obstacle does not concern so much the insults and the contempt but the fact that man must want these: why the *desire* for them? Why is it not enough that man accepts insults when they come his way? To understand Ignatius on this point, one must go back to the exercise "del Rey" and the contemplations that follow it. In the "offering of great value" at the end of the exercise "del Rey," Ignatius writes about "an earnest desire and deliberate choice . . . to imitate Thee in bearing all wrongs and all abuse and all poverty, actual and spiritual" ("pasar todas injurias y todo vituperio y toda pobreza así actual como spiritual," 98). In the parable and its application there is only question of toil, vigil and pain (93, 95, 96, 97). At that stage, the exercitant was not asked to commit himself, as was explained in the chapter on this exercise. Matters change when the contemplation on the Nativity brings out the fact that Christ's Incarnation and mission into this world will actually involve a great deal of suffering. In addition to toil and poverty, hunger and thirst, heat and cold, Ignatius mentions insults and outrages (injurias y afrentas, 116). It must not be forgotten that the exercitant in the third prelude asked for the grace of faithfully following (not imitating) his Lord (113, 104). He is being prepared to follow Christ even where He will be slighted, despised, ignored, and so forth. Now, on this fourth day of the second week, "deseo de opprobrios y menosprecios" suddenly turns up, and the exercitant is not ready for it, as most directors will have experienced. Here it is of decisive importance to remember that the exercise on Two Standards is not a contemplation. It is a meditation, and the meditation rather objectively informs the exercitant what the sacred doctrine of his Lord implies. Or, more accurately, those who will help Christ will spread this doctrine of spiritual poverty, of the desire for insults and contempt, and of humility. There is, of course, an appeal to the exercitant to practice what he is going to preach. But it is an indirect appeal, and not even in the colloquy does Ignatius, as it were, hurry on and increase the pace. After all, the exercitant is thinking about a plan, a scheme, and in the colloquy he does not move beyond the request that he might be placed under the standard of Christ: it is a favor he begs for, not a generous resolution he makes here and now. Furthermore, it is the favor of being received under Christ's standard in poverty, and in *bearing* insults and wrongs (en pasar opprobrios y injurias, 147). The *desire* for insults and contempt has made way for a *readiness* to bear insults and wrongs. It does not mean that the sacred doctrine is set aside; but a certain mellowness asserts itself as soon as the exercitant has actually been confronted with the doctrine. This gentle method is sensed in the phrase immediately following, where the humble exercitant restricts his readiness to bear insults: he adds, "if I can suffer these without sin on the part of another." Ignatius continues in the same gentle way when in the meditation on Three Classes of Men he does not even refer to either the desire for insults or the readiness to bear them. He confines himself to the subject of poverty, thus giving the impression that for the present the exercitant has plenty to think about.

The desire for insults returns, and with a vengeance, in the exercise on three kinds of humility. At that point the exercitant cannot even stop short at the desire: he will have to *choose* insults. Even there the same mellowness and gentleness are found: the motive for desiring and choosing things that go against nature raises the problem to another level altogether, namely, to that of following and imitating Christ, who endured insults for the exercitant (167). The subject will be dealt with in a later chapter.

The main point, then, on this fourth day of the second week is the extension of the exercitant's composition, based on a more fully extended vision of God, Satan, and this world, and of himself as drawn into the conflict that is raging. The director should see to it that in accordance with the meditation on Two Standards there is a call made to the exercitant by Christ, who wishes to be helped. There is a rather shy answer to it, expressed in the form of a request (the colloquy). The exercitant asks for the grace to be received under Christ's standard, which means, if the imagery is dropped, the grace to be won over by Christ and the grace to assist Him in winning over his fellow men; all this in poverty, and in bearing insults and wrongs uncomplainingly. He does not worry about the conditions implicit in the appeal made to him, neither does he shut his eyes to these conditions. He prays and even adds "in order to imitate the Lord especially in these, that is, in poverty and in bearing insults" (por más en ellas le imitar, 147).

The exercise on Two Standards is marked not by enthusiasm but by seriousness. The new dimensions which the exercitant has to integrate into his composition are not only very extensive and almost too wide to hold within his grasp, they will also penetrate deeply into his very being. But there is as yet no question of making a personal offering to Christ the Leader. The fact that the word "Leader" (Capitán) is dropped as soon as it has been used in the preludes—in the points and the colloquy Christ is called "Señor"—should prevent the exercitant from making any hasty decisions: the wisdom of the fourteenth and fifteenth annotations guided Ignatius in the composition of this exercise on Two Standards. So in the end, the exercitant, realizing the seriousness of the new situation in which he finds himself, begs the favor and prays for the grace to be permitted to help Christ, for that is what is meant by being received under His standard. He can only help Christ on Christ's conditions, and these are not light. This explains the elaborate form of the colloquy: one does not rush into poverty, into the desire for insults, and so on. The exercitant goes to his *Señora* first. He made the same cautious advance when he was faced with the future in the first week. He was then much preoccupied with what truth, harmony, and order might have in store for him in days to come. Now his thoughts again turn to the future, seen in much wider perspectives. It is no longer a question only of detesting and avoiding sin, any form of disorder, and its cause, but of embracing a life of poverty, of patience in bearing injustice, and of true humility. As in the first week, the exercitant next goes to the Son and finally to the Father. Each time he makes a colloquy, the subject of which is a request: it is a question of talking over and discussing the favors desired.

The meditation on Two Standards is repeated three times. It is unavoidable that meditation turns into contemplation. It is no slip of the pen when Ignatius refers to these exercises as contemplations (156). Contemplation implies that the attention is shifted from the battlefield and the battle to the Leader, is shifted from simple historical fact to the mystery behind it, from the way in which the battle is fought to God who has an enemy, to God who is being thwarted in His designs and who is in need of help. Almost naturally the exercitant will turn his thoughts toward choosing what is better (149), toward what is more pleasing to the Divine Goodness (151). The contemplative elements of this exercise will play their own important part in the contemplations of the second half of this week.

## Three Classes of Men

In the seventh annotation the director is advised not to drive the exercitant too hard. So far from showing severity he should be kind and gentle, inspiring the exercitant with courage and strength for the future. This surely does not apply only to the times of desolation and temptation but also to the time when for whatever reason the exercitant yearns for encouragement. It would appear, however, that Ignatius himself hardly observes this rule, for he forces the exercitant, probably still somewhat dazed by the prospect of spiritual poverty and the desire for insults and contempt, to make the exercise on Three Classes of Men. The traditional interpretation of this exercise suggests severity: the time for decisions, and hard decisions at that, has come. There must be no trifling with the great sum of money that is a burden and an impediment, and the exercitant must seriously examine what his own *ten thousand ducats* consist in. It must be observed, however, that the exercise that closes the fourth day of this week is no more than a meditation, in a certain sense a step back, because the exercise on Two Standards had certainly reached the level of contemplation in the second or third repetition. Moreover, the meditative element of this exercise is slight. The word itself is not used, nor is "to consider," "to reflect," "to watch," (mirar) or similar verbs. All this is difficult to reconcile with the opinion that important decisions are now about to be made.

The body of the exercise is an elaboration of the first prelude, the history. There are no points in the usual sense of the word. Contrary to normal practice, the history is not introduced by "cômo."[6] Apparently, it is simply a matter of recalling everyday facts, which are further dwelt upon in the three parts of the exercise. Six people are involved in this piece of history, and the six fall into three groups. They are all rich and have worked hard for their riches. They are good Christians who would not think of risking eternal salvation for whatever reason, and they sincerely wish to find God in peace. The love of God plays its part in their lives, and they admit that they have failed insofar as this love of God has not been their only motive in becoming rich (no pura o dêbitamente por amor de Dios, 150). They feel somehow burdened and hampered, and they know the cause of the trouble: they are too much attached to their ten thousand ducats. And so the exercitant continues to watch what happens around him in this world. It is all straightforward enough, and there is no need to give any further explanation. It cannot escape the exercitant that the first group does not go to hell, although they really do nothing to get rid of the attachment for the sum of money they possess. The second class are in a worse disposition than the first, because they want God to come to what they desire: weakness is not so bad as cool calculation. The third class do not as yet give up their money; they keep it, awaiting God's decision. Meanwhile, they try to arrive at the necessary degree of detachment: they will rid themselves of the money *en affecto,* in desire (155).

The exercitant recalls this piece of human history, and he observes. He is not asked to judge, certainly not, to condemn. He merely notices that there are degrees and different ways of wanting a thing. He is faced with the fact that there are degrees of wanting to find God in peace, and degrees of wanting to get rid of the burden and impediment that riches constitute. It is on the one hand a matter of end and means, on the other one of weakness and calculation over against downright honesty and common sense. As far as the exercitant is concerned, nothing as yet happens. It is only in a note that follows the exercise that the meditation proves to be slightly more personal than was thought. There Ignatius writes: "When we feel any affection or repugnance to actual poverty, when we are not indifferent as regards poverty or riches . . ." (157). The text must be read correctly. Ignatius places a special stress on the personal pronoun "nosotros," thus indicating a personal application of this history. Besides, the sentence is not introduced by the conditional conjunction *if* but by the temporal conjunction *when* (quando). So, any commitment on the part of the exercitant is put off to some time in the future, probably to the days that lie ahead in this second or third week. We will return to this note later in this chapter.

There is great gentleness and patience in the exercise on Three Classes of Men. There is no trace of a violent attack launched against the poor exercitant. He is not asked to top the four exercises on Two Standards with some sort of vital decision. But the meditation has not yet been given in full. No mention has been made of the second and the third preludes, and there has been only a passing reference to the title of the exercise "in order to embrace what is better" (para abrazar el mejor, 149). As the title is meant to be a piece of advice for the director concerning the purpose of the exercise and does not immediately affect its structure and contents, it is wiser to begin a further investigation of this meditation with the second prelude.

The neutral position of the exercitant as a kind of spectator is badly shaken by the composition. This should be everybody's impression as soon as the text is read: "The second prelude is the composition by seeing the place: it will be here to see myself, how I stand before God our Lord and all His saints, that I may desire and know that which is more pleasing to His Divine Goodness" (151). It is well to give the autograph text, which states: "El 2º preámbulo, composición viendo el lugar: será aquí ver a mí mismo cómo estoy delante de Dios nuestro Señor y de todos sus sanctos, para desear y conoscer lo que sea más grato a la su divina bondad."

The exercitant is asked to make this composition by seeing the place. The place itself has evidently nothing to do with the history, which (as first prelude) precedes it; so far the composition always completed the history. The place in this composition is myself: there can be no doubt about it. Ignatius uses the verb "ver" twice, and its object is both "lugar" and "mí mismo."[7] It can only mean that somehow the exercitant makes himself a spectator of himself, an outsider to himself. Hence, there may not be that discrepancy between the first and the second prelude which seems so obvious at a first reading of the text. The object of the verb is the exercitant himself "how he stands in the presence of God and all His saints." The phrase lends itself to misinterpretation. Ignatius does not want the exercitant to make what is called an act of the presence of God. He must make an effort to realize that God and all His saints are present to him and that he moves in their presence. This is nothing new. The exercitant is made aware of it at the beginning of each exercise (75), has meditated upon this aspect of reality many a time in the first week (60), and on this day, the fourth day of the second week, he has been made familiar with the vision that the world he lives in is not merely peopled by men of various races, civilizations, and so forth, but is like the plain of Jerusalem, where Christ is seen, beautiful and attractive (144), surrounded by many persons, apostles, disciples, and so on (145). If, then, it is asked why in this composition the exercitant be not permitted to see Christ and those surrounding Him, to see God and all His saints, the answer is that the exercitant is making a meditation, not a contemplation. Thus, the second prelude does fit in with the first. Indeed, on the level of external events, those six people, the three classes, are really of no concern to the exercitant. But they move about in the same reality of the presence of God and all His saints as the exercitant: for those six people seek God in peace, as we are told in the history, and so does the exercitant.

The composition differs in another aspect from those that have gone before. Its purpose is given, namely, "in order to desire and to know what is more pleasing to the Divine Goodness." The choice of the words "pleasing" and "Goodness" is not unexpected, as was pointed out above. That the desire and knowledge goes hand in hand with the wish to receive the grace to choose in accordance with this desire and knowledge similarly causes no difficulty; in other words, the third prelude logically joins on to the second. The crucial point is that the exercitant appears to be faced with the notorious "magis." If Ignatius is seemingly so gentle and patient at this stage of the exercises, why then this urge towards what is better? He hammers it home, three times: in the title "to embrace what is better," in the second prelude "to desire and know what is more pleasing," in the third prelude "to choose what is more to the glory of God." It almost looks like an obsession.

One ought to remember that Ignatius did not write the text for the exercitant but first and foremost for the director. Accordingly, the two clauses introduced by "para" in the title and the second prelude (para abrazar el mejor; para desear y conoscer) contain advice meant for the director. Ignatius does not often indicate the purpose of an exercise or composition,[8] but then the meditation on Three Classes of Men is in nearly every respect so extraordinary and so uncommon that explanations are evidently needed. As far as the exercitant himself is concerned, the three thrusts are now reduced to one: he must ask for the grace to choose what is more to the glory of God. The director can keep silent about the purpose of the exercise and of the composition, but he should not in any way change or distort the third prelude. However, all this does not explain why Ignatius should introduce the "more" and the "better" at all.

A simple solution of this problem might be given by pointing out that in the introductory remark to the meditation on Two Standards, the word "perfection" was used: the exercitant will consider how he ought to dispose himself in order to arrive at perfection in whatever state or way of life (135). It will be objected that this remark has had little influence on this fourth day. The exercitant has been occupied not with perfection but with the battle that is raging around him and which he himself cannot escape. This is the clue wanted. For four full hours the exercitant has turned his mind to the intention of Christ and the intention of Satan, and all through the day he has been occupied with snares, deceits, and frauds as well as with doctrine that is subtle, high, and sublime. In the triple colloquy he has asked that he might be received under Christ's standard, but the prayer is not enough. Even when meditation has reached out to contemplation, there will always be a question left: what am I to do, and to do now, with this fight going on around me, at this very moment, and God needing my help? What the exercitant wants is guidance. As he has not got the knowledge nor, in all likelihood, the time or the ability to find out the frauds, snares, and deceits of the devil, Ignatius will help him with very practical advice, and it is: choose what is better, and do it wholeheartedly. He gives the exercitant a simple principle that will see him through the difficulties and problems that beset him. The same advice may be given in a negative form; it amounts to "do not calculate." (Cfr. the second class of men.) Consequently, the "aim high" of this exercise is meant to be a safe light to guide the exercitant through darkness and confusion, which are inseparable from the battle that constitutes in no mean measure the reality of the exercitant's composition. It is not the highest motive. Later the urge to desire, to know, and to choose what is better will be given a more perfect and more solid foundation.

Is what has been said about the urge toward what is better really an advance upon what is contained in the fifth and sixteenth annotations? It looks as if the desire to know and choose what is more pleasing to God is part of the initial disposition of the exercitant. Indeed, but by the end of the fourth day the exercitant cannot content himself with a right disposition. For, this very disposition is receiving only too careful attention from Satan. It is being explored and even attacked, as is explained in the last rule for the discernment of spirits, first series (327). Normally, the exercitant is not aware of this, and he certainly does not know how and where he is being attacked. He needs an effective weapon against these attacks, and this is now placed in his hands. Incidentally, the weapon has already been alluded to in the meditation on Two Standards. Ignatius there did not speak of spiritual poverty merely. Each time he wrote "*summa* pobreza spiritual" (146, 147), and the highest spiritual poverty entails embracing what is better, what is more pleasing to God.

Once again, not much happens in this exercise on Three Classes of Men, or on this fourth day as a whole. This is as it should be on a day of meditations in which the contemplative element is slight and unobtrusive. This is further illustrated by the last colloquy of the day: it is the same as the first. It is hard to agree with those who want the exercitant to make decisions, who want him to adapt the exercise by substituting health or success for the ten thousand ducats of the three classes. The official *Directory* changes the three groups of rich merchants into three groups of sick people: they all wish to be cured, but the first group do not take the medicine—it is too bitter; the second know better than the doctor and they abstain from wine or something of the kind; the third leave everything to the doctor and subject themselves entirely to him (cap. 29). Gagliardi talks of soldiers, Lancisius of religious, Pinard de la Boullaye about sculptors. In all these examples, the central problem of being inordinately attached to a good thing has been greatly weakened, and the exercise has been turned into a reflection on wanting the end and not wanting the means. More harmful is the implication that the exercitant has to decide, and decide here and now, without delay. The cause of these faulty interpretations may easily be traced. It is a preoccupation with the election of a state or way of life, especially in actual poverty. Indeed, actual poverty is mentioned in the meditation on Two Standards, but each time as a possible actualization of spiritual poverty (146, 147). The exercitant is not really much interested in actual poverty, nor primarily even in spiritual poverty. It is the way in which he can be of service to God that holds his attention. Dealing with the third class of men, Ignatius writes of their desire "de mejor poder servir a Dios" (155). In this phrase, "mejor" does not qualify "servir," it belongs to "poder." The desire that is uppermost in the exercitant's heart and mind is the desire to be better able to serve God.[9]

The Note

We return to the note that follows the meditation on Three Classes of Men; we referred to it briefly above. From the way in which "nosotros" and "quando" are stressed, it is clear that the contents of the note apply to some future moment in the Spiritual Exercises or even after them. One must not exaggerate the true tenor of what Ignatius writes. To give a not very elegant but close translation of the autograph text: "When we ourselves feel any affection or repugnance to actual poverty, when we are not indifferent to poverty or riches, it will help much in order to extinguish such inordinate affection to ask in the colloquies (even though it be against the flesh) that the Lord should choose us to actual poverty" (". . . quando nosotros sintimos affecto o repugnancia contra la pobreza actual, quando no somos indiferentes a pobreza o riqueza, mucho aprovecha para extinguir el tal affecto desordenado, pedir en los coloquios (aunque sea contra la carne) que el Señor le elija en pobreza actual;" 157). So far the note is clear and shows only one irregularity: Ignatius changes from the first person plural (nosotros) to the third person singular (le). It is a change that causes no difficulties. There is another irregularity which is of greater importance: "mucho aprovecha" is followed by the infinitive form "pedir," which is what one expects. The object of *pedir* is introduced by the conjunction "que," which again is regular. Ignatius then continues: "y que él quiere, pide y suplica, sólo que sea servicio y alabanza de la su divina bondad." One may be inclined to place the two clauses introduced by "que" on an equal footing and to make them both dependent upon "pedir" ("pedir que el Señor le elija . . . y que él quiere, pide y suplica"). But the verbal forms form an argument against it, and there does not seem to be much sense in asking that one should ask and pray. The other alternative is to accept the irregularity that Ignatius has "mucho approvecha" followed first by an infinitive construction and next by a dependent clause; that no subjective form is used has to be accepted as another irregularity.

The *versio prima* and the *versio vulgata* are not of much help here, although the *versio vulgata* seems to favor the reading that "multum confert" has a double subject, namely, "petere a Deo" and "hoc ipsum optare, petere et flagitare" (*Sp. Ex.*, 362). Roothaan inserts another verb so that his translation reads: "Multum iuvat petere in colloquiis ut Dominus ipsum eligat ad paupertatem actualem, et protestari se id velle, petere et supplicare." It gives the note a harshness which is not found in the original. The grammatical and syntactical irregularities have to be accepted. There can be no doubt, however, that in order to extinguish an inordinate attachment, it is a great help to beg and plead for God's assistance.

One more point must be stressed. In the note Ignatius advises the exercitant; he makes a wise suggestion; he does not impose anything. He refrains from using the word "menester" (necessary), which is found in the First Principle and Foundation. He points out that it will be a great help and that it will be very profitable to pray that God may choose the exercitant for a life of actual poverty, always presupposing that the exercitant is not, or not yet, indifferent. The expression "mucho aprovecha" is proof of that mildness and gentleness which characterize the fourth day of this second week.

In conclusion, the exercises of the fourth day show us the exercitant in surroundings partly familiar to him (through the contemplations of the first half of this week) and partly new. They contain a strong appeal, not in the least to the apostolate in a very wide sense of the word: "the Lord recommending to him to seek to help all" (146). But there is as yet no reply to this indirect appeal; there is the readiness and there is the desire. Hence, this fourth day is not a day of vehement agitations or momentous decisions. It is a day of new visions and new convictions, which undoubtedly give the retreat a rather serious turn, for the reason that grave consequences will be in store for the exercitant. All this does not take away peace and tranquillity. At the end of the day the exercitant will want to return to his Lord's life in contemplation, he will feel the need for more intense and more intimate prayer.

ten

# THE SECOND WEEK: THE SECOND HALF

On the fifth day the exercitant resumes the contemplations of Christ's life. One might expect Ignatius to weave of set purpose the contents of the meditation on Two Standards into the fabric of the contemplations on the public life of Christ, and to ask his exercitant to concentrate on the life of the great Leader and Captain who is fighting His battle against Satan. But Ignatius drops the word "Capitán" as soon as he deals with the second part of the meditation on Two Standards, and never uses it again. There is no reference to battle or battlefield anywhere in the exercises that follow. He proceeds with his contemplations as if there had been no fourth day devoted to any intention of Christ or any intention of Satan. Not only does he keep clear of what might be deemed to be golden opportunities to clarify and enforce the contents of the meditation on Two Standards, such as contemplations on Christ driving out devils, on Christ being accused of acting in the name of Beelzebub, on Christ going to His Passion in order to fight and overcome the Prince of this World; but it looks as if Ignatius is anxious to eliminate whatever may remind the exercitant of the fourth day. Thus on the sixth day, the exercitant will contemplate how Christ went from the River Jordan to the desert (161). Ignatius leaves out any reference to Christ being tempted by the devil. Indeed, "inclusive" is added and one might think that this refers to all that happens in the desert, the temptations not excluded. It must be admitted that in the section of the points following the exercises (261-312), mention is made of "how Christ was tempted by the enemy" (274). The curious fact, however, is that Ignatius here does not refer the exercitant to the points in this section, and it is the only time that the exercitant is not referred to this section. Similarly, Ignatius does not anywhere specifically point to the designs of

Christ or those of Satan. The conclusion is clear: the contemplations on the life of Christ must continue without any preoccupation with the contents of the meditation on Two Standards.

Christ's public life is dealt with, if the expression be allowed, in eight episodes, the supposition being that the second week is to last twelve days.[1] If, as is normal, it is reduced to ten, or even eight days, only six or four events in Christ's life are subject matter for contemplation. For in contrast with the first three days of the second week, the exercitant now concentrates on one event each day. He is to make three repetitions, which are followed by the exercise called the application of the senses. It proves that any event is of relative unimportance, it always yields first place to the Person of Christ. Another point must be noted. If the exercitant returns over and over again to those parts of the contemplation where he felt consolation or desolation and where he experienced greater spiritual relish—this is of the essence of all repetitions (62, 118)—the supposition is that he is being moved by various spirits and more so now than in previous days. It is here that the meditation on Two Standards asserts its influence.

There is another reason why the exercitant will confine himself to one event in Christ's life each day. Ignatius gave two ways of making a contemplation, as was shown when the contemplations on the Incarnation and the Nativity were examined. There is no reason why both methods should not be used in contemplating the same mystery. By giving one mystery only, Ignatius appears to suggest that both methods are to be used in order to penetrate the mystery more deeply. It is not because there is more visible or audible *material* in, let us say, Christ's Baptism than in the Nativity, but the dimensions of the exercitant's composition have become considerably widened since he spent a day meditating on life in this world, considered as a battlefield. Here the meditation on Two Standards once again indirectly asserts its influence. It is likely that the exercitant will make the first contemplation, followed by a repetition, after the pattern of the contemplation on the Incarnation; the third exercise, again followed by a repetition, will be made after the method given in the contemplation on the Nativity. The fifth and last contemplation will always be an application of the senses.

Although the many repetitions point to an increase of consolation and desolation, this must not be taken to mean that undue pressure is brought to bear on the exercitant or that an element of disquiet creeps in. On the contrary, the many repetitions reveal the single-minded purpose of Ignatius, namely, that the exercitant should experience satisfaction and should come to rest (2, 76, 118). In a sense, days of great intimacy and sanctity lie ahead, days too of tranquillity and peace (333).

The exercitant will now remember the third annotation: as the intimacy grows, so must the reverence on the part of the exercitant. He must not put obstacles in the way by careless behavior during the exercises. It is the reason why Ignatius brings up the subject of the particular examination of conscience. It was mentioned at the end of the first week. There he wrote, to quote the autograph text: "El examen particular se haga para quitar defectos y negligencias sobre exercicios y addiciones; y ansí en la 2ª, 3ª y 4ª semana" (90). Now he writes: "El examen particular después de comer y después de cenar se hará sobre las faltas y negligencias cerca los exercicios y addiciones deste día . . ." (160). The following points must be noted: the exercitant is explicitly told that this examination is to be made twice daily;[2] the times when it is to be made are now given; there is a change in the wording of this exercise. Since the purpose of this examination is not repeated, it must be assumed to remain the same, namely, "to remove defects and negligences" (para quitar defectos y negligencias).

The subject matter shows a subtle but not unimportant shift from "sobre exercicios y addiciones" to "sobre las faltas y negligencias cerca los exercicios y addiciones desta día." The new wording presupposes that faults are being made and that the exercitant is somewhat careless, evidently now more than before. This is understandable, if only for this reason that, as the retreat proceeds, he will be moved by various spirits, and not always pleasantly. Desolation and tedium set in and may easily cause a slackening of attention and application. Accordingly, now even *faltas* must be sedulously detected. Where there is greater intimacy of contemplative prayer, faults cannot be considered of slight importance. Once again, Ignatius impresses upon the exercitant that no risks can be taken where God is at work and wants the full cooperation of the exercitant (15). The mention of the frequency, time, and contents of the particular examination of conscience, together with the insistence that five exercises are made each day, with no concessions granted by way of change to those who are less strong,[3] indicates that the second half of the second week is a time of higher and more intense prayer.

Since Ignatius wants his exercitant to be on his guard against faults and infidelities in his contemplations and even in the observation of the additions, we may correctly assume that his advice for the remainder of the second week is significant. Consequently, there must be very good reason for these three points: the deviation from Scripture when he inserts the departure from Nazareth and Christ's farewell as matter of contemplation on the fifth day, the additional consideration placed immediately after the contemplation on the Vocation of the Apostles, and the selection of mysteries proposed for contemplation in the second half of this week.

Taking the second point first, one notices that only the contemplation on the Vocation of the Apostles has a consideration added to it. The link between this contemplation and the second part of the meditation on Two Standards is evident. While in the latter he uses "escoje" (to choose), he now prefers "llamar" and "llamamiento," and while in the former the apostles and disciples were being sent in order to spread the sacred doctrine, the apostles are now said to follow the Lord (161, 275). In the consideration added to the contemplation, the exercitant should observe that all the apostles were uneducated and from a humble condition of life, and he should pay attention to the dignity to which they are so gently called, and to the gifts and graces by which they were raised above all the Fathers of the Old and New Testaments. The exercitant considers more closely what is implied in the call of the apostles. No more than this; there is no suggestion that he should come to any decision regarding his own vocation.

More important are the reasons why Ignatius added the non-Scriptural departure of Christ from Nazareth. He writes: "First point, after Christ our Lord had bidden farewell to His blessed Mother, He went from Nazareth to the River Jordan, where St. John the Baptist was" (273). Ignatius refers to St. Matthew's Gospel: "Then Jesus came from Galilee and stood before John at the Jordan." The farewell scene stresses Christ's loneliness. In a literal sense of the word, He will not have a roof over His head: this in contrast with the birds, which have their nests and the foxes, which have their dens. Loneliness is accompanied by poverty; "Not a stone on which to lay His head" comes almost spontaneously to mind when Christ's departure from Nazareth is contemplated. Is Ignatius here thinking of the doctrine given in the meditation on Two Standards? Did he for this reason insert the incident of Christ leaving His Mother? It is unlikely: the incident is not included to illustrate the meditations of the previous day. Such a utilitarian function would detract from the true value and purpose of contemplation. One might then reasonably expect that sooner or later, directly or indirectly, the desire for insults and contempt would emerge in the contemplations, and there is no trace of it. The explanation must be sought elsewhere.

### Mysteries Selected

In the fourth chapter of this study, each exercise, and indeed each day, was shown to be marked by the recurrence of a certain rhythm. The question arises whether or not a similar rhythm occurs within the week. It is our contention that a close examination of the mysteries chosen by Ignatius reveals such a rhythm.

The starting point of this investigation is the rather unexpected part played by the Mother of Christ on this, the fifth day of the second week. The Gospels make no mention of Christ bidding farewell to His Mother: it has been inserted by Ignatius. On this same day, the exercitant contemplates the mystery of the Blessed Trinity, revealed at Christ's Baptism. Now on the first day of the second week, the exercitant is similarly spending the day in contemplating the mystery of the Blessed Trinity (the first contemplation on the Incarnation), while the Mother of Christ might be said to dominate the incidents of both contemplations (Incarnation and Nativity). On both days, the journey from Nazareth to the South is contemplated. The beginning of Christ's hidden life and of His public life comes to the fore, and another parallelism is given with Christ's birth and the rebirth that is essential to baptism. If, moreover, the week is lengthened and Mary's visit to Elizabeth is taken as the second contemplation of the first day (263), the person of John the Baptist is placed before the exercitant on both days. Finally, both the first and fifth day lay special stress on poverty and suffering.

If we compare the second and the sixth days, we notice that Christ's stay in the desert shows a certain affinity with His flight into Egypt (161, 274). Regarding any parallelism between the presentation in the Temple and Christ's dwelling and fasting in the desert, points of similarity might be found, as, for instance, the part attributed to the Holy Spirit in these two mysteries, but for fear of reading things into the text we refrain from doing so. On the third day, the exercitant is indirectly occupied with the question of various states and ways of life and, consequently, with the possibility of a vocation to the priesthood or the religious life. The seventh day is entirely taken up with contemplations on the Vocation of the Apostles. The correspondence between the fourth and the eighth days is obvious: the Sermon on the Mount is an elaboration of the mind and intention of Christ as set forth on the fourth day.

Having established the somewhat frail outlines of a rhythm between the first and the second quartets of days, one might, all the time treading carefully, discern that the rhythm repeats itself in the third and final quartet. On the ninth day, corresponding to the first and the fifth, the exercitant contemplates Christ working a miracle. It is not a truly spectacular one, like His healing all the sick of a village, or feeding five thousand people with a few loaves, or raising someone from the dead. Ignatius' choice is a miracle that took place on the lake. He could now choose between the mysteries of Christ calming the storm and Christ walking on the waters. The former is more impressive, since it reminded the apostles at once of divine powers; the latter, Ignatius' choice, is marked by a certain simplicity and humility. And although Ignatius does write "and the wind ceased" (280), there can be little doubt that his full attention is directed to Christ walking on the waters *to meet His apostles*. This element of condescending goodness also distinguishes the mysteries of the Incarnation and Nativity, as it does Christ's Baptism, which marked Him as the Lamb that carries the sins of all mankind. It is of interest to note that the fear and anguish of the apostles is entirely passed over but that special mention is made of Christ's going to pray by Himself, which reminds us of "Jesu baptisato et orante" in St. Luke's Gospel. Another link between these three days is found in the use of the boat tossed by the wind as a well-known symbol of the Church. Both the first and the fifth days concentrated on the human family (the Church) to be won back to the love of God.

At first sight there appears to be only a slight similarity of subject matter between the contemplations on the Flight into Egypt, the Presentation in the Temple (second day), Christ's Stay for forty days in the Desert (sixth day) and His Preaching in the Temple (tenth day). The fact that the presentation and the teaching both take place in the Temple carries no conviction; besides, it cannot be fitted in with the fast in the desert. It must be observed, however, that the preaching in the Temple, which is the first point of the contemplation, is immediately followed by Christ's loneliness: He left Jerusalem because no one received Him there (161, 288), and He proceeded to Bethany. The common element in the contemplations of the second, sixth and tenth days now shows itself to be the Lord's solitude, His not being wanted, either in Bethlehem or in Jerusalem, of His not belonging anywhere.

At this point there is a very significant deviation from the chronological order, which otherwise Ignatius maintains rather scrupulously. The preaching in the Temple takes place in Holy Week, after Palm Sunday, as is correctly pointed out in the sequence of mysteries briefly outlined after the fourth week (287, 288). The contemplation on Palm Sunday is given for the twelfth and last day of the second week. Ignatius must have had a good reason for this change. An obvious motive would be that he preferred to place the contemplation on Palm Sunday on the last day as a suitable transition to the third week, the week devoted to contemplations on the Passion. This solution leaves another question unanswered: why did Ignatius not place the contemplation on the Preaching in the Temple on the eleventh day? He moved it to the tenth day, and assigned the contemplation on the Raising of Lazarus to the eleventh day. There can be no doubt that this miracle preceded the preaching in the Temple. It certainly did not take place in Holy Week, as is correctly pointed out in the series of points given later in the book of the *Spiritual Exercises* (285, 287). These changes involve Ignatius in a certain lack of logic, for the return to Bethany following the unaccepted preaching in Jerusalem cannot be very well explained if one loses sight of what had happened to Lazarus more than a week before.

The reason for this shifting about of the mysteries might be discovered if the subject matter of the contemplations for the third, the seventh and the eleventh days is placed side by side. On the third day, the exercitant is indirectly occupied with various states of life; on the seventh, he contemplates the vocation of the apostles; on this eleventh day, he mainly dwells upon the mystery of Mary and Martha. In the first point we read: "Mary and Martha inform Jesus of the sickness of Lazarus; when He heard of it He stayed away for two days so that the miracle might be more manifest." In the second point we read: "Before He raised him, He asked each of them to believe." It is only in the third point that the miracle itself is made the subject of contemplation. Traditionally, Mary and Martha represent the two different states of life, and, consequently, there is a clear parallelism of subject matter in the contemplations of the third, seventh and eleventh days. This has been established by moving around the mysteries. There is, moreover, a close connection between the Holy Family in their hiddenness of Nazareth, the apostles who were only fishermen, and Martha, busily engaged in household duties; a similar connection exists between "to devote Himself exclusively to the service of His Eternal Father" (135), "to follow Christ forever" (275), and "the best part chosen by Mary which shall not be taken away from her" (285; Lk. 10.42).

Ignatius now achieved a striking similarity between the contemplations of the fourth, the eighth and the twelfth days. The contemplation on Palm Sunday gathers together the exercises on Two Standards and the Sermon on the Mount. The heart of the meditation on Two Standards is, on the one hand, Christ our Lord standing in a lowly place in a great plain about the region of Jerusalem, His appearance beautiful and attractive (144), and, on the other, His intention to have His sacred doctrine of poverty and humility spread over the whole world, a doctrine rehearsed in the Sermon on the Mount and, even more clearly, in the mystery of Christ riding into Jerusalem, a King, but seated on a donkey.

This recurrent rhythm deserves close study. If it were established beyond doubt, much insight would be gained into what was uppermost in Ignatius' mind when making his choice of mysteries. To relate the first day to the fifth and to the ninth imparts a deeper meaning to each of these three days, and the same holds good for the other three triplets. Further evidence in favor of what has been tentatively suggested might be discovered by looking at some other features of the mysteries chosen by Ignatius. Contemplation, as has been shown, implies living in the nearness of God-made-Man. The selection of mysteries made by Ignatius allows the exercitant to spend a day with Christ and His Mother, with Christ and John the Baptist, with Christ and the apostles, with Christ and the common people, with Christ and His enemies, with Christ and the family of Bethany, and with Christ in solitude (respectively, on the third, the fifth, the seventh, the eighth, the tenth, the eleventh and the sixth days). The exercitant will pass a day with Christ in the desert, on the lake, in the town, in the country, in the village, and in the Temple (respectively, on the sixth, the ninth, the twelfth, the eighth, the eleventh and the tenth days). The scene changes continually, the Person of Christ is always the same, and it is He whom the exercitant contemplates. The matter will not be pursued any further. The possibility that there is much wisdom in Ignatius' selection of mysteries deserves attention.

### Mysteries Omitted

If Ignatius left nothing to chance and did not select at random the matter for contemplation, an investigation into which mysteries he omitted may be significant. The section that contains the points for prayer contains fifty subjects for contemplation or meditation.[4] Ten of these deal with Christ's hidden life (262-71) and they cover all the incidents narrated in the Gospels: the Annunciation, the Visitation, the Nativity, the call of shepherds and magi, the circumcision, the presentation in the Temple, the flight into Egypt, the hidden life at Nazareth and the finding in the Temple. The visitation and circumcision, together with the call of shepherds and magi, are omitted in the contemplations of the first three days of the second week. Leaving out for a moment the mysteries of Christ's public life, one observes that ten sections are given to the contemplation of Christ's Passion (289-98). All of them serve as matter for contemplation in the third week. There are some slight irregularities of very minor importance regarding the way in which the mysteries are distributed over the six days of the third week. The fourth week is made up of fourteen sections (299-312); the points are at times very brief. There is no saying how many of the mysteries are to be contemplated, as Ignatius gives no indication whatever how long the fourth week should last. This leaves sixteen sections for the whole of Christ's public life (273-88).

Of these sixteen, the first four and the last four may be said to cover the first beginnings and the final phase of the public life: namely, Christ's Baptism, His stay in the desert, the vocation of the apostles, and the first miracle, which took place upon His return to Galilee (273-76), the raising of Lazarus, the supper at Bethany, Palm Sunday and Christ's preaching in the Temple (285-88). Of these eight, all but two, the miracle at Cana and the supper at Bethany, were chosen by Ignatius. The remaining eight mysteries embrace by far the greater part of the public life. They are: Christ casting out the sellers from the temple, the Sermon on the Mount, Christ walking on the waters and calming the storm, the mission of the apostles, the conversion of Mary Magdalen, the feeding of the multitude and the transfiguration. Of these eight, only two, the Sermon on the Mount and Christ walking on the waters, found their way into the second week.

A survey of the sixteen mysteries covering Christ's public life reveals that, among other mysteries, Ignatius omitted the healing of the sick, the blind, the lame, and the lepers, the casting out of devils, the forgiveness of sins, and the explanation of the Kingdom by means of parables. Having thus drastically reduced, so to speak, the public life to sixteen mysteries, Ignatius further reduced this number to eight. The choice cannot have been very hard, for a fair number of mysteries chose themselves. Against the background of the fourth day and the new dimensions there given to the life of the exercitant, Christ's Baptism, together with the revelation of the Blessed Trinity, Christ's stay in the desert, and His desire to be helped by apostles and disciples were almost inevitable choices. The same must be said of the subject matter of the last day of this second week: the contemplation on Palm Sunday, as a transition between the second and third week, could not be omitted. So, there remained four contemplations. The Sermon on the Mount seems an obvious choice, because the vocation of the apostles will concentrate on spreading Christ's sacred doctrine, mentioned in the meditation on Two Standards. Understandably, Ignatius now omits the mission and preaching of the apostles, as to a certain extent this would be a repetition of the contemplation on their vocation and the Sermon on the Mount. Moreover, it would have meant another day spent with Christ and His apostles, and here Ignatius prefers the miracle of Christ walking on the waters.

Six out of eight contemplations assigned for the second part of this week have thus been accounted for without any great difficulty. The two remaining contemplations are devoted to the raising of Lazarus and the preaching in the Temple followed by Christ's rejection. We have suggested reasons why Ignatius fixed his choice on these two contemplations when we discussed the recurrent rhythm of this second week. We must register a mild surprise that Ignatius omitted the contemplation on the Transfiguration. One might have expected Ignatius to grasp with both hands the opportunity of contemplating the Self-revelation of the Blessed Trinity, seeing how intense his devotion was for this mystery. Yet, he preferred the raising of Lazarus and the preaching in the Temple, or more accurately, the rejected teaching in the Temple. This rejection effects a transition to the third week. At the same time, it continues a subject indicated as early as the second contemplation of this week, that of the Nativity, with its emphasis on toil, labors and failure (116).

A few facts stand out when we survey the question of mysteries chosen and omitted by Ignatius. Evidently, the contemplation of the Person of Christ is more important than that of any incident or event, and even more important than any doctrine taught. The eight mysteries chosen for the second half of this week seem to point to a kind of obsession with the dark side of Christ's life. This theme was introduced in the contemplation on the Nativity, and it was consequently continued throughout the first three days of this week, as the contemplation on the Nativity was given as an example. It was intensified by the clash between darkness and light in the meditation on Two Standards. It now apparently dominates the rest of the week, what with Christ's Baptism, His stay in the desert, Palm Sunday, and the failure of His preaching. One might perhaps accuse Ignatius of gloom and pessimism. Bright, cheery incidents, such as the healing of the sick, the feeding of the multitude, the blessing of mothers and children, are discarded. Ignatius is very serious; there is little light and joy in these contemplations, or so it seems.

There is no getting away from the fact that God's decision to regain the love of the human family is a dreadfully serious matter. It must not be forgotten that the light was rejected and that His own received Him not. There is with Ignatius the unabated amazement that Christ should have been so attractive and lovable and yet have met with insults, wrongs, and contempt. At the same time, he leaves no one in any doubt that the servant is not greater than his Master. In other words, Ignatius is deeply convinced of the truth of the doctrine of Christ, as set forth in the meditation on Two Standards, which we shall meet again and in a more sublime form in the third kind of humility and the third week.

There is another reason why great stress is placed on what we called the dark side of Christ's life. The starting point of the Spiritual Exercises is Ignatius' passion for order. It implies removing any disorder in man's desires, actions, operations, intentions, and so forth (16, 46). Being a man who knew well what was going on in the world and in the Church, Ignatius was not blind to the rush for benefices, offices and high, well-paid positions; he was not blind to the urge everywhere around him to climb the social or ecclesiastical ladder. He was never blind to the absence of any real concern to be a Christ-like Christian. It is not surprising that God should have shown one of those whom He had destined to be a true reformer the terrible discrepancy within the Church between the Master and the servant.

The prudent director will be on his guard against any one-sidedness when he tries to help the exercitant to achieve order and harmony. He must not over-accentuate the dark side of Christ's life in order to force the exercitant into removing any disorder in his thoughts, his desires, and his behavior. It might easily lead to an opposite kind of disorder. Nothing is gained by substituting the disorder of too little for that of too much in matters of poverty, or fame, or success, and so on. Hence, it should never be overlooked that, when all has been said about this dark side of Christ's life and Ignatius' apparent predilection for it, the whole of the second week is based upon the fact that God has forgiven all the exercitant's sins. Ignatius might have rubbed this in by inserting a contemplation on the prodigal son, on Christ's encounter with the woman taken in adultery, on His meeting with Zachaeus, or even on His casting out of a legion of devils; he even omits a contemplation on the conversion of Mary Magdalen. A return to these and similar subjects would only detract from the *tanta piedad y misericordia,* which has filled the exercitant with unbounded joy ever since he made the fifth exercise of the first week (71).

Besides, there is much light and joy in the vocation of the apostles, in the Sermon on the Mount, in the mystery of Christ walking on the waters, and in the raising of Lazarus. Above all, one cannot forget that the contemplations themselves are marked by an ever-increasing familiarity between Christ and the exercitant. It is not only that God-made-Man is gentle and attractive (143), not only that the exercitant longs to know Him better that he might love Him more (104), but with the apostles and disciples the exercitant is now called friend (146), and if he is called to help Christ, he is made to realize how gently he has been called and to what dignity (275) and how he is taken into the Lord's confidence and may count on His gifts and graces just as could the Fathers of the Old and New Testaments (275). The whole of his life is made meaningful, and there is a tremendous joy in this knowledge. On top of all this, God is ever communicating Himself and even seeking to embrace the exercitant (15). Hence, whatever may be the outcome of the exercitant's desire and decision to compose himself, that is, make himself one with Christ in His fight against Satan, be it even actual poverty, insults, and contempt, it will always be based on and inspired by love. There will also always be deep humility, in perfect balance with love. The favorite combination for Ignatius in his letters and *Constitutions* is "amor et reverentia," and most precious to him is the "humildad amorosa."[5]

Discernment of Spirits

The exercitant will make the triple colloquy of the meditation on Two Standards (159) or make a colloquy in accordance with the note that follows the meditation on Three Classes of Men (*ibid.*), a colloquy that is closely akin to that of the meditation on Two Standards. With each contemplation he will talk over (razonar, hablar) his own position within the mystery of God having an enemy and needing help, and five times a day he will reflect upon the highest spiritual poverty, possibly even actual poverty, upon insults and wrongs to be borne, and upon the close imitation of and likeness to Christ (147). His own inclinations, expectations, mentality, spirit,—whatever word is preferred—will not be in accord with what is put before him in the colloquy. He has been told about this at the very beginning of the retreat (16), and it has been made clear to him in the note after the meditation on Three Classes of Men (157). A clash of spirits will be unavoidable, and behind this Ignatius discerns a clash between Spirits. The exercitant will undergo various spiritual motions, even agitations, and it is not always easy to determine what exactly is happening. To analyze at any length the rules given by Ignatius as a help to discern the various spirits at work and the motions they cause would be beyond the scope of this study. A few observations that make for a better understanding of the final days of the second week must suffice.

Ignatius speaks of rules more suitable for the first week and of others more suitable for the second week (9, 313, 328). The expressions "mâs proprias" (313) and "conducen mâs" (328) suggest that there are no hard and fast rules either for the first or second week exclusively. The foundation of the two sets of rules is taken from what happens generally, as a rule, *comúnmente* (10). Ignatius restricts himself to the first and second weeks, and makes no mention of the third and fourth weeks. The reason is not that there will be no motions in these latter weeks, but that by then so much clarity will have been gained in what is taking place and such dexterity in discerning the various spirits that no further guidance is necessary.

Ignatius judges the second set of rules as of particular importance to the exercitant contemplating the public life of Christ. As we have said, the clash between various spirits is made inevitable by the exercitant's natural aversion to a life of the highest spiritual, perhaps even actual poverty. He will feel drawn asunder. On the one hand, he will be "harassed with anxiety, afflicted with sadness, faced with obstacles that disturb his soul" (315) and on the other, he will feel encouraged to go forward in doing good (*ibid.*). The evil spirit will fill the exercitant's imagination with delights and gratifications, which he will have to forego if he should respond to the constant appeal of dedicating himself to Christ (314). This appeal threatens to be drowned by voices suggesting that such a life of poverty cannot possibly be lived by him. Even apparent pleasures of a life completely after his own choice will enter his mind, and these he finds very hard to dismiss (313).

The last four sentences paraphrase the opening paragraphs not of the second set of rules but of the first set, and, hence, are more suitable for the first week. There can be only one conclusion: in the second week the exercitant has moved quite beyond this stage, and the collision between various spirits will not occasion the fear of a difficult future. In contrast with the traditional interpretation, there is no question of making firm resolutions regarding such a future. This can only be because the exercitant is comforted and consoled by God and His good angels, and because all sadness and all disturbance is banished (328). What he must pay careful attention to are fallacious reasonings, subtleties and, continual deceptions (*ibid.*), to evil designs and hidden snares (333), to holy and pious thoughts that may be suggested by the devil in the appearance of an angel of light (*ibid.*). He must check his own dispositions and thoughts (17, 332, 335). In the end, he will distinguish what comes from the good angel from what proceeds from the evil spirit by the experience of peace, tranquillity, and quiet (329, 333). What makes matters even more difficult is that in souls progressing to greater perfection the action of the good angel is delicate, gentle, and sweet, like a drop of water penetrating a sponge. The action of the evil spirit upon such a soul is violent and noisy, like a drop of water falling upon a stone (335). Unfortunately, the soul progressing steadily will often hardly discern the gentleness with which the good angel acts, and conclude that nothing happens. Very significantly, Ignatius does not say that the movements caused by the evil spirits have to be rejected, as he did when he gave the first set of rules. They are too tenacious to be rejected offhand. It is a matter of detecting and discerning them, and then turning a deaf ear to them so that there will be no unrest and no confusion and the clarity of the good angel may remain.

The second week, and especially the second half, is not a time of strain, stress and pressure. On the contrary, peace, tranquillity and quiet in the Lord and Creator are increasing and deepening as contemplation, and with contemplation, the exercitant's composition, move toward completeness and perfection. The third prelude, in which he asks for what he wishes and desires, has received a too ascetical emphasis in the traditional interpretation of the Exercises.

Ignatius always insists on asking for an intimate knowledge of the Lord. This knowledge contains the gift of light, peace, and joy in the Lord. Similarly, Ignatius' advice or exhortation "sacar algún provecho," frequently found in the points of the contemplations (106-08, 114-16, 122-25), allows more room than is suggested by Roothaan's translation "fructum capere," which has, moreover, been interpreted as meaning that practical resolutions are to be the fruit derived from the exercise. "Provecho" means, indeed, profit, advantage, even progress, but no greater profit can be derived from any contemplation than a greater knowledge of Christ, more love, and consequently more light, more joy, more peace, and all the other good things enumerated by Ignatius when he describes the nature of consolation (314).

eleven

## "MATERIAS DE ELECCIÓN"

The paragraphs dealing with the examination of conscience, which precede the exercises of the first week, are not discussed in this study, the reason being that they were written not for the exercitant of the long retreat but for an altogether different group of Christians. For the same reason, the *materias*, or *materia, de elección* (18, 338) could be silently omitted. This does not imply that the exercitant of the twentieth annotation may not want to make an election about some matter or other, possibly even about an immutable state of life. Ignatius is aware of this possibility when at the end of the contemplations of the second week he introduces a note with the words: "The matter of the elections will begin from the contemplation of Christ's departure from Nazareth to the Jordan, inclusive, that is from the fifth day" (163). The help he gives to the exercitant of the complete Spiritual Exercises bears little resemblance to that contained in his "materias de elección" (169-89).

Tradition has been so strong in this matter of making an election or a reformation of life that no one can act as if this tradition and this practice were nonexistent. Moreover, the exercise on three kinds of humility, which Ignatius made preparatory to a sound election, is often considered to contain the quintessence of Ignatian spirituality. Hence, we can no more ignore the elections than the three kinds of humility.

With care Ignatius looked for those who were suited to make his Spiritual Exercises. A time of preparation preceded, and this period might last months, even years, as for instance, in the case of Francis Xavier. During this time of preparation, the future exercitant received guidance about various subjects, now gathered together in the annotations, the additions, the paragraphs dealing with the First

Principle and Foundation, various methods of prayer, examination of conscience, regular confession and Communion. It is almost unthinkable that in this preparatory period nothing was said about various aspects of the election and the reformation of life. For one thing, the reformation of life did not begin in the third week of the long retreat but long before the retreat: how can there be a desire to make as much progress as possible (20) without a true reformation of life, and what else is the contents of the sixteenth annotation but a reformation of life? We know, moreover, that certainly in the case of Francis Xavier the election of a state of life was made before and not during the retreat that was to come: he took his vows, as has been pointed out before, in August, 1534, and began the Spiritual Exercises a month later. If the First Principle and Foundation were diligently explained during those weeks and months of preparation, it is hardly likely that its bearing upon the choice of a state or way of life would have been omitted (cfr. 169, 172, 173, 178-82, 189).

Besides, not a single point of the paragraphs dealing with the matter of the elections asks for an explanation at the time of the exercises. Ignatius knows "three times for making a good and sound election" (175-78). The long retreat will by itself take the exercitant into the second time, "when considerable light and knowledge is obtained by experiencing consolations and desolations, and by gaining experience in the discernment of various spirits" (176). An exposition of the second time is consequently superfluous. But neither need the first and third times be explained. The former is as unexpected as it is exceptional, and is by no means confined to the time of the retreat. The latter lies outside the retreat altogether, as will be shown presently. Ways of coming to a good election in any of these times consequently need not be discussed in the long retreat. It is now easy to understand why Ignatius does not once speak of "him who makes the exercises" or "him who exercises himself." It is not surprising that he should fall back upon a terminology that is irresistibly reminiscent of the text of the *First Principle and Foundation.* Reading through the paragraphs in question is like moving into a spiritual climate totally different from that of the second week. There is no trace of the contemplations in which the exercitant has been spending at the very least four days, nor is there any trace of influence of the meditation on Two Standards. The instructions lie completely outside *las varias agitaciones y pensamientos, que los varios spíritus le traen* (17). They are very businesslike, both in form and contents. In the past, the second week and the election have been forged into an unbreakable whole; there seems to be no foundation for this in the text itself. Accurately, Ignatius speaks in the eighteenth annotation of "matters of election" *and* "any other exercises that are outside the first week."

Three Kinds of Humility

The election is preceded by the exercise on "tres maneras de humildad." The classical translation is "three degrees of humility." Rickaby prefers "modes of humility," while Puhl has chosen "kinds of humility," which we have adopted, not because it is entirely satisfactory but because we prefer it to modes or degrees. A more exact but rather cumbersome rendering would be "three ways of humbling oneself," as is clearly borne out by the description of the three parts of this exercise.

The purpose of the exercise is given in the words: "Before one enters on the elections, that he may be well affected toward the true teaching of Christ our Lord, it will be profitable to consider and notice the three following kinds of humility, considering them from time to time during the whole day" (164). The following points must be noted. Ignatius speaks of "elecciones," not of the choice of a state of life. The exercitant is not mentioned, the subject being "hombre," which becomes "quien" in the note following the exercise (164, 168). The exercise is not obligatory; it is introduced by "aprovecha," it is profitable; Ignatius does not even say that it is *very* useful.[1] No day is assigned to the exercise. The considerations take place all through the day, but there is no indication that contemplation discontinues or that even one contemplation is omitted. Not much time and energy remain for considerations throughout the day if the exercitant spends five hours in contemplation, attends Mass and Vespers (20), makes his examination of conscience twice (160), frequently recalls the mysteries contemplated (130), and conducts himself in accordance with the mystery on which he is engaged (*ibid.*). The exercise on the kinds of humility is a consideration (164); "to contemplate," "to meditate," even "mirar" are avoided. It seems hardly possible for an exercitant who spends the day in contemplative prayer to combine this with repeated matter-of-fact considerations. Finally, the exercitant is asked in a note following the exposition of the third kind of humility to make the triple colloquy of the meditation on Two Standards: he has made this five times already (168). All these observations point to one conclusion: the exercise on three kinds of humility is not meant for the exercitant of the thirty days' retreat.

The end in view when this exercise is made, is that "man may be well affected toward the true teaching of Christ our Lord" (para afectarse a la vera doctrina de Christo nuestro Señor, 164).[2] This cannot be called a step forward for the exercitant. He has been concentrating on and praying for knowledge and an ever-increasing love of Christ for at least seven days. It is a step back to occupy himself now with Christ's doctrine. For the exercitant, the doctrine is exemplified in the Lord (139), and through contemplation the exercitant desires to arrive at greater love of the Master as exemplifying His sacred doctrine. The situation is different if a person (hombre) has to be guided toward making a sound choice in whatever matter. If there is aversion to the doctrine of Christ and to His predilection for poverty and humility, there is little chance of the exercitant's choosing the right thing; such a person must first be brought to a certain appreciation of and affection for Christ's doctrine.

By looking at each of the three kinds of humility the same conclusion emerges, namely, that the exercise was never meant for the exercitant of the twentieth annotation. The first kind does not measure up to the disposition which Ignatius presupposes to be present when the thirty days' retreat begins. The fifth, fifteenth, sixteenth and twentieth annotations contain higher perfection than the first kind of humility. Anybody making himself as humble as he can in order that he may not give in to mortal sin (165) is not the same as one who wants to make as much progress as possible (20), leaves all his liberty and his whole will to God (5), and seriously seeks to rid himself of all inordinate attachments (16). To the exercitant, who has been thinking about the greatest spiritual poverty, and if God wills, actual poverty, and this for some five or six days, the suggestion that "even if I were made lord of the whole of creation" must sound out of place and even slightly ridiculous. If it is answered that the person making this exercise is considering that in the first kind of humility he does not even *enter into deliberation* to break a Commandment, the plain reply is that the exercitant of the long retreat is deliberating about altogether different matters.[3] For this reason there is no need to go any further into the description of the first kind of humility; the reader is referred to a note on the subject.[4]

With regard to the second kind of humility, there is a certain correspondence with what Ignatius wrote in the meditation on Three Classes of Men. The second kind of humility is an attitude of mind in which a person neither desires nor is inclined to have riches rather than poverty, to seek honor rather than dishonor, to desire a long life rather than a short life (166). The disposition of the third class of men implies that they want neither to retain nor relinquish the money acquired; they wish to consider that they have left everything in desire, striving to wish neither for this nor for any other thing, unless it be only the service of God that moves them to this wish (155). The correspondence is of slight importance. First of all, the three classes of men do not stand for three classes of exercitants, as has been pointed out before. There must be no identification of the exercitant to anyone who has made a great amount of money and tries to find God in peace. Secondly, the exercise on Three Classes of Men was a meditation, and the exercitant played the role of a spectator; in fact, he had moved quite beyond the disposition of the three classes and was only checking whether he took the enterprise of making progress in the spiritual life with sufficient seriousness. Thirdly, as with the first kind of humility, a comparison between what is written in the annotations mentioned above (5, 15, 16, 20), and especially in the sixteenth annotation, and the description of the second kind of humility, will show that the exercitant was supposed to have reached this second kind when the retreat began, or even to have passed beyond it.[5] Fourthly, the second kind of humility is very like indifference as is evident from a comparison of what Ignatius writes here, in the First Principle and Foundation, and the second point of his first method for making a good choice in the third time.[6] Both the First Principle and Foundation and the third time are not for the exercitant. Finally, we repeat that "never to enter into deliberation about committing a venial sin, neither for the sake of all created things nor even if on that account man should deprive me of life" sounds inappropriate for the exercitant who for the last four or five days has been asking to be received under Christ's standard in the *greatest* spiritual poverty, and who has been praying for more than a fortnight that all his intentions, actions, and operations may be *purely* ordained toward the praise and service of God (46). For these reasons the exposition of the second kind of humility is given in a note.[7]

The description of the second kind of humility contains the phrase "when the service of God our Lord and the salvation of my soul are equal" ("siendo igual servicio de Dios nuestro Señor y salud de mi ánima," 166). In the description of the third kind of humility this becomes: "when the praise and glory of the Divine Majesty are equal" ("siendo igual alabanza y gloria de la divina majestad," 167). This can mean one thing only: where such a condition does not obtain, man ought to choose what is more to the service and glory of God. If this inference is not drawn, the service of God would take second place to what man prefers, which implies that he cares more about his own good in whatever shape than about God's service and honor. This would involve a sinful attitude, one that is excluded in the second kind of humility, as well as in the first. But the inserted phrase "where the service of God, the salvation of my soul, and the honor and glory of the Divine Majesty are equal" introduces an element of unreality. In actual fact, one of two alternatives *must* be the will of God, and consequently must be *more* to the service and honor of God. So, a fictional case is used by Ignatius to check man's attitude, disposition, and affections; the fiction is introduced so as to make the consideration of humility both easier and clearer.

This explains why *hombre*, who, emphatically, is not the exercitant of the twentieth annotation, can yet turn his mind to the third kind of humility. Man considers and studies a fictional case, and takes notice of a further possible perfection of humility; that is all. Certainly he is not asked to practice it; that question is handled in a note (168). A striking difference from the first two kinds of humility must be noted. Whereas in the first and second kinds of humility the reference is only to "God our Lord," Christ is now mentioned by name no less than four times. The third kind evidently implies a personal relationship with Christ, and with Christ as a Man of sufferings. It is no longer a matter of humility only; love enters, which is proved by the change from "service and salvation" to "praise and glory," as was pointed out in a previous chapter. The third kind of humility is "humildad amorosa," and it comes to this, that man would feel ashamed to lead a more comfortable life than Christ led, that man desires to resemble Christ in actual fact, "más actualmente."[8]

If this third kind of humility were meant for the exercitant, one would have to conclude that, as was the case with the first and second kinds, it has wandered from its proper place. Not that the third kind of humility belongs to the time of preparation, as the first and second do; it is part of the third week. This becomes clear as soon as the words used by Ignatius in the third prelude of the contemplations of the third week (203) and in the second addition as adapted to the third week (206) are placed by the side of those employed in his description of the third kind. The texts are given in a note.[9] The exercitant will be faced by the third kind of humility in the third week, not in the second. He will be faced by it irrespective of any choice or election; and when it comes before him it will be infused with love. At that time he will find himself deep in contemplation, and not in considerations of certain modes of humility.

In the second note Ignatius writes that "the matter of the elections (materia de las elecciones) begins from the contemplation of Christ's departure from Nazareth to the Jordan." The objection might be raised that surely Ignatius now wants his exercitant to turn his thoughts to the election of a state of life or way of living. It must be observed that the very vagueness of "materia de las elecciones" makes any restriction to the choice of a state or way of life impossible. According to this note, the exercitant will from now onward not only be concerned with greater knowledge and love of Christ by continuing the contemplations on His life (135), but also with His teaching, exemplified in His life (*ibid.*), and with His teaching, not as a thing merely to be listened to but to be put into practice. While in the first half of this week the main accent fell on knowledge and love of the Lord, now "seguir y imitar" is equally stressed. This involves deliberations, elections, decisions. These do not exclusively refer to the exercitant's state of life, by any means. The object is *vida o estado,* and the two are at once superseded by nothing less than perfection in whatever God gives the exercitant to choose (135). Elections and decisions do not dominate the second week; they are not restricted to the second week. If Ignatius does indicate the beginning, he nowhere indicates where the *materia de las elecciones* should conclude. It can only come to an end when the will of God has been found, and this will not be during the second week. As will be shown, it is more likely to happen in the course of the third week, and even then the will of God is not found in all its fullness. This is a task that involves all the time to follow after the retreat.

## Instructions

Anyone approaching the instructions given by Ignatius at the end of the second week (169-89) will be struck by the utter difference of tone and contents from what has preceded, so much so that it is almost impossible to give the exercitant who has reached the end of the second week the instructions as written down in the Spiritual Exercises. They would have little effect, except perhaps that of drawing him rather violently away from contemplation down to calculation, from grace to cool reason. There appears to be little point in reminding him at this stage that "man is born for the praise of God and the salvation of his soul" (177, 179) without any indication that this God came down from eternal life to undergo death for him (53) and that this God has appealed to him to follow and help Him (145). There is hardly any sense in arguing about means and ends, about advantages and disadvantages, when the exercitant has possibly been asking for insults, wrongs, and contempt (147, 157), which lie altogether outside the categories of means useful to a certain end. Consequently, as these instructions are not meant for the exercitant of the twentieth annotation, except perhaps as matter to be treated during the months or weeks of preparation, we shall confine ourselves to a few points that deserve attention.

Ignatius knows "three times for making a sound and good election" (175). The third time is a time that lies outside the long retreat. It is described as "a time of tranquillity, when the soul is not agitated by different spirits and enjoys the use of his natural powers freely and quietly" (177). The exercitant, however, is a person who is moved and agitated by divers spirits (6), who experiences consolations and desolations, and who is guided by interior clarity and knowledge (2, 176). If no spiritual motions, such as consolations and desolations, are experienced in the soul of the exercitant, and if he is not agitated by divers spirits, there is something wrong, and the director is told to find out what has gone wrong (6). Ignatius never at any time has great confidence in a choice made in the third time. It should only be resorted to when the choice is not made in the first time, which, as a direct gift from God, is outside any man's power, nor in the second time (175, 178). Besides, no choice that is immutable must be made in the third time. This is expressly stated both in the first point of Ignatius' first method (its object being "qualquier cosa que cae en elecciŏn *mutable*," 178) and of the second method, where *la tal cosa* can only refer to the office or benefice, or whatever falls under a mutable election, as earlier mentioned (184, 187). Even when there is only question of a matter that falls under a mutable election, Ignatius shows a marked hesitancy regarding its result, for the sixth and final point of the first method advises the person who has made his choice to begin to pray with great diligence in the presence of God, offering Him the election, that His Majesty may be pleased to receive and confirm it, if it be to His greater service and praise ("siendo su mayor servicio y alabanza," 183). A similar note of diffidence is heard in the phrase at the very beginning of the introductory paragraph, "en quanto es de nuestra parte." Evidently, because this does not bring sufficient certainty, it must be supplemented by "de parte de Dios." Any person relying on his own natural powers will never be quite sure of having found the will of God. In the end he will have no choice but "ir con mucha diligencia a la oración delante de Dios nuestro Señor." The seriousness of this advice is stressed by the wording of the phrase. In the Exercises themselves God is no less than five times spoken of as "giving us to choose" a state or way of life (135, 146, 147, 157, 168).[10] It will come as no surprise to hear that many of Ignatius' letters end with the request that the recipient will join him in praying for the grace to know, or sense, the will of God and faithfully to accomplish it ("ruego a Dios nuestro Señor a todos quiera dar su gracia, para que su santísima voluntad siempre sintamos, y aquella enteramente la cumplamos").

The election made according to the methods of the third time has come to be considered a valuable contribution of Ignatius to the Christian life. It has even taken precedence over a choice in the second time. The tradition goes back a long time. The second time, according to the official *Directory* of 1599, may be "sine dubio excellentior et altior," but the third time "nempe per ratiocinationem et discursum est securior et tutior" (*Dir.*, 701). Polanco, too, calls the second time "excellentior," but he adds that it might be wise to check, as it were, the result of an election made in this time by one of the methods of the third time (*ibid.*, 309-11). González Dávila agrees with Polanco, as is clear from his detailed exposition of the second time, but judges the third time to be "más seguro" (*ibid.*, 518). Mirón, too, thinks the second time "excellentior," but his difficulty is that usually there will be some doubt both with the exercitant and the director "an sit illa motio a Deo" (*ibid.*, 401). This is a remarkable observation, because by definition the second time gives the exercitant "asaz claridad y cognoscimiento" (176). Ignatius would never have run into trouble with the Inquisition and would never have been under suspicion of being an *alumbrado* if he had propagated the third time as the most suitable for discovering the will of God.

Ignatius gives two methods for making a good choice in the third time. The first is well known: it is by weighing the advantages and disadvantages of two alternatives. It contains six points, which are really six different activities performed by him who is to make a choice: proposing the matter, keeping before his eyes the end for which he was created, begging for grace that God may move his will, considering the matter, that is, reasoning about the advantages and profits of the matter proposed, weighing the matter to see to which side reason most inclines, and finally betaking himself to fervent prayer (178-83). Such a structure reminds one of meditation. The second method knows no points; instead four rules are given, just as rules are given for the distribution of alms and for the discernment of spirits. They allow greater liberty to the person who is to make a choice. In this second method, he starts from a certain predilection for one of the two alternatives. From the outset there is "the love which urges and causes him to choose such or such a thing" (184).

He is asked to remember that the first rule must be that this love should descend from on high, from the love of God. Where there is an outspoken love or predilection for a certain matter, the will influences the intellect to the extent that the objective weighing of pros and cons is made difficult. So, Ignatius has recourse to a method which for the moment paralyzes this predilection, and this in four different ways: rather theoretically, by stressing the right order between various loves (185); more practically, by asking the person to think about someone he does not know who needs advice in a situation exactly corresponding to his own (185), by asking him to imagine himself at the point of death (186) and finally by asking him to see himself in the presence of God on the day of judgment (187).

In contrast with the first method, the second twice speaks of perfection, once even of greater perfection (185). In the first method, praise and service of God, together with the salvation of one's soul, are the dominating motives, although the combination "alabanza-gloria" occurs twice (179, 180). In the second method, the corresponding words are love, glory and perfection, pleasure and joy (respectively, 184, 185, 187). Indeed, in the note following the four rules, Ignatius refers to salvation, but this is now joined immediately to "quietud eterna" (188). The expression not only points to the removal of the burden and impediment which follow in the wake of any attachment, as was Ignatius' presupposition in his meditation on Three Classes of Men, but also suggests consolation, especially when found in the vicinity of pleasure and joy (316). The whole coloring, then, of this second method is quite different from that of the first. This is also mirrored in the interesting fact that in the second method Ignatius avoids the word "affección" (attachment); it does not sound very favorable, and points to the object to which a person is attached, whereas love, the word used now, lays more stress on the inner motive that moves a person. Relevant is the recurrence of the word "affección" in the rules for distributing alms (342, 338).

### Reformation of Life

Ignatius closes the section of instructions with a paragraph headed "to amend and reform one's whole life and state" ("para emendar y reformar la propria vida y estado," 189). The interpretation sometimes given, that this paragraph is meant for those who have already chosen an immutable state of life and are now advised to consider a reformation of life as a kind of substitute for such an election, cannot well be maintained. Ignatius does not have in mind the exercitant. He speaks of "those who hold high office in the Church or are in the state of matrimony and who have not an occasion or any prompt will to make an election with regard to matters which fall under mutable elections"; such persons can in no way be identified with the exercitant of the twentieth annotation. A little further on, Ignatius makes the suggestion that such people be brought "to think and consider by means of exercises . . .," a phrase not applicable at all to the exercitant. Regarding resolutions hinted at by Ignatius: the person will have to examine how great a house and estate he ought to keep up; how he ought to govern and rule it; how he ought to instruct it by word and example, and with regard to his means, what part he ought to take for his family and household and how much for distribution among the poor and other pious objects. Such examinations will hardly appeal to the exercitant. The interesting point is that no resolutions are mentioned in connection with prayer and spiritual practices, and even more striking, that poverty, the desire for insults and contempt, and the humility of being esteemed a fool for Christ's sake (167) would look out of place in the context. The reformation of life, as it is usually called, is certainly not meant for the exercitant and does not belong to the second week.

If then, to bring this chapter to an end, it is asked why Ignatius inserted the "materia de las elecciones" into the second week, it must first be pointed out for the sake of accuracy that Ignatius does not *insert* it: he makes the instructions concerning this matter *follow* the exercises of the second week. Secondly, there is no other reasonable place to put them. Because the election matter demands a certain maturity, as is clearly indicated in the eighteenth annotation, he could not very well place it before or within the framework of the first week, which, moreover, already contains a fair amount of instructive matter. Any choice, whether immutable or not, will always contain an element that is closely akin to what is the focal point of the meditation on Two Standards, and, to a less extent, of that on Three Classes of Men. The exercitant will be faced by decisions and elections, but from the second half of the second week onward (135, 163). It is only natural that Ignatius gathers together the *materia de las elecciones* at the end of the second and before the third week, in which it will play its own important role.

twelve

# THE THIRD WEEK

In studying the third week, a different procedure has been chosen from the one we have followed so far. The starting point will not be the new dimensions added to the exercitant's composition as a further unfolding of order and harmony, but some noteworthy points in the text.

First, the title of the first exercise of this week states that the contemplation takes place during the night: "la primera contemplación a la media noche" (190). This happens in no other week. It does not mean that no exercise was made at midnight in the course of the other weeks. Now the night exercise is mentioned in the title, and it is no less than six times referred to when Ignatius gives the subject matter for the various days (208).

Second, Ignatius insists that five exercises be made every day (205, 209). He allows a lessening of this number for reasons of health, age, and physical constitution only.[1] In the first and second weeks he permitted some change in the number of exercises for the sake of variety; in the third week this is no motive. A good case might be made for a similar strictness in the second half of the second week as was pointed out in the third note to the tenth chapter.

Third, the exercitant is now called "persona que se exercita" (205) whereas in the second week he was called "persona que hace los exercicios" (129); in the fourth week he is "persona que contempla" (228).

Fourth, Ignatius describes in rather elaborate detail the way in which the exercises are made. The exercitant has been exercising himself, has been meditating and contemplating for almost three weeks. One would expect that by now he has mastered the art of praying, or at least, knows how to contemplate. Yet, Ignatius returns to the subject of the preparatory prayer, the three preludes, the points, and the colloquy, adding, apparently rather superfluously at this stage of the exercises, that the preparatory prayer and the preludes must always precede the exercise and should never be omitted. The text in question runs as follows: "In this second contemplation, after the preparatory prayer has been made, as well as the three preludes already mentioned, the same form of proceeding will be observed for the points and the colloquy as was given in the first contemplation on the Supper; and at the hours of Mass and Vespers two repetitions will be made on the first and second contemplations, and afterward, before supper, an application of the senses on the above-mentioned contemplations, always first using the preparatory prayer and the three preludes according to the subject matter, in the same form already laid down and explained in the second week" (204).

Fifth, there is the frequent occurrence of the word "mystery." Ignatius always refers to the subject matter of this week as mysteries. Where he gives points, he writes: "de los misterios hechos desde . . ." (290-98). As soon as the fourth week begins, he writes: "de la resurrección . . . ." (299).

Sixth, in connection with this it must be observed that the exercitant passes quickly through the first three points of every contemplation, which are the same as those in the contemplations of the second week, namely, to see the persons, to hear what they say, and to watch what they do (194). He then concentrates on three other points, all of them introduced by "considerar," the object being how Christ suffers in His humanity, how His divinity hides itself, and how He suffers all this for man's sins (195-97). Clearly, the exercitant tries to understand and enter more deeply into the mystery of all the sufferings undergone by God-made-Man. The shift from contemplation to consideration in these three points takes place, be it noted, within the contemplation. The shift is already discernible in the composition, where "considerar" replaces "ver."[2]

Seventh, Ignatius writes about the colloquy as if the exercitant required elementary instructions. The text reads, in the translation of Morris: "It is to be noticed, as has been before in part declared, that in colloquies we ought to reason and make supplication according to the subject-matter; that is to say, according as I find myself in temptation or in consolation, and according as I desire to have one virtue or another; according as I wish to dispose myself to one side or another; according as I desire to grieve or rejoice in the matter which I contemplate; finally, asking for what I more vehemently desire with regard to any particular matter" (199). To make the impact of this description stronger, it must be placed beside what Ignatius wrote when dealing with the colloquy for the first time: "The colloquy is made properly by speaking as one friend to another, or as a servant to his master; at one time asking for some favour, at another blaming oneself for some evil committed, now informing him of one's affairs, and seeking counsel in them" (54). Two questions have to be asked: why does Ignatius return to the subject of the colloquy at such length, and what is the reason for the change of contents? The answers to these two questions will at the same time suggest the explanation of the other striking points noted in the text of this third week.

The answer to the first question is that a higher degree of contemplative prayer is expected of the exercitant. In the third chapter we have seen how the colloquy, borne up by *hablar,* points to a great intimacy and how it becomes the climax to which meditation and contemplation move. That Ignatius returns to the subject at some length and dwells upon its definition proves that he is somewhat apprehensive lest in this third week the colloquy might lag behind the increased intensity of contemplation; the exercitant needs further guidance.

The answer to the second question can only be given if the contents are accurately examined. The word "hablar" has disappeared. Ignatius substitutes "razonar." Roothaan translates this by "ratiocinari," but the translation given by Puhl "to talk over motives" is much to be preferred.[3] It is a word that lacks the simplicity and intimacy of "hablar." If it be pointed out and objected that "hablar" was not used in the triple colloquy of the second week either (147), it must be remembered that there Ignatius is not giving a description of what a colloquy should be. *Razonar* is followed by *pedir;* the latter verb is found in every description of the colloquy. The two words must be taken together (hablar pidiendo, 109, and razonar y pedir, 199).

Attention must now be paid to the quartet of possible subjects about which the exercitant is to talk and to present petitions. The quartet is preceded by "según la subiecta materia." One would expect that in the week of the Passion the subject matter would be the sufferings of Christ, or Christ suffering. In fact, the phrase refers to what the exercitant undergoes: he finds himself in consolation or desolation, he desires to have this virtue or another, he wants to dispose himself this way or that, or he wants to grieve and rejoice over the matter he contemplates. These four topics emphasize two things: first, the exercitant is no outsider or spectator; on the contrary, he is much more deeply committed than he was in previous weeks. One need only compare the rather vague "según que en sí sintiere" of the contemplation on the Incarnation with the detailed possibilities indicated here. Second, Ignatius steers the exercitant toward decisions. The difference in this respect with the first colloquy of the Spiritual Exercises is obvious. There the exercitant asked himself the questions: what have I done? what am I doing? what ought I to do for Christ? (53). In this colloquy it is a question of this virtue or that, or being disposed this way or that. The final phrase of the colloquy strikes hard: "asking for what I more vehemently desire with regard to some particular matters." The autograph text uses "que más efficazmente desseo," which is more meaningful than the translation just given. Ignatius *steers* the exercitant to decisions, no more. The colloquy is not a time of making resolutions and taking decisions: it does not move beyond "razonar y pedir." It does not lose its true character of intimate conversation with God, but there can be no doubt that the conversation will turn upon practical matters. It is as if Ignatius is afraid lest the exercitant be merely interested in what he contemplates or contemplates in a receptive mood or frame of mind, satisfied when he feels drawn to pity and compassion.

This leads to another observation concerning the care taken by Ignatius to make sure that this week is made with the utmost concentration and surrender. From the early morning and throughout the day, the exercitant will rouse, even force, himself to sorrow, suffering, and anguish, always making an effort to be sad and grieve because of the Lord's Passion (206), and each contemplation will be marked by a similar effort (195). On the one hand, this seems to indicate that the exercitant must not be satisfied with watching what is happening in Holy Week: he must draw profit (sacar provecho) from what he sees and hears (194, 195, 196). On the other hand, it seems to imply that the exercitant will be tempted to skim the mysteries of this week so as possibly to be content with sadness and grief because of the shameful way the Lord is treated by His enemies. But it is quite another thing to have it repeatedly pointed out that Christ suffers and dies for him and for his sins: *por mí* and *por mis peccados* (193, 197, 203). Nobody likes to be continually reminded of the fact that God suffered for *his* sins and died for *him*. Ignatius makes this aspect of the truth a central factor in the third week, so much so that nowhere does he suggest that Christ is the Redeemer of the whole human family: in this week He is the Saviour of the exercitant. The wide dimensions of the contemplation on the Incarnation and the meditation on Two Standards may be said to recede somewhat into the background. The exercitant is very much thrown back upon himself and upon his relations with the *Criador puesto en cruz*.

Another matter that recurs insistently in every contemplation makes heavy demands upon the exercitant. It is the consideration of what he ought *to suffer* for Christ (197). The sixth and last point of all contemplations reads as follows: "The sixth point is to consider that He suffers all these things for my sins, etc. and what I ought to do and suffer for Him" ("Considerar cómo todo esto padesce por mis peccados etc., y qué debo yo hacer y padescer por él"). Rather unexpected and difficult to explain is the *etc.* which follows "por mis peccados." Be it noted that the autograph text shows no sign of a comma preceding *etc.* There appear to be three explanations for its use. The first makes *etcetera* into a tacit extension of "peccados," such as faults, defects, negligences. This explanation is to be discarded, as it would only weaken the impact of the sixth point, giving a descending scale of wrongs committed. The second possibility is that *etcetera* refers back to "todo esto"; its meaning would now be that the exercitant considers how Christ suffers *all this*, does not destroy His enemies, does not call upon twelve legions of angels, allows His sacred Humanity to undergo so much pain, and the like. The objection to this explanation is that *etcetera* is entirely superfluous, and is made superfluous exactly by "todo esto": *all this* leaves no room for *etcetera.* Moreover, the absence of the comma would be very hard to justify. The third and most likely interpretation is that *etcetera* stands for an extension of "por mis peccados." The exercitant will consider how Christ suffers all this for his sins, and then adds, in order to save him from eternal damnation, to make him happy for all eternity, and above all, in order to win his love. In other words, "por mis peccados" almost stands for "por mí," which is found in the third prelude of the second contemplation of this week (203).

Neither "por mis peccados" nor "por mí" is entirely new. On the contrary, "por mí" has played its part ever since the contemplation on the Nativity, in which the exercitant considered how the Lord was born in extreme poverty, that after many labors, hunger, thirst, heat and cold, after insults and outrages, He might die on the cross, and all this *for me* (todo esto por mí, 116). In a similar way, "por mis peccados" has played its unobtrusive part since the first exercise, in which the exercitant began to ponder why God became Man in order to die for his sins (53). Precisely because of this "por mí" and "por mis peccados" the impact of the verb "padescer" is now so much the stronger. This matter of suffering for Christ cannot be deferred to some future time. Ignatius did not have the future primarily in mind, or he would have used "para adelante", or he would have pointed to matters that need ordering and amendment, as he did in the first week (63). The retreat is not a time of reflection upon what one ought to do afterward. Suffering for Christ does not belong to a future date. It is part of the third week and part of all true order; hence, a great effort must be made to suffer for Christ and with Christ.

*With Christ,* and here another difficulty comes to the fore. Suffering for Christ means suffering *with* Christ, *now* undergoing His Passion. In the third prelude of the second contemplation, the exercitant will "beg for sorrow with Christ in sorrow, for anguish with Christ in anguish, for tears and deep grief because of the great affliction Christ endures for me" (203). The prayer recalls the third kind of humility, in which a person chooses poverty with Christ poor, insults with Christ loaded with insults, and to be esteemed useless and a fool for Christ's sake, who was first held to be such, in order to imitate Him and to be like Him *más actualmente,* the correct translation of which appears to be "here and now" (167).[4] The mystery of suffering with Christ here and now is underlined in the sixth addition; Ignatius speaks of the mystery in which the exercitant is now engaged, or more accurately, in which he now finds himself, in which he now stands (206). This, too, is not entirely new. In the contemplation on the Nativity he contemplates "as if he were present." Very significantly, "as if" has now been omitted.

From the various observations made on the text so far it emerges that the central point of the third week is the great mystery of the close union between the suffering Christ and the exercitant. This one-ness is so alarming that the exercitant is warned not to try to evade it, and he is told more than once to exert himself to live this one-ness with all its consequences. It is high time to turn to the contemplation itself, and see how its structure bears out the same fact.

## Preludes

In the second week, Ignatius gave two sets of preludes and points, thereby indicating that a contemplation may be made in two different ways. In this third week, once again he deals with the first two contemplations rather extensively, but the reason cannot be the same. For there appears to be very little difference between the exercise on the Last Supper and the one on the Agony in the Garden (191-99, 200-03). What difference there is, is confined to the three preludes, because the six points and the colloquy of the second contemplation "have the same form of proceeding" as the first (204). Comparing and contrasting the exposition of the two sets of preludes, one soon discovers that there is no question of two different forms of contemplation. At first sight, the only difference to be discovered appears to be that the first contemplation deals with "Christ *going to His Passion* for the exercitant's sins" (193), while the second, and consequently all the contemplations following, deal with Christ *suffering* for him (203). Thus, the first contemplation looks like a transition from the second to the third week or like an introduction to the contemplations on the Passion. This finds a certain confirmation in that Ignatius writes of the contemplation "de la cena," omitting the word "mystery" (289). So, all the contemplations of the third week appear to have for their model the contemplation on the Agony in the Garden. The necessary inference from this observation is that the contemplations of the third week have no composition, although they have a second prelude. This sounds startling, and the statement needs clarification and certain qualifications.

The difference between the two sets of preludes is not only that between "Christ going to His Passion" and "Christ actually suffering." A second difference is that in the second contemplation the word "composición" is omitted. It is the only time that it is missing. Ignatius does use the phrase "to see the place," but immediately replaces "ver" by "considerar." Should the omission of "composición" be explained as due to slovenliness or oversight, or was it left out on purpose and for good reasons? The first alternative must be set aside: Ignatius spent too much care on the text, and this for many years, to permit us to accept this, especially as the composition is of such fundamental importance in his Exercises. If he left it out on purpose, it may be explained in two ways: either because the composition was to be discarded as something useless and out of place, which is rather unlikely, or because the composition had already been achieved, so that a second prelude of composing oneself had become superfluous. If this is the case, the task usually assigned to the composition must have been taken over by the first prelude, that is, the history.

In giving the history of the second contemplation, Ignatius deviates from normal practice in three points. First, when the history of the contemplations on the Incarnation and the Nativity is given, after a few introductory remarks, the exercitant is referred to the section containing the points, placed after the four weeks (103, 111). In the third week, there is no such reference. All the material is packed in this first prelude, and it is given in detail. In the second contemplation, no less than thirteen incidents are enumerated, and there are no less than seven references to the place where the incidents happen. It looks as if the *shape* of the mystery in time and place is more intricately bound up with the mystery itself than before.

Second, Ignatius inserts two non-Scriptural words into the history of the first contemplation, namely, "sanctíssimo" and "preciosa," preceding "cuerpo" and "sangre" respectively. This cannot be a question of historical embellishment, as was the case with the maid and the donkey, introduced as objects of pious meditation in the first prelude of the contemplation on the Nativity (111). The unexpected choice and insertion of these two words suggest that the exercitant respond to the historical events to which he is made present; he is engaged already.

Third, whereas in the second week the past tense is used in the history ("miraban," 102;[5] "salieron," 111), Ignatius shows a preference for the present tense, the final clause for instance of the prelude of the second contemplation being "how they drag Him down the valley and up the slopes" ("cómo le llevan el valle abajo y después la cuesta arriba," 201). Ignatius will soon write of the mystery "en que al presente me hallo" (206).

These three observations show that the history, as the first prelude, has to a considerable extent taken over the task normally assigned to the composition as the second prelude. Hence, it is not quite accurate to maintain, as we did above, that the contemplations of the third week have no composition; they have, but the first and second preludes are now so closely merged into one that Ignatius purposely dispenses with the word "composición." All this is foreshadowed by what we read about the second addition. The impression is once again given that Ignatius had never spoken of it before and that the exercitant had never been told what to do on rising during the night or in the morning, whereas careful instructions have been given both in the first and the second week (74, 130). The exercitant will on rising turn his thoughts to the subject matter of the exercise he is to make. In the first week, the expression "advertir luego a lo que voy a contemplar" is used. In the second (and also in the fourth, 229), Ignatius writes "poner enfrente de mí la contemplación que tengo de hacer." In the third week, he prefers "poniendo delante de mí." This appears to be more apt because more concrete or more strictly local than "enfrente de mí," as is shown from its use elsewhere in the Exercises.[6] Besides this, we find that the object changes: "poniendo delante de mí adónde voy y a qué, resumiendo un poco la contemplación . . ." (206). The exercitant shall, while rising and dressing, make a resumption of the contemplation he is going to make. This is a first approach to the contemplation itself, and this idea of approach is underlined by both "poniendo delante de mí" and by its object "whither I am going and for what purpose." Approach seems to be too weak a word, because the exercitant is told at the same time to exert himself to grieve and sorrow over so much grief and suffering of Christ.

Another important observation must be made regarding this second addition. Its wording corresponds with what Ignatius writes in the fifth note of the second week: "Immediately on my perceiving that it is the hour of the exercise I have to make, before proceeding to it, I will place before my eyes whither I am going and in whose presence I am, and I will shortly pass over in my mind the exercise which I am about to make." ("Luego en acordándome que es hora del exercitio que tengo de hacer, antes que me vaya, *poniendo delante de mí adónde voy* y delante de quién, *resumiendo un poco el exercicio que tengo de hacer,*" 131). This advice concerns the repetitions to be made in the second week. It recalls the fourth exercise of the first week, entirely devoted to the resumption, with its stress upon "cosas contempladas" which, as we have shown, is closely connected with consolation, desolation and spiritual feeling (64, 62). Evidently, then, the approach to the morning contemplation in this third week is almost in the nature of a resumption; it is as if contemplations and repetitions have gone before. This can only point to one thing: the subject matter of the contemplation which the exercitant is about to make is of relative unimportance. The mystery of Christ completely dominates the mystery of what He is enduring. It emphasizes the fact that to a large extent the composition of the exercitant with the suffering Christ has already been accomplished; this is the reason why he could leave out the word.

Some other irregularities in the text of the second prelude are not difficult to understand. The verb "ver" is still used, but it is immediately replaced by "considerar." The object of the verb also changes. In the contemplation on the Incarnation, the exercitant pays special attention to the room and house of Our Lady ("particularmente la casa y aposentos de Nuestra Señora," 103); in the contemplation on the Nativity, he sees the way from Nazareth to Bethlehem, considering its length, its breadth, whether level or through valleys and over hills; similarly, he looks closely (mirar) at the place and the cave where Christ is born, how big, how small, how high, how low and how it is arranged (112). Now the composition reads: "to consider the way from Bethany to Jerusalem, whether narrow or wide or level, and similarly, the place of the Supper, whether great, whether small, whether of this appearance or that" (si de una manera o si de otra,

192). In the second contemplation: "to consider the way from Mount Sion to the valley of Josaphat, and similarly, the garden, whether broad, whether long, whether of this appearance or that" (si de una manera, si de otra, 202). We notice that "cómo" and "quan" have disappeared in the preludes of the third week. Details no longer matter, hence, "si de una manera, si de otra." Details might now become a hindrance instead of a help. The role of the senses in the composition is not nearly as important as it was in the second week.

In connection with the composition we usually spoke of new dimensions being added, of a widening of the reality in which the exercitant moves. In the third week there is no question of an expansion of the exercitant's composition. Horizontally, so to speak, not much happens. The exercitant moves smoothly from the second week into the third. But the brief phrase to which we have alluded above must not be overlooked by the exercitant: the Lord is going to His Passion for *his* sins. This might be called the new dimension that is now added. The mystery of Christ winning back the love of the human family does not only involve Christ waging a fierce battle against Satan but also His taking upon Himself the sins of the exercitant and deleting them completely. It is not so much a widening of the composition as a narrowing and deepening of it.

Points

This deepening of the composition accounts for both "suffering for Christ" and "suffering with Christ" in this third week. It also explains why the exercitant will penetrate the mystery of Christ suffering far beyond what is presented to his senses. The first triplet of points is of minor importance. The second, consisting of three considerations, contains the marrow of this exercise. Ignatius makes the rhythm of contemplation recur not three times but four times. In the preludes the theme is given. It is played through a second time in the first three points, and the resumptions finally repeat it. For the third time it is found in the second triplet of points. The exercitant considers the same theme and the same scene, but this time he concentrates on what is invisible, namely, on what Christ suffers and is prepared to suffer in His humanity (195). Humanity is not identical with body. More painful than all bodily sufferings is the contempt, the derision, the disappointment, the betrayal, the failure. That is what He suffers in His humanity, as Man, as this Man. Next the exercitant will consider how the divinity hides itself (196). Ignatius explains what he means: Christ, being God, could destroy His enemies and, we might add, could prevent and thwart their wickedness, or could call upon twelve legions of angels, but He "allows His sacred humanity to suffer in such a cruel way" (196). This immediately prompts the question, "why"? The answer is given in the sixth point: how else would the exercitant be saved?

The whole of the third week is inspired by the intimacy that develops between the exercitant and Christ suffering. The words "dolor, quebranto, pena, lágrimas, tormento, doler and entristecer" form an awe-inspiring group, especially when followed by "con Christo."[7] The subject matter of the mysteries matters less, the number of mysteries matters less; it does not even matter whether the exercitant makes repetitions. It is all the same whether he makes one contemplation, which he repeats a number of times, finally adding an application of the senses, or whether he takes five distinct mysteries for his five contemplations (209). For the heart of any contemplation and any repetition is the same: Christ suffering for the exercitant and for his sins. Prayer becomes very affective as is clear from the guidance given by Ignatius to the exercitant on rising, and in the third prelude together with the colloquy. As a result, at the end of the week he is not primarily filled with gratitude because he has been saved (as at the end of the first week), nor primarily moved to compassion because of the great sufferings of God-made-Man, but first and foremost he is drawn to love. Notwithstanding the many tears (llorar mucho sobre las penas y dolores . . . 87), he is not brokenhearted. The change from "por mis peccados," which occurs twice in the first contemplation and never again after that (193, 197), to "por mí," which takes its place in the second contemplation and, consequently, in all the other exercises of this week, may now be seen in its true perspective, and how weighty a change it is. The resting point is once again "humildad amorosa."

Rules with Regard to Eating

Depths of mystery and heights of prayer are characteristic of the exercises of the third week, which are at the same time notably practical and businesslike. In the sixth point of every contemplation the exercitant considers what he must do and suffer for Christ, and in every colloquy he will talk things over "according as he desires to have one virtue or another, wishes to dispose himself to one side or another, always asking for what he more vehemently desires with regard to any particular matter" ("más efficazmente cerca algunas cosas particulares desseo," 199). Even the colloquy of the meditation on Two Standards, which he has made some twenty-five times, may be continued, "together with the note that follows the meditation on Three Classes of Men" (199). The impression is thereby given that the *quando* of that note may be very well placed in this third week. Besides, there are the rules with regard to eating, "reglas para ordenarse en el comer para adelante" (210-17). Could there be any greater contrast than between the many tears shed with Christ (87) and the down-to-earth advice about the quality and quantity of one's food?

In the third chapter, the question was put whether or not these rules belong to the third week or whether they are primarily meant for a different class of persons altogether, just as the instructions given in the first week (24-44) and in the second week (169-89) were not given for the exercitant of the thirty days' retreat. We recall that the reference to "internas noticias, consolaciones y divinas inspiraciones" in the fourth rule is quite in keeping with the high degree of prayer that marks the third week. Another question might be asked: why does Ignatius give practical rules with regard to eating, and why not with regard to other forms of penance? One must be careful here. Ignatius is not giving rules for some form of penance; eating is not a penance and it is not to be turned into penance. A better question would be why Ignatius did not formulate rules with regard to sleeping, to recreation, to social contacts, and so forth. The answer was given in our third chapter, though rather hesitantly. It was suggested that the contemplation on the Last Supper may have reminded Ignatius of the whole matter of meals. We are less hesitant now. The colloquy is meant to be practical in this third week, as has been shown; "más efficazmente," which Roothaan translates by "magis efficaciter," must on no account be overlooked. But Ignatius leaves the exercitant free to make the triple colloquy of the meditation on Two Standards "if the matter or devotion moves him to do so" (199). So the matter may suggest the contents of the colloquy, or it may urge the exercitant now to become practical. Ignatius gives a self-explanatory example of what he means. In the first contemplation, the exercitant is present at the Last Supper, and this *matter* prompts him to dispose himself this way or that with regard to food and drink. In the fifth rule, Ignatius appears to point to the link between the rules and the Last Supper.

The important conclusion is that these rules are meant to be exemplary, and this in a threefold function. First, regarding the matter itself: The exercitant should not confine himself to ordering his life with regard to eating and drinking. When he spends the day contemplating Christ in prayer during the night, it would not be out of place if he turned his attention to the question of prayer at night and vigils. When he contemplates Christ derided by Herod, it would not be out of keeping with the true contents and purpose of the third week if he considered his own future with regard to his eagerness to be appreciated and praised, to be esteemed and honored. Secondly, regarding the principles given by Ignatius: The real value and importance of the rules relating to eating lie in this, that they are rules, or directions, and these go back to certain fundamental principles, which have a far wider application than merely to eating and drinking. The principles fall outside the scope of this study. It is enough to point out how firmly they are imbedded in the twofold trend of the Spiritual Exercises, namely, the removal of anything that is inordinate (210, 212, 217), which should always be identical with achieving right order (211, 213), and shaping one's life after that of Christ. As for this latter trend, it should be noted that Ignatius is not opposed to one's continuing considerations and even contemplations while one is occupied with matters that have little directly to do with prayer, such as eating (215). This leads us to speak of the third function of the rules with regard to eating, the breadth and depth of their application.

The widening, and especially the deepening, of the exercitant's composition during the third week emphasize how order and harmony lead to higher prayer. The exercitant does not make the Exercises that he might think about order and about ordering his life but that he might achieve these and continue them in his daily life. The third week, containing the second and first week, and as we shall see, also the fourth week, has to be carried into the future and must become part and parcel of the exercitant's life. It is untrue and dangerous to maintain that his future life is a question of living the second week. Hence, his life will be marked by prayer and by penance. The composition reached in the third week is impossible without a high degree of contemplative prayer. Neither can it exist without "parescer mâs actualmente a Christo pobre, lleno de opprobrios, etc." (167). This involves penance, but penance always stands for harmony between inner disposition and external behavior, both being inspired by the desire for a life shaped after the model of Christ. The rules with regard to eating give clear expression to this marriage between contemplation and the motives and methods of practicing penance.[8]

Structure of the Week

The exercitant moves gradually through the whole story of the Passion of Christ. On the fifth day he contemplates Christ's death on the cross. The sixth day is spent in contemplating the burial of Christ and what happens to Our Lady in "the house to which she retired after the burial of her Son" (208). On the seventh and last day the contemplation at midnight is devoted to the whole Passion, as is that made on rising. There are no repetitions on this last day. The exercitant will consider as frequently as possible ("quanto mâs freqüente podrâ") how the most sacred body of Christ remained detached and separated from the soul, and where and how it was buried; he will consider also the solitude of Mary, her great sorrow, and weariness; and in a similar way, he will consider the loneliness of the disciples (208). Two days are thus devoted to the mystery of Christ dead and buried and to that of our Lady's loneliness and, to a lesser extent, to the loneliness of the apostles. But this is not entirely true. On the day following the last day of the third week, the exercitant once again makes himself present to the mystery of Christ dying on the cross, of His body remaining separated from His soul, but united with His divinity. Again, the exercitant will see the holy sepulchre, and the house of our Lady, beholding all the parts of it, in particular, her chamber and oratory; in this way he will make his composition (220). It is evidently another day spent with Christ buried and with His lonely Mother. This day is actually the first day of the fourth week: we have just now given part of the two preludes of the contemplation on the

Resurrection. Here we have to anticipate the fourth week in order fully to understand the third week, especially in its closing phase.

The end of the third week does not differ from the beginning of the fourth. Ignatius does not use the word "day" when dealing with the fourth week. He does speak of "first contemplation," but never of any day. He gives no contemplation on the Resurrection of Christ. The first contemplation has for subject matter Christ's first apparition, namely, to His Mother (aparesció, 219; paresce y se muestra, 223). There is no break whatever between the third week and the fourth. The first day of the fourth week might just as well be called the eighth day of the third week, or the last day of the third week might be called the beginning of the fourth week. If the preludes of history and composition are as important as throughout this study we have made them out to be, there can be only one conclusion, namely, that as the last day of the third week is the first day of the fourth, similarly the death of Christ is at the same time His resurrection. It would be even more in accordance with the text to hold that Christ's being dead is His risen life. A contemplation on the Resurrection would disturb and distort the essential oneness between Good Friday and Easter Sunday. In Christ's burial, body and soul are separated (desatado, apartado, 208; separado, 219), but both are *unido con la divinidad* (219); this fact manifests itself visibly in Christ's risen life, which clearly is the translation of "resurrección" in the fourth point of the first contemplation of this week. Ignatius expresses this tremendous mystery in his own simple, perhaps even primitive way, but his vision of the mystery of death and resurrection is well ahead even of modern theological opinion.

The problem of adapting the Spiritual Exercises is not dealt with in this study in any exhaustive way. But the main objection to the contemplations of the third week cannot be by-passed: they appear to be fairly useless for modern man. This, not merely because Christians today are not easily moved to tears and grief, but also because they think it untruthful to weep with Christ, who, in fact, is risen, and whose sufferings are a thing of the past. The objection sounds plausible, yet betrays a considerable lack of insight into the mystery of the risen Christ. For Ignatius, it was always a dead Christ who was raised to life; for him the Resurrection is not the undoing by the Father of what the Jews did to His Son. If it is Christ dead and buried who rose again, the risen Christ will always be the Christ who was rejected, is still rejected, and, to a certain extent, is rejected by the exercitant through his own sinfulness. In the letter to the Hebrews, this is called "crucifying Him again" (6.6). There is, then, good reason for grieving with Christ full of grief.

Another way by which modern man might overcome the difficulty in question is by concentrating on the wonderful things that happen when he listens to a story, to any story, but especially to a story told by God about His own Son. We refer the reader to the chapter on meditation and contemplation.

Ignatius was a great mystic and the book of the *Spiritual Exercises* is the work of a mystic, and it contains his mystical experiences. Hence, only a mystic will be able fully to comprehend the unfathomed depths of contemplative prayer in this third week and fully understand the language used by Ignatius. It is a good director's task to penetrate what Ignatius had in mind and then to open the road for the exercitant to the heights of prayer and the depths of affliction with Christ. He must on no account make the third week into a series of exercises on the Passion of Christ and reduce it to a time in which resolutions made in the second week are confirmed.

thirteen

# THE FOURTH WEEK

The outline of the last phase of the Spiritual Exercises can confidently be surmised. The intimate relationship between the exercitant and Christ, crucified but alive, will increase. There will be a greater union with the crucified Lord in His risen life. The incidents of this risen life will be of secondary importance, not only because incidents became of less importance in the course of the third week, but mainly because the apparitions bear quite a different relation to Christ's risen life from that of incidents in His hidden and public life in the mystery of God-made-Man. Since all the apparitions are meant to be proofs that Christ is alive, the way in which this is manifested will always take second place. Furthermore, we expect that affective prayer will develop. The cooperation between the exercitant and God, who wishes to communicate Himself to him (15) will become deeply mysterious, because the obstacles that hinder it may be presumed to have been cleared away in the third week. The question, "what must I do and suffer for Christ?" will have dispelled any seeking after *provechos y intereses temporales*, which form the principal hindrance in this matter (16).

In all likelihood, there will be little desolation and few, if any, temptations. The director will withdraw more and more, giving a bare minimum of advice and guidance. If the purpose of the Exercises is to approach and be united with God (20), communication and unity will be nearing perfection. At this peak of intimacy, anything schematic is to be handled with the greatest circumspection. There will be probably little of this regarding preludes, points, colloquies, number of exercises, number of days, and so on.

Such features of the fourth week, gathered together a priori, are borne out by the text. The number of exercises is reduced from five to four (227). There is no indication how long the week should last; in fact, as was pointed out in the previous chapter, the word "day" is not even used. Ignatius does not insist upon repetitions. From the second note it appears that he does not even leave room for them, with the exception of the application of the senses; we will return to this point later. Because incidents are of little importance, points are hardly given. The exercitant has to be satisfied with "after that He appeared to five hundred brethren at once" (308) and "after that He appeared to James" (309), not to mention "Joseph of Arimathea, as may be piously believed and is read in the lives of the saints" (310). Details of time and place matter little. Indeed, Ignatius does refer in the first three points to seeing, hearing, and watching, but no words are wasted: the exercitant is reminded of what is written in the contemplation on the Last Supper (222). That the first prelude, which is the history, is confined to what happens to Christ and to what actions He performs, is also understandable. A comparison with the histories of the previous weeks will show that now other persons appear only insofar as they are in need of comfort and are comforted by the risen Lord (219).

In the second prelude, which is the composition, the exercitant is not asked to make use of "vista imaginativa," he is permitted to see and watch ("ver y mirar"). A rich choice of objects is opened up for the exercitant: the holy sepulchre, the place or the house of our Lady, its different parts, her oratory, her room (220). This is followed by "etc.", which should not escape attention, nor should the absence of details. The "how large, how small, and so forth," of previous compositions is missing, and even the "whether great or little, and so on" of the third week can now be dispensed with. There is no guidance in the matter of the colloquy, and the particular examination of conscience is passed over silently. Naturally, the exercitant is not called "persona que se exercita" but "persona que contempla" (228). For the first and only time, the contents of the exercise are not mentioned in the title. Ignatius indicates the subject matter but does not tell the exercitant that the contemplation consists of preparatory prayer, preludes, points, and a colloquy.

Ignatius leaves no room for repetitions, as was pointed out above. The exercitant will make a contemplation in the early morning, another at the hour of Mass, instead of the first repetition, a third at the hour of Vespers, instead of the second repetition, and before supper he will make the application of the senses (227). The function of the repetitions is taken over by the application of the senses. It is instructive to see how accurate Ignatius once again is.

Dealing with the repetitions in the first week, he writes: "notando y haciendo pausa en los punctos que he sentido mayor consolación o desolación o mayor sentimiento espiritual" (62). Returning to the subject in the second week, he writes: "notando siempre algunas partes más principales, donde haya sentido la persona algún conoscimiento, consolación o desolación" (118). The text of the application of the senses in the fourth week reads: "notando y haciendo pausa en las partes más principales, y donde haya sentido mayores mociones y gustos spirituales" (227). Comparing and contrasting these three texts, we notice that "desolación", occurring in the texts of the first and second weeks, does not appear where Ignatius deals with the fourth week. "Sentimiento" and "conoscimiento" of the first two weeks have been replaced by "mayores mociones y gustos spirituales." Knowledge and feeling undoubtedly form part of more intense stirrings and spiritual relish, but at the same time, *mayores mociones y gustos spirituales* cover a far wider field of spiritual experiences. The expression reminds one of the closing phrase of the second annotation.

One more point needs attention. In the repetitions of the second week, the *partes más principales* are those where the exercitant derived some knowledge, consolation, or desolation. In the application of the senses of the fourth week, Ignatius clearly distinguishes these parts from those where the exercitant experienced greater motions and spiritual relish. He now writes: "partes más principales y donde hay sentido mayores mociones y gustos spirituales" (227). The autograph text has no comma before the conjunction *y*. The principal parts of the contemplations of the fourth week are given in the fourth and fifth points; they will be discussed later in this chapter.

Affective Prayer

"Mayores mociones y gustos spirituales" points to affective prayer. In a sense, this form of prayer is not new to the exercitant, but a significant change is taking place within this affective prayer. The first week is a time for affective prayer, as is evident from the shame, confusion, contrition, and tears for which the exercitant insistently begs. The affections and motions have for their source the situation in which the exercitant finds himself as a sinful, ungrateful, deeply fallen man. There is affective prayer in the second week. There has been the earnest wish and desire to know the Lord better and love Him more, and it may be safely assumed that there has been more ardent love based on greater knowledge. That the exercitant keeps on praying for knowledge that leads to love implies that he knows himself to be ignorant and insensible, and that he remains apprehensive lest knowledge should remain sterile; in other words, his affections are not yet detached from his own plight. In the third week, affective prayer increases considerably. One recalls the effort which the exercitant is asked to make repeatedly in order to be sad and to grieve. The affections are in no small measure inspired by "por mí" and "por mis peccados," which again proves that the affections are not yet detached from his own situation. In the fourth week, one soon discovers that there is complete self-forgetfulness: the affections are entirely outgoing. They are inspired by the Lord, irrespective of the exercitant's own wishes, condition, and so on.

The fourth week is immersed in joy. As soon as he awakes, the exercitant will strive to feel joy and happiness, and in the course of the day he will call to mind and think on what causes pleasure, happiness and spiritual joy; he will make use of light and the pleasures of the seasons, if these help him to rejoice (229). At the beginning of every contemplation, he will ask for the favor to rejoice and to be intensely glad (221). This joy has one cause only, namely, the joy and happiness of the Lord together with His glory (tanta gloria y gozo de Christo, 221; tanto gozo y alegría de Christo, 229). The exercitant's own redemption is passed over in silence as a possible source of joy. No mention is made of his joyful hope of following in glory Him whom he followed in labour and in pain (93). Even Christ's victory is not mentioned, which is remarkable, because in the exercise "del Rey" the ensured victory of the King played an important part in His call (*ibid.*). The exercitant's joy does not spring from what the Lord did for him nor from what He achieved by His Passion and Death, but from what He is now. It is the Person of the risen Christ that dominates everything. The joy and happiness of the Lord cannot, of course, be isolated and separated from the glory with which the Father has endowed Him. For Ignatius the glory and triumph of Christ are in strict harmony with the words of St. Paul: "He emptied Himself and became obedient unto death; *hence* the Father gave Him a Name," and so forth. This means, once again, that in the Spiritual Exercises the Lord of the fourth week is always the Lord who died. There is nothing more disastrous in understanding the Spiritual Exercises than to separate the third and fourth weeks.

The joy and happiness of the Lord lie at the root of the exercitant's joy. No matter what his own sufferings are and, consequently, how great his need of comfort is, his is a most unselfish joy. There is an intense closeness of affections between the risen Lord and the exercitant. Instead of closeness, the classical expression "vida unitiva" could be used. It does not occur in the Exercises, but where Ignatius associates the first week with the purgative life and the second with the illuminative life—Ignatius prefers "life" to "way": it is more expressive (10)—he suggests that the other weeks move the exercitant toward the unitive life. It is then understandable that the relationship between Christ and the exercitant is now one of friendship (224). The exercise "del Rey" speaks of "todos los suyos" (93) and of servants (señalar en todo *servicio,* 97). In the contemplation on the Nativity, the exercitant made himself a poor little servant, unworthy at that ("un pobrecito y esclavito indigno," 114). In the meditation on Two Standards, Christ addresses His apostles and disciples as servants and friends ("sus siervos y amigos," 146). In this fourth week, the exercitant is called friend.

There is no need to stress the fact that amazement accompanies the joy of the exercitant. When reading the text, parts of which we have quoted, one will notice the use of "tanto." What may escape attention is that Ignatius does not refer to the risen Lord as Saviour or Redeemer. This fits in with what has been said about the unselfish character of the exercitant's joy. At the same time it shows how the four weeks are not a question of re-enacting salvation-history. The final resting point of the fourth week is not that the exercitant has been saved, but that the name of Christ is "Señor," the name given Him by the Father (221, 222, 224, 229). This explains why Ignatius has no contemplation on the exercitant's own resurrection or on heaven. It would turn his mind away from Christ to himself. Resurrection and heaven and similar subjects only have a place in the Spiritual Exercises as a form of Christ's *officio de consolar* (224).

A few remarks must be made with regard to this "office of comforting His friends", which should be carefully looked at (mirar) in the fifth point of all contemplations. We observe first of all that no persons are mentioned. In the third week, and to a less extent in the second week, the figure of the exercitant was always hovering somewhere behind the words of the text; we need only recall "por mí" and "por mis peccados." Now, no trace of any person can be found. It is Christ's task to comfort. It does not matter whether He comforts the exercitant here and now: the exercitant is fascinated by the fact that His office is to dry tears, to encourage, to console, to give more faith, hope and charity, and so forth (316). Secondly, for Ignatius, the apparitions intend no more and no less than to show that He is alive, and that to be alive means to fulfill this office of comforting His own. Thirdly, one can now understand why Ignatius does not mention the historical event of Pentecost. This mystery no doubt presents emphatic proof of Christ's comforting powers, for He sends His Spirit. At the same time it fixes the attention upon those who are, so to speak, at the receiving end of His comfort. But Ignatius wants the exercitant to find his rest in the Comforter Himself, who is always comforting, whose office it is to comfort, and always does so by sending His Spirit. It explains why Ignatius fails to round off the fourth week, as many wish he had done.

This supplies a clue for understanding why Ignatius deviates from the chronological order of mysteries and events. In the fourth annotation, the fourth week is said to be the week of the Resurrection and the Ascension. In the series of points given after the three methods of prayer, the exercises are flanked by the opening exercise on the Resurrection and the closing exercise on the Ascension (299, 312). The apparition to St. Paul, which certainly took place after the Ascension, now precedes it (311). Evidently, it makes no difference whether the apparition takes place before or after the Ascension; the office of comforting His friends is fulfilled as much during the forty days preceding the Ascension as after it. The Spiritual Exercises are not what might be called a "closed circuit." This interpretation could follow if Ignatius had placed the apparition to St. Paul in its right historical place, an exception implying that Christ's office as Consoler had ceased with the Ascension. We need not point out that the danger of adding contemplations on Pentecost, the Last Day, and

Heaven similarly is this idea of a closed circuit. But if the Exercises aim at ordering the exercitant's life, there must be no closed circuit suggestion at all: part of right order is that he knows himself to be moving toward the Parousia, all the while being comforted by the risen Lord.

## To Rejoice in His Creator and Redeemer

One would not expect the seventh addition to be uncommonly important in this fourth week. In the first week, Ignatius tells the exercitant that darkness might be a help toward achieving what he desires (79). He returns to the subject in the second week and now makes mention of darkness and light, of fine weather or the opposite (130). This advice holds good for the third week (206). Surprisingly, he becomes rather wordy about it in the fourth week. Darkness is not mentioned; but besides light, he now speaks of the pleasures of the seasons, the refreshing coolness in summer, the sun and the fire in winter (229). He then adds—and the autograph text is indispensable here—"en quanto el ánima piensa o coniecta que la puede ayudar, para se gozar en su Criador y Redemptor" ("insofar as the soul thinks or conjectures that they can help it to rejoice in its Creator and Redeemer"). The clause merits careful consideration: why "ánima," why "coniecta," why "gozar en," why "Criador y Redemptor"? Why did Ignatius not write: "insofar as these things help, or are thought to help the exercitant to rejoice because of the great joy of Christ the Lord"? (Cfr. 221, 199).

The verb "coniectar"[1] suggests a certain vagueness and uncertainty. It contains a warning lest the exercitant should tie himself down to any one thing; he must allow himself much freedom. Fixed rules and a definite way of proceeding will now, more than before, hamper the unhindered conversation of the exercitant with God, and might even obstruct God's activity toward him. Contemplation has clearly reached a height which demands the exercitant's courage to be most receptive and responsive to God communicating Himself. This tallies with the choice of the word "ánima," which takes the place of "persona que contempla" (228). It occurs a good number of times in the rules contained in the Spiritual Exercises,[2] but when, as is the case here, it refers to a person, Ignatius always has in mind someone specially devoted or dedicated to God. Its use points to closeness with God. This is easily illustrated by what Ignatius writes in the fifteenth annotation (15) and in his brief description of the first time to make a safe choice (175); in both cases he adds "devota." Further evidence is found in the description of what consolation is (316).[3]

"Gozar en" is unexpected, because after the third prelude "gozar de" would seem to be the logical expression. ("para me alegrar y gozar intensamente de tanta gloria y gozo," 221). It fits in well with the wording of the fourth note of this week: "affectar y alegrar de tanto gozo y alegría de Christo nuestro Señor" (229). One might say that as "gozar" is followed by both *de* and *en* without much difference in meaning, a simple answer should be given to a simple question. The objection to this solution is that the advice given in the seventh addition cannot be separated from what is written in the second addition and in the third prelude of the contemplations of this week. The use of the verb "gozar" in this seventh addition immediately suggests the preposition *de,* because this is found in the two other passages just mentioned and also in the third week (199). The text of the seventh addition would now read: "En quanto el ánima piense o coniecta que la puede ayudar, para se gozar 'de tanto gozo y alegría de Christo nuestro Señor' en su Criador y Redemptor." In order to discover why Ignatius here, and here only, uses the preposition *en,* the combination "Criador y Redemptor" will be examined.

The question to be answered is whether "Criador y Redemptor" refers to the risen Christ. There are sound reasons to believe that it does not. If it did, the exercitant would be asked to rejoice *with* Christ ("gozo con Christo gozozo," 48), to rejoice *on account of* Christ ("gozar de Christo," 221), and to rejoice *in* Him: there is a certain redundancy about this. Besides, outside the first colloquy of the retreat, Christ is never referred to as the Creator, and a careful reading of this colloquy shows that even here Christ is given the function, more than the title of "Creator." Neither is He called "Saviour" or "Redeemer" anywhere in the four weeks.[4] The title given to Him is always "Señor," the use of "Rey" and "Capitán" being strictly confined to the exercises "del Rey" and on Two Standards. It is very unlikely that He is given two new titles in this seventh addition. The conclusion is that "Criador y Redemptor" stands for the Blessed Trinity.

Expressions of the type of "en Dios" are very rare. The first time this expression or its equivalent is found is in this seventh addition. In the rules for the discernment of spirits "en Criador" occurs three times. Giving his description of consolation, Ignatius writes: "The soul is so strongly inflamed to love its Creator and Lord that it cannot love any created thing in itself, but only in the Creator of all things" ("ninguna cosa criada puede amar en sí, sino en el Criador de todas ellas," 316). Toward the end of the same paragraph we read that by consolation is meant every increase of hope, faith, and charity, and every interior joy "filling the soul with quiet and peace in its Creator and Lord (quietándola y pacificándola en su Criador y Señor)." This example is valuable because it retains traces of the almost local meaning of *en:* in the presence of. This is confirmed by the eleventh rule of the first series of rules for the discernment of spirits. The person who is in desolation is advised to reflect that he can do much with the help of God's grace "tomando fuerzas en su Criador y Señor" ("finding strength in his Creator and Lord," 324). The temptation to consider the *en*-expression a pious addition must be resisted. In the tenth rule, Ignatius also speaks of "tomando fuerzas," but omits the phrase "en su Criador y Señor."

The subject of the sentence of this tenth rule is not a person in desolation, as is the case in the eleventh rule, but one who enjoys consolation, that is by definition, a person who has found peace and quiet in and with the Lord. There is, consequently, no reason to advise this person to gain fresh strength in his Creator and Lord, who at that very moment is the source of peace, joy, faith, hope, charity, and so on. Very different is the situation of the person in desolation who, again by definition, finds himself slothful, tepid, and as it were separated from his Creator and Lord (317). This person must gain strength by overcoming his sense of separation, and, hence, by approaching and being with his Creator and Lord: "tomando fuerzas *en* su Criador y Señor."

This meaning of *en* is intended by Ignatius where he asks the exercitant to be full of joy *in his Creator and Redeemer*. The expression stresses close, almost local proximity; it conveys a sense of being in the presence of, and of being one with, the Creator and Lord, and of having come to rest in Him. It points once again to a high degree of contemplative prayer.

The phrasing itself of the concluding line of the seventh addition with "ánima," "coniecta," "gozar," and "en su Criador y Redemptor" strongly suggests that the exercitant's composition has now developed toward the spiritual condition of the twentieth annotation: he is so closely united with the Lord and Creator that he is disposed to receive graces and gifts from His infinite Goodness (20). Naturally, he will now turn his attention to these gifts and graces, which will be described as those of creation and redemption, given by the Creator and Redeemer (234); this constitutes the link between the fourth week and the next contemplation to attain the love of God.

The above analysis and explanation of "gozar en su Criador y Redemptor" have not yet accounted for the circumstance that it is found in the seventh addition. Why did Ignatius not use this or a similar expression in the third prelude? In every week the seventh addition is always inspired by the need for the exercitant to achieve harmony of body and soul, and thus he will sometimes make use of bodily comforts, sometimes forego them. Even in this fourth week Ignatius sounds a warning when, in the tenth addition, he points out that the exercitant should attend to temperance and moderation in all things ("mire la temperancia y todo medio," 229). There is some danger that in his great joy he may forget to attend to harmony not only between body and soul but between himself and external circumstances. One is reminded of the dimensions of the exercitant's composition as indicated in the fifth point of the second exercise of the retreat. These wide dimensions are again suggested by the choice of the combination "Criador y Redemptor." The risen Christ immediately reminds Ignatius of the Father, who now gives Christ a new name, having first sent Him into this world; all this is inspired by Love, who is the Holy Spirit. The exercitant finds his final joy and rest in the Blessed Trinity.

At the risk of repetition, some final observations on the text itself will now be gathered together. The second week opens with a first day and with a first contemplation (101), the third week similarly has a first contemplation with "$1^o$ dia" written in the margin of the page (190). The first week has a first exercise, but no first day is mentioned. This is very accurate because the first exercise normally does not take place on the first day: indispensable days of preparation precede the first exercise. Now, in the fourth week, there is only "primera contemplación"; it is as if Ignatius loses every sense of time. The number of days was noted in the second and third weeks, and in the first week there is at least a fixed number of exercises. Now, neither the number of days nor exercises is mentioned. The impression is given that the fourth week has little of a beginning as there is no break between the contemplations on Good Friday and Easter Sunday, and that it has no end. In fact, not much is laid down. There are a few additions and these mainly purport to restrain the exercitant from becoming self-confident. He must prepare himself for every exercise, he must remain recollected, and he must make his review (additions 1, 3, 8, 9, and 5). It is doubtful whether Ignatius expects him to make his particular examination of conscience. Whereas he is careful to impose this in the other weeks (90, 160, 207), he is silent about it in this week. It all points to one thing: the Creator and Lord communicates Himself to the devout soul in quest of the divine will, embracing him and disposing him for the way in which he will better serve the Divine Majesty in the future (15). The part of the director is confined to seeing that nothing is done hastily or inconsiderately by the exercitant (14). Some other points are best dealt with in the contemplation to attain divine love in the chapter that now follows.

fourteen

# CONTEMPLATION TO ATTAIN THE LOVE OF GOD

It is generally taken for granted that the last exercise of the Spiritual Exercises is the contemplation to attain the love of God. It is very rewarding to examine whether this is true and why and in what sense this exercise rounds off the retreat.

The contemplation shows traces of having been added at a late date. An expression such as "id est se habet ad modum laborantis" (236) speaks for itself. The juxtaposition of to be, to live, to feel, and to understand (235) smacks not a little of the textbook, and the same holds good of the group: dando ser, conservando, vejetando y sensando (236). The autograph text appears to place the contemplation outside the fourth week and outside the retreat. The usual indication of the week in the top left-hand corner of the page is no longer there. This has never happened before, not even when Ignatius gave his presupposition (22), the First Principle and Foundation (23), and the instructions on the examinations of conscience in the first week (24-44), those on making a sound election in the second (169-89), and those concerning food in the third (210-17). At the top of the page, not, as has been Ignatius' practice, in the righthand corner, but in the center, the title is given "de amor." The same deviation from normal practice is found when the annotations (1-20) and the three methods of prayer (238-60) are presented.

Nowhere does Ignatius tell the exercitant that he must make this contemplation. One can only say that, if the contemplation is included in the book, it is meant to be made. Both the director and the exercitant are left in the dark as to when and how often the exercise should take place. It is found between the end of the fourth week and the description of the methods of prayer. The second and third methods of prayer conclude the retreat. Hence, it is safe to assume that this contemplation follows the fourth week and precedes the methods of prayer. This point was discussed in our second chapter.

The exercise itself betrays a certain looseness of construction. To begin with, as in the exercises of the fourth week, the title does not say anything about its contents; there is no "y contiene en sí." The preparatory prayer is mentioned, but for the first time "preparatoria" is omitted (231).[1] Though the exercise is a contemplation, there is, again for the first time, no history as first prelude. It is the first contemplation (notice: contemplation) in which the composition is not made "by seeing the place." Ignatius writes: "Composición, que es aquí ver cómo estoy delante de Dios" (232). The second prelude, which is the introductory prayer, shows a change from "demandar lo que quiero," consistently used so far, to "pedir lo que quiero."[2] The colloquy is mentioned, but not a word is added; even "según subiecta materia" has now gone (237; cfr. 109, 199, 225). Another novelty is that notes precede the exercise; up to this point they had always followed the exercises (230, 231).[3] In this case, the notes could not very well be placed elsewhere, as they explain the title and contents. After these preliminary observations upon some obvious deviations from normal practice, the title itself will require close inspection.

## Title

The title "contemplación para alcanzar amor" unexpectedly reveals the purpose of the exercise.[4] The verb "alcanzar" means both "to obtain" and "to attain." The former meaning is found, for instance, in the triple colloquy of the first and of the third week (63, 147). In its latter meaning the verb occurs in the fourth rule with regard to eating, where the exercitant is advised to diminish the amount of food that suits him in order *to arrive at* the mean he should observe (alcanzar el medio, 213).[5] Morris and Rickaby, among others, translate "alcanzar" in the title of this exercise as "to obtain," but Puhl's translation "to attain" is to be preferred. The reason is that the love of God is not contemplated as given or infused but as a great good that man can *attain* when he has a deep understanding of the favors received that are so many proofs of God's love for him.

Why does Ignatius prefer "amor" to "caridad"? The three theological virtues are called: fee, esperanza y caridad (316), and the rules for thinking with the Church speak of "fe formada en charidad" (368). Except for one other instance, which will soon be mentioned, "amor" is used throughout the Spiritual Exercises. The difference between these two words poses no difficulty: "caridad" stands for the virtue of love, "amor" for the act of love. As an illustration the fifteenth annotation will serve: the exercitant is embraced by God "en su amor y alabanza," which means "so that he may come to love and praise Him." As soon as there is question of motive or movement, "amor" is used; thus, in his description of consolation, speaking of interior movements, Ignatius explains how the Christian is inflamed toward loving God (inflamar en amor, 316), and in dealing with the election he speaks of "el amor que me mueve" (184).[6] But St. Peter is three times asked about his *caridad.* This is very accurate, since there is little need to ask him about his *amor* after the threefold denial of his Master. Where *amor* fails, *caridad* need not have necessarily departed at the same time (306). Confirmation of the meaning of "amor" is given in the note preceding the contemplation. Ignatius connects it with *obras,* with deeds, and with the act of communication and sharing. The purpose, then, of this contemplation is that the exercitant may attain to loving God in deed.

The correct understanding of the title contains the answer to the possible objection that this exercise is superfluous. One may point out that the exercitant at the end of the fourth week, having asked and implored God that he might know the Lord better in order to love Him more, and having considered how his Lord suffered for his sins, and so forth, has surely come to love Him by this time; if not, the Exercises are a failure, and it is an illusion to think that what thirty days spent in prayer have failed to achieve can now be accomplished by an additional contemplation "to attain the love of God." It must be admitted that the exercitant does undoubtedly love God. Order and harmony have been gradually unfolded and realized, and this implies that the exercitant's affections and desires have been duly ordered (16). The consolation that is typical of the fourth week stands for an increase of faith and hope, but especially of love, so much so that the verb "to inflame" is not thought to be unfitting (316). But it is quite another question whether this love of God will show itself in deeds and will be realized *en todo,* in everything (233). The contemplation directs attention to the practice of loving God, and, consequently, looks to the days ahead. It joins the fourth week to the first day of everyday life and all the days following it, in which *caridad* must manifest itself in *amor.* The contemplation carries the fourth week, and with it the three other weeks, further into the future. In this respect it joins the second and third methods of prayer, as will be shown in our final chapter.

Preludes

The prelude, called the history, is not presented to the exercitant. The history of the contemplation is, consequently, the *here and now,* the reality in which he finds himself. The very absence of this prelude is an invitation to concentrate upon the mystery of his own existence. What this implies is made explicit by the composition. Ignatius writes: "Primer preámbulo es composición, que es aquí ver cómo estoy delante de Dios nuestro Señor, de los ángeles de los sanctos interpelantes por mí" (232). The text recalls the composition of the meditation on Three Classes of Men: "Composición viendo el lugar: será aquí ver a mí mismo, cómo estoy delante de Dios nuestro Señor y de todos sus sanctos . . ." (151). Three points in which these two compositions differ must be noted, as they are rather relevant.

In the present contemplation there is no reference to any place and the exercitant is not asked to look at himself. The composition is very straightforward: composing himself means realizing that he is, or moves, or lives, in the nearness of God (delante). The second point to be observed is that now not only are the angels mentioned, but the conjunction *y* following "Dios nuestro Señor" is lacking; moreover, there is no comma in the autograph text after "ángeles." In contrast with the composition of the meditation on Three Classes of Men, the exercitant is here enumerating groups of persons. The impact of this enumeration will be more striking if a comparison is made between what Ignatius writes here, in the exercise "del Rey," and in the second addition of the first week. In the oblation of the exercise "del Rey" the text reads: ("I make my oblation with Thy favor and help") "delante vuestra infinita bondad, y delante vuestra Madre gloriosa y de todos los sanctos y sanctas de la corte celestial," (98). In the second addition of the first week, the text reads: "así como si un cabellero se hallase delante de su rey y de toda su corte" (74). The absence of *y* and of any commas in the composition of the contemplation to attain the love of God gives the impression that the exercitant should take time to look around in order to realize that he is in the presence of God, of the angels, of the saints, and we are almost inclined to add "and so forth." The composition is not as static as it was in the other instances given, it comes alive. The seriousness of the composition elsewhere has given place to the thrill of it in this exercise. The angels and saints pray for the exercitant. There is no comma following "sanctos," so "interpelantes por mí" is to be taken as a predicate to both "ángeles" and "sanctos." The phrase itself recalls the second exercise of the first week, where the exercitant ponders how the angels, who are the sword of God's justice, have borne with him, have guarded him, and prayed for him, and how the saints have been interceding and praying for him (60); the exercitant states a fact which is beyond his understanding, hence, the exclamation of wonder with which this fifth point of the second exercise opens. Now, in this contemplation, it is merely a question of observation. The phrase is not added for any other purpose than that the truth should be placed before him. One might perhaps look for other motives, as, for instance, of encouraging him against despondency about the future, but none are given or added for utilitarian purposes.

Taken together, the points of difference between the composition of the meditation on Three Classes of Men and the composition of the contemplation to attain the love of God bring out the fact that the composition in the former exercise operates like a device. It serves a very definite end, namely, to influence the exercitant to regulate his desires and discover what is more pleasing to God. It is not so much intended to make him one with God and His saints as to remove from him the good things of the world insofar as he has not acquired them for the love of God. In this contemplation, on the other hand, the composition serves no further purpose than to make the exercitant fully aware of God's nearness to him and of the nearness and prayerful interest of angels, saints, and so on. He is made to see what *to exist* really means. No one will be surprised to hear that the next step to be taken by the exercitant is to see how his true composition will embrace the whole of creation: the heavens, the elements, the plants, the fruits, the herds (236), as well as whatever in this world is good, just, merciful, and so on (237).

The exercitant, in composing himself, will see himself "delante de Dios nuestro Señor." It was shown how this expression referred to Christ in His risen life in the fourth week; hence, the question whether "Dios nuestro Señor" in this exercise immediately following the fourth week refers to the risen Christ or to the Blessed Trinity. In the fourth week, the exercitant frequently gave his attention to the divinity which concealed itself in the Passion, but showed itself most miraculously in the Resurrection with its true and most holy effects (223). A better translation of "Divinidad" would be "being God," and "risen life" is to be preferred to "resurrection" as the rendering of "resurrección." There is in this fourth point of the contemplation of the fourth week a twofold use of "sanctíssima - sanctíssimos" in quick succession. This cannot be explained as verbosity, yet at first reading, not much would be lost if the superlative were omitted in either case. It should be noted, however, that the superlative of "sancto," with the exception of standard expressions such as "sanctíssimo cuerpo" (191) and "sanctíssimo sacramento" (44), is in the exercises themselves exclusively used with reference to the triune God, as, for instance, in "sanctíssima voluntad" (5, 180), "sanctíssima majestad" (90), "sanctíssima incarnación" (108). Its twofold use, consequently, in this fourth point gives one the impression that in Ignatius' vision, the risen life of Christ merges into that of the Blessed Trinity and that no conclusion whatever can be drawn from the fact that Christ is called "nuestro Señor" in the fourth week.

In the same week, "el officio de consolar" is attributed to the risen Christ. But to every Christian the Holy Spirit is the Comforter, the Paraclete. The rules for the discernment of spirits attribute true consolation to the good angel, but only God gives consolation without any previous cause: "Sólo es de *Dios nuestro Señor* dar consolación sin causa precedente" (330). The same second rule teaches that the end of consolation is to draw one wholly to the love of the *Divine Majesty,* and Ignatius explains that it belongs solely to the *Creator* to come into the soul, to leave it, to act upon it. In defining consolation Ignatius restricts himself to the use of "Criador y Señor" (316). Thus, the office of consoling is freely attributed to the Creator and Lord, to the risen Lord and, according to sound Christian doctrine, to the Holy Spirit. Hence, the fact that the fourth week speaks of the task of comforting others indicates that from this fourth week onward the Trinity dominates the life of the exercitant and that Ignatius wants his exercitant to realize how he lives in the presence of *Dios nuestro Señor*, who is Father, Son and Holy Spirit. For further confirmation we refer the reader to our investigation into the expression "gozar en su Criador y Redemptor" in the previous chapter.

The second prelude, which is the introductory prayer, cannot be properly understood without recalling the second note that precedes the preludes. Love is not a static quality; it consists in a mutual sharing of goods. Any act of communication is always accompanied by the desire that it might find a response (231). The exercitant readily admits that God loves him: it was the gist of the contemplations of the four weeks. His difficulty is that he may fail to see that and how divine love communicates itself. There is a real danger that he might accept the gifts and favors without ever realizing that these gifts are modes of God communicating Himself. It is only the perfect, so Ignatius says, who, due to constant contemplation and the enlightenment of the understanding, consider, meditate, and contemplate that God our Lord is in every creature by His presence, power and essence (39).[7] The exercitant, then, will feel the need for an intimate knowledge of so much good received, so that filled with gratitude he may love and serve the Divine Majesty in all things; and that is what he prays for (233). The text is charged with meaning and, once again, deserves close attention.

The autograph text reads: "Pedir lo que quiero: será aquí pedir cognoscimiento interno de tanto bien recibido, para que yo enteramente reconosciendo, pueda en todo amar y servir a su divina majestad" (233). The exclusive choice of "pedir" has already been noticed; "to beg" would be a satisfactory translation. The combination "cognoscimiento interno" (and its verbal equivalent "conoscer interiormente, internamente") was formerly used with reference to sin (44, 63), and with reference to Christ in the third prelude of every contemplation on His hidden and public life (118). Its true meaning and import are clearly indicated in the second annotation; on the one hand, it should be contrasted with extensive knowledge (mucho saber), and on the other, closely linked with "to understand, savor and relish" (sentir y gustar) and with "gusto y fructo spiritual" (2) and, hence, with pure contemplation. There is a kind of natural association with the second time for making an election, and consequently "cognoscimiento interno" goes hand in hand with clarity of vision and insight (176). This is corroborated by the use of the adverb "enteramente" which modifies the verbal form "reconosciendo." Translations such as "thoroughly grateful" or "filled with gratitude" do not do full justice to the text. They tend to obscure the connection between "cognoscimiento" and "reconosciendo." Courel preserves this in his French translation "connaiscance-reconnaisance." The fundamental meaning of "reconosciendo" is to know a thing again, to know a thing for what it is, and it is this meaning that is strongly suggested by the choice of the adverb "enteramente." Ignatius uses this adjective and adverb elsewhere, when he speaks of the full hour that must be spent on the exercises (12, 13), of the whole day that must be devoted to the contemplation of the Passion (209), and of the complete abstinence from certain kinds of food (212). The phrase "enteramente reconosciendo" points to a thorough knowledge of the good gifts of God as such: they are known in their true character, as proofs, that is, of God's love.

Roothaan renders "tanto bien recibido" by "tot ac tantorum bonorum acceptorum." He seems to have been influenced by the *versio prima,* even perhaps by the *versio vulgata,* which has "beneficia." Ignatius uses the word "dones" in the first and fourth points of this contemplation; in the fourth point it is used together with "bienes." Where "bien" is used in the singular, the quality of goodness is stressed, whereas in "dones" and in "bienes" the gifts themselves, and hence the act of giving, come to the fore. The exercitant, therefore, begs for a thorough knowledge of so much good, or even goodness, received. There is a certain urgency behind all these words. There are the two doublets, "cognoscimiento-reconosciendo" and "interno-enteramente," there is the choice of "bien," which, be it noted, is preceded by "tanto," which expresses admiration. This is followed by "recibido." We shall see how "to give" will dominate the points of the contemplation, and one might reasonably expect that the exercitant begs to be grateful for such great goods *given* to him by God. Ignatius prefers "recibido," thereby indicating that the exercitant received and accepted the good things, irrespective of whether or not he realized what their goodness in fact implied. It is as if Ignatius is afraid that the exercitant might misunderstand what is actually taking place around him and within his own life.

The cumulative driving force of Ignatius' own conviction gives the clue to a proper understanding of the closing clause. One might have expected Ignatius to be satisfied with a simple sentence, such as "in order that he may henceforward love God." He inserts "pueda" (to be able), "en todo" and speaks of "amar y servir." Hence, the profound knowledge of so much good received will *enable* the exercitant to love God as He should be loved; it is an indispensable condition as well as the moving force. Wedged in between "pueda" and "amar y servir" stands "en todo." It refers back to the good that has been received.[8] The participle "recibido" not only points to the person receiving the gifts but also to the Person who gives. In the cause or source of so much good received by the exercitant, God manifests Himself (337). Logically, the prayer in which the exercitant begs for awareness of God in all the good things he has received (cognoscimiento interno) is followed by the prayer begging for the love of God in all these things, thus preventing the gifts from being wrenched away from the Giver. But "en todo" does not modify only "amar" but "servir" as well. There may be some difficulty in understanding what exactly is meant by "en todo servir," but this disappears as soon as one recalls the warning of Ignatius that love is not a question of words but of deeds (230). If "servir" is paraphrased by "to remain the servant" or "to do God's will," the expression becomes very meaningful. For the exercitant has always strong motives for imploring God that he may be able to remain His true servant in the midst of the goods received or, more accurately, to fulfill the will of God in the goods given to him. He will ever be tempted to indulge in the gifts themselves, forgetting that these are given as proofs of God's love for him and, consequently, as an invitation to love God in return and as a help to be faithful in His service.

Just how inseparable for Ignatius are *amar* and *servir* appears from the last paragraph of the Spiritual Exercises, where he speaks of "el mucho servir a Dios nuestro Señor por puro amor" (370). The combination, together with "en todo," is used again when he states that the characteristic of the positive doctors, such as Augustine, Jerome, Gregory, and others, is that they arouse affections "para en todo amar y servir a Dios" (363). It might be profitable to recall once again the exact wording of the second part of the fifteenth annotation.

First Part

The four points or parts of the contemplation are as always a further extension of the composition of the exercitant. He knows himself to be in the presence of God, angels, and saints, and looks around in order to see how God manifests Himself. Looking around is not enough. The cooperation with God communicating Himself involves rather strenuous concentration. So, he uses his memory, he ponders, considers, and reflects, is moved by intense affections, and in the end he will make offerings and pray ("traer la memoria, ponderando con mucho afecto, reflectir en mí mismo, considerando con mucho razón y justicia, offrescer y dar affectándose mucho," 234). This process is repeated in the other three parts of the exercise. The field of vision now embraces the whole world, the whole of creation, the present and the past, and above all the whole of God's activity in creating and redeeming man. In the end it takes in God's infinite justice, goodness, power, and mercy. Indeed, the dimensions of the exercitant's composition know no limits.

Just as the words of the second prelude proved to be charged with meaning, so the first part almost collapses under the weight of what it has to convey. The autograph text is indispensable: "El primer puncto es traer a la memoria los beneficios rescibidos de creación redempción y dones particulares, ponderando con mucho afecto quánto ha hecho Dios nuestro Señor por mí y quánto me ha dado de lo que tiene, y consequenter el mismo Señor desea dárseme en quanto puede según su ordenación divina" ("The first point is to call to mind the benefits received, of my creation, redemption, and particular gifts, dwelling with great affection on how much God our Lord has done for me, and how much He has given me of that which He has; and consequently, how much He desires to give me Himself in so far as He can according to His Divine ordinance." Translation, Morris). The exercitant calls to mind the benefits *de creación redempción y dones particulares.* There is no comma anywhere in this phrase according to the autograph text. This suggests a certain parallelism between the nouns used. "Creación" does not mean the created universe;[9] if this were so, the parallelism would disappear. "Creación" stands for the act of creating, just as "redempción" stands for the act of redeeming. They are referred to when the exercitant considers how much God has *done* for him.

The parallelism also involves that "dones particulares" is, just as are "creación" and "redempción," dependent upon "beneficios." The exercitant calls to mind the benefits or blessings of being created, of being redeemed and of the special favors given to him. "The blessings of special favors" is not a pleonasm. The construction lays stress on the fact that these special favors are indeed blessings, good deeds done and good gifts given by God. Ignatius uses the word "dones," which by itself emphasizes that God is the Giver, and consequently it brings out the relationship of love that exists between God and the exercitant, as was pointed out by Ignatius in the second note (231). Having recalled the benefits of being created and redeemed and of the special gifts, the exercitant ponders

how much God our Lord has done for him
how much He has given of what He has
how much, insofar as He can, the same Lord desires to give Himself.

The subject of each of these sentences is God. We have said above that what God has *done* for the exercitant is summed up by the benefits of having been created and redeemed. The key word in the second and third sentence is "dar"; it corresponds to "*dones* particulares" and reminds one at once of "dar y comunicar," which is the expression of true love (231). It follows that the exercitant contemplates in all the goods received his *Creator,* his *Redeemer,* and his *Lover.*

The second part of this point follows. Communication on the part of God demands communication on the part of the exercitant. He reflects upon himself and considers, according to all reason and justice, what he ought to offer and give: all things that are his and himself with them. Ignatius then suggests, and it is no more than a suggestion, the well-known prayer: "Take, O Lord, and receive . . . ."

Notwithstanding the great seriousness of this prayer, there appears to be a certain playfulness, or at least a kind of matter-of-factness, about it. The verbal form "recibid" might easily mean that, as the exercitant has been good enough to receive God's gifts ("tanto bien recibido, los beneficios rescibidos"), so God will be good enough to receive his in turn. A similar sense of humor can be detected in the phrase: "Thou hast given it all to me, to Thee I return it all." An example of perfect communication! Or, again, in the closing sentence: it all begins with God's initial giving, it develops when the exercitant gives in return, and it ends with God's renewal of His gifts: "Give me Thy love and Thy grace."

The verb "disponer" no one can afford to overlook. Ignatius writes: "Todo es vuestro, disponed a toda vuestra voluntad." We discussed its meaning when the fifth and first annotations were examined in our first chapter. The prayer recalls the fifth annotation. The exercitant began the retreat with magnanimity and generosity, "offering God his entire will and liberty, that His Divine Majesty might dispose of him and all he possesses according to His most holy will." It looks as if after thirty days the exercitant finds himself where he began, perhaps returns to where he began. However, the difference between the fifth annotation and the prayer in question cannot be minimized. The enumeration in the prayer is much more elaborate; "ofreciéndole todo su querer y libertad" now becomes "tomad y recibid toda mi libertad, mi memoria, mi entendimiento, y toda mi voluntad, todo mi haber y mi posseer." Such a long enumeration, lavishly interspersed with "todo" (no less than five times in this prayer), is evidence of the seriousness of the exercitant, as if he were afraid to keep something to himself; hence, the wonderful choice of "todo mi haber y mi posseer." Generosity and magnanimity are now replaced by poverty: todo es vuestro. Above all, it is no longer service that dominates but love. The offering is said to be the result of self-reflection and takes place with much reason and justice. Why is Ignatius so verbose, almost complicated?

"Reflectir" and especially "reflectir en mí mismo" only occurs in contemplations. One looks for it in vain in the first week. Even in the instructions for making a good election, where one would think there would be much room for self-reflection, the verb is not used; "pensar," "ruminar," "discurrir," "raciocinar" are preferred. As soon as the exercitant begins to contemplate, the verb is used at the end of each of the three points of each contemplation (106-08, 114-16). We find it again in the repetitions of these contemplations (123, 124) and in the contemplations of the third and fourth weeks (194, 222). In the present contemplation it occurs no less than four times; each time the verb is followed by "en mí mismo." It carries the clear implication of turning one's thoughts away from a certain object and of directing them toward oneself. The reason for this is clearly seen in the contemplations on the Incarnation and Nativity, where Ignatius appears to be well aware of the danger lest the exercitant lose himself and indulge in the wonderful things brought before him through the preludes properly made. Thus, he is told in all three points "to bend back upon himself" and to try and gain some profit from what he has seen and heard. Consequently, "reflectir," whenever it is used in the contemplations, involves an unmistakable reminder to become committed, *engagé*. The verb does not appeal to his intellect but to his whole person. Nowhere is this more evident than in the first part of this contemplation, where it is followed by "considerando," by "affectándose mucho," and by "offrescer." Intellect, affections, and will all play their part in this self-commitment.

But this is not really the end. If self-reflection leaves no escape but forces the exercitant to become committed, this does not mean that a clear insight into what he ought to do will be automatically followed by his act of self-commitment. Hence, Ignatius does not and cannot command the exercitant to make the prayer. He does not and cannot guide him beyond the point where he, the exercitant, admits that he *ought* to give and offer to the Divine Majesty all that he has and himself together with it ("lo que yo *debe* de mi parte offrescer"). It is again a sign of Ignatius' wisdom and mildness that he inserts the phrase "as one would offer who is moved by great feeling" ("así como quien offresce affectándose mucho"). Faced with what he on his part ought to do, the exercitant in all likelihood will turn to the colloquy. Ignatius gives no indication what the colloquy should be about; any information would be useless and superfluous. But the words used elsewhere take on a new meaning: the colloquy is made by speaking exactly as one friend speaks to another (54), in colloquies one ought to talk things over and beg for favors, according to the subject matter, according "as I wish to dispose myself to one side or another, according as I desire to grieve or rejoice in the matter I contemplate" (199). It is not improbable that in this colloquy he will beg a favor according to the subject matter, and the favor will be that he may be able to say: "Take, O Lord, and receive . . . ."

Second Part

The exercise under discussion is a contemplation of God. In the first part, the exercitant perfects his composition by realizing how much God desires to give Himself to the beloved. He moves from what God has done for him and has given him to what God wants to do and to give out of love. The second part takes its beginning from here; there is no longer room for the past tense. The exercitant will contemplate God giving here and now. It is not a question of deep thinking but of careful observation. The verb used is "mirar," which is followed, significantly, by "cómo." Ignatius writes: "mirar cómo Dios habita en las criaturas dando ser, en las plantas vejetando, en los animales sensando, en los hombres dando entender; y así en mí dándome ser . . ." (235). It is important to determine whether the stress should be laid on "habita" or on "dando" (and parallel with it on the other gerundial forms). Is the exercise a contemplation of God's presence in His own creation, or is it an exercise in discovering God's gift of Himself in all things? The verb "habitar," which does not occur anywhere else in the text, appears to bring a new element into the contemplation, but the threefold use of "dando", coming after the phrase "cómo Dios desea dárseme" of the first part and irresistibly recalling the twofold use of the same verb together with "comunicar" in the note preceding the contemplation, leaves no doubt that this verb must receive all emphasis.

It may not be unprofitable to point out how Ignatius separates the exercitant, as it were, from all the rest. He moves from the universal, comprising elements, plants, animals and men, to the individual. The exercitant is asked to see himself as what nowadays we might call the top of the evolutionary process, for the various ways in which God gives being, life, sensation, and understanding to different groups of creatures are all realized in him. Besides, he has been made God's temple, created as he is after the image and likeness of the Divine Majesty (*ibid.*). At the root of whatever is and at the root of his own existence, the exercitant discovers God and contemplates how He is always giving in the things and persons in which He dwells. The whole of the universe becomes transparent: God is seen in all things, and is experienced within the exercitant himself.

The composition of the exercitant now reaches perfection. An impressive distance has been travelled since the first exercise when he composed himself by considering that his soul is imprisoned in his body, and this whole self ("todo el compósito," 47) is in this vale of misery, as it were, in exile among brute beasts. All this remains true, but it is not the whole truth. The composition of fallen man also implies the conviction and experience of God within him, giving life, understanding, and so forth, as in His temple; he knows that he carries within himself the image of the Divine Majesty. This is in fact the end: God sharing His majesty with the exercitant. Except for one thing: the communication must be mutual. Once again, the exercitant will reflect upon himself, and again Ignatius does not provide any further guidance.

### Third Part

The third part does not add anything new to the contemplation or the vision. So much is at once clear from the verb "considerar", with which it opens. It asks that the exercitant directs his attention to an aspect of his vision or his composition that might have escaped him. Employing a simple metaphor, one might say that after the first two parts the picture is there in all its brilliant glory; it will be worth while to concentrate for a moment on the coloring. This stands for the costs entailed by God's love for man, and in a very special way, for this man, for the exercitant. Ignatius writes: "considerar cómo Dios trabaja y labora por mí en todas cosas criadas sobre la haz de la tierra." None of the expressions is new to the exercitant. There is no need to speak of "por mí" nor of "todas las cosas criadas sobre la haz de la tierra." The verb "trabajar" was used in the exercise "del Rey" both in the parable and its application (93, 95), and in either case the toil refers to the King and him who is to follow Him. All those who listen to the call of Christ, those who are guided by judgment and reason and those who are moved by love, offer themselves to this toil, which is always *trabajar comigo*, toil with Him (95-97). Verb and noun are found in the third point of the contemplation on the

Nativity: Christ's life is a life of *tantos trabajos* (116). It is well once again to remember that this contemplation on the Nativity was meant by Ignatius as an example of future contemplations. In the third week, "trabajos" is found together with fatigue and sorrow (206). The exercitant has, then, been familiar with Christ's *trabajos* ever since the beginning of the second week, or even since the first colloquy, where His death on the cross is mentioned (53); the word has been given a certain slant. This is corrected in this third point. Ignatius now adds the verb "laborar" and he explains it by "habet se ad modum laborantis"; it is less stringent than "trabajar."

The triple function of God, which was mentioned in the first part of the contemplation, now emerges anew, though the same words are not repeated. "All the things on the face of the earth" recalls the Creator; the choice of "trabajar" points to the Redeemer; and God as the Lover is emphasized in the expression "por mí." Again, it is of interest to notice the distance that has been covered since the beginning of the retreat. "Las otras cosas sobre la haz de la tierra son criadas para el hombre" has lost its vagueness: the heavens, the elements, the plants, the fruits, the herds, with a significant *etc.*, are now distinctly recognized. Instead of the less personal "para el hombre" we find "por mí"; instead of the passive voice "son criadas" we now find "Dios trabaja y labora." A new element appears: God is now seen as *giving* being, sensation, and so forth.

To conclude: the third point makes no advance upon the second part but brings out a certain detail of what the exercitant contemplated before. It is not surprising that Ignatius repeats a good deal of what he said in the second part in order to stress that communication on the part of God involves toil and work. The exercitant will reflect upon himself and consider what he will give "de mi parte" (234). No one can mistake the implication that toil, even pain, ought not to deter him.

The contemplation to attain the love of God has now reached its end. The composition, or union with God, Creator, Redeemer, and Lover, has been achieved. Everything now depends upon the final communication "de mi parte." This only will bring complete fulfillment; the composition will be lived and realized in the days to come, in the everyday life of the future. Hence, there is no indication how often and when the contemplation should be made. Henceforth it should be *lived* continuously. The exercise is not a question of a contemplative act lasting an hour or a number of hours, but of a contemplative vision, which undoubtedly needs to be nourished by contemplative acts explicitly and purposely made, and which in the end will always be rounded off and completed by the decision of the exercitant to communicate to God all he has, and himself.

## Fourth Part

The fourth part is not a contemplation of God. The object of the opening verb "mirar" is the world surrounding the exercitant. With his habitual accuracy, Ignatius does not now use the expression "todas las cosas criadas sobre la haz de la tierra" or something similar. This would have been well-nigh impossible, since the whole of the created universe is to the exercitant one great collection of *bienes y dones*, of good things and gifts (237). Everything has become transparent, revealing God as the Giver. Everything is directly and spontaneously seen as good, and as a gift descending from above: "mirar cómo todos los bienes y dones descienden de arriba."

The fourth part does not consist in gathering the fruits of the three preceding parts. It is not a question of having reached the top of the hill and looking down into the valley below, now seen in a different light. It is a warning not to take things for granted and thereby to become blind to what truth, harmony, and order really are. To use another image: the exercitant has discovered the sun and knows why everything is bathed in light. The danger is that, like the spoiled child he is, he should take the light for granted without giving any thought to why there is light, and what its source may be. It is an image used by Ignatius, and he adds another, that of the river and its source.

It is very striking that in this fourth part of what is a contemplation, the word "Dios" or "Señor" is not found at all. It almost sounds like a pagan phrase in the mouth of Ignatius when he asks the exercitant to observe how all these good things "descend *from above* ("descienden de arriba"). Both "descienden" and "arriba" occur twice, and it seems almost incomprehensible why these words should be used in a contemplation the heart of which is the intimate encounter between the Lover and the beloved in all created things. It is most astonishing, too, because this fourth part undoubtedly derives from Ignatius' own vision when he was watching the waters of the Cardoner. There surely must be a good reason why Ignatius' choice of words seems rather chilly at the height of contemplation.

"Bienes y dones" presupposes that the exercitant, since he considers and experiences all created things as gifts and favors, is attached to them, or in the words of the Exercises, feels an affection for them. Ignatius prefers "amor" to "affección," as for instance, in the instructions for making a good election when he writes of the "amor que tiene a la cosa que elige" (184). In connection with this love for a thing or a person, the expression "descienda de arriba" is used in the first rule for making a good choice (184) and in the application of this rule to the giving of alms (338), and nowhere else does it occur. In both cases the expression is immediately explained; as might be expected, it means the same as "descienda del amor de Dios." This posits the question why Ignatius should insert "de arriba" at all; would there be any loss if it were omitted? The answer appears to be that its omission would make the transition from the natural to the supernatural far too sudden; man would be asked to connect his love for any person or thing at once and directly with the love of God. The insertion of "de arriba" marks a kind of intermediate stage. Man should transcend this natural love or affection, he must be on his guard against any merely natural attachment. Thus the expression primarily warns the exercitant that his love for persons and things should not be a matter of egotism or sensuality, of worldly or carnal love, of selfishness and self-love.[10] To extend the metaphor behind "descienda de arriba," it expresses the principle that man's love for persons and things must not be *pedestrian*.

All this is applicable to the use of the same expression in this fourth part. Ignatius does not and cannot warn the exercitant against loving created things, as they are so many proofs of God loving him and of God communicating Himself. Ignatius points out that they are good things and gifts, and that their goodness derives not from themselves but from another source. "From high above" suggests "down here below." That is where Ignatius wants his exercitant to start in order that he might transcend it. The contemplation takes for its beginnings the normal life of the exercitant, all the things that surround him and that he uses every day. He must see all this as *bienes y dones*, which means that he must live his daily life with his eyes open in order to discover that the things here below do not in themselves contain the explanation of their existence and their goodness. Hence, this fourth part belongs less to the retreat in the strict sense of the word than to the days after the retreat: it should be part of the exercitant's daily life.

So far the first half of this fourth part has been examined. The starting point of the second part comes as a great surprise: the exercitant will realize that he is a man of capabilities, of justice, goodness, piety, mercy, *and so forth*. True, Ignatius adds "limited" (medida), but all the same, it is rather unexpected to find these virtues in one who began the Exercises as an insignificant being, full of corruption (58). It should be added that this is not quite accurate, because the exercitant will also see himself at the very beginning of the retreat as a knight who has received many gifts from God (74). The second half of this fourth part will, however, not be nearly so surprising if it is remembered that the exercitant is completing the contemplation to attain the love of God. He has learned to see himself as made after God's own image in whom God dwells, giving His great gifts and favors. Just as the universe around him speaks of *bienes y dones* and *is* a great collection of gifts and favors, in a similar way the exercitant gathers within himself justice, goodness, piety, mercy, and so on. This is a very optimistic view of man, but the introductory "mirar cómo" indicates that it is not the whole story. His own good points, to use this vague expression, never find their explanation in themselves or in the exercitant; with an irresistible immediacy they demand "de arriba." The name of God is not mentioned, but the exercitant's own everyday existence is completely inexplicable unless attention is turned from *here below* to *yonder, high above*. The parallelism with the first half of this fourth part is evident. There appears to be one point of difference; now there is a marked contrast between man's *limited* goodness and the *supreme* and *infinite* Goodness ("summa y infinita"). One must not stress the adjectives "summa y infinita" in such a way that the contemplation is turned into an act of worship of God's infinite perfections, shining forth, though weakly (medida), in man and in the whole created universe, so much so that man's perfections are completely negligible. This is not Ignatius' intention at all. The attention given to oneself, and, in general, to created things, is far from being a device for ascending far above them, presumably even forgetting all about them as soon as possible, in order to arrive at the contemplation of God's goodness, justice, and so forth. On no account must matters be reversed in this exercise. It is essentially a question of enjoying the light and enjoying the waters, but it is pointed out that the light and the waters must have a source. Is Ignatius somewhat afraid lest the exercitant may move away from the light to the sun that he refuses to use words such as "Dios," "Señor," and "Criador"? The purpose of the fourth part of this exercise is for the exercitant to see and experience that he himself and all things around him are "charged with the grandeur of God," to use a well-known phrase of Gerard Manley Hopkins. God's grandeur is the exercitant's power, justice, goodness, piety, mercy, and so forth.

Throughout this fourth part we hear clear echoes of what Ignatius writes in his description of consolation: (la ánima) ninguna cosa criada sobre la haz de la tierra puede amar *en sí* (316). The contemplation to attain the love of God leads not only to mutual communication but also to consolation. Love, communication, and consolation then are closely linked together. One is reminded once again of the fifteenth annotation, where Ignatius also speaks of "ánima," of "comunicar," and of "amor." As we know, in this annotation Ignatius writes of the *ánima devota* as he does when he explains the first time for making a good election (175). For Ignatius, however, *devoción* is the facility of finding God in everything, as we read in his own *Pilgrim's Story* (*Autobiography*, 99).

The reflection will be the same as in the three preceding points. To give a literal translation: "I will reflect in myself what I, on my side, with great reason and justice, ought to offer and give to His Divine Majesty, that is to say, all things that are mine, and myself with them, saying, as one who makes an offering, with great affection: take, O Lord, and receive." The reflection turns upon what the exercitant *ought to* offer ("lo que yo debe offrescer"). This reflection is really the end of the exercise. However, sooner or later, it will be followed by 'Take, o Lord, and receive' as the exercitant's own oblation. Ignatius writes: "acabar reflictiendo en mí mismo según está dicho" (237). The sentence is immediately followed by "acabar con un coloquio y un Pater noster." The conclusion to be drawn from this twofold use of "acabar" is that the reflection is its object only in a certain sense, with certain qualifications. What one *ought* to do can never be the final resting point. What follows is that God and the exercitant talk things over, and, as has been said before, most likely the subject matter of this conversation will be what the exercitant on his side is going to give to God as Love.

The twofold use of "acabar" might also indicate a certain hesitancy on the part of Ignatius to put an end to the Exercises, or better, where exactly to put it. We shall soon see how the verb returns no less than five times in the second method of prayer, which appears to show that it is not easy to say where the Spiritual Exercises actually have their ending.

fifteen

# THREE METHODS OF PRAYER

In the fourth annotation, Ignatius states that the three methods of prayer belong to the fourth week. They are part and parcel of the thirty days' retreat. The statement is modified by Ignatius himself when he eliminates the first method at once. It is a method of prayer on the Ten Commandments, the seven deadly sins, the three powers of the soul and the five senses of the body. It is more suitable for the exercitant of the eighteenth annotation and it is there that we find it mentioned. This way of praying is "rather to give form, method, and exercises enabling the soul to prepare itself and profit thereby, and in order that its prayer may become acceptable, rather than in order to give any actual form and method of prayer" (238). The awkward translation brings out the awkward way in which Ignatius tries to explain what he means by this "manera de orar." It is worth noticing which verbs and expressions are used. They are: conoscer, considerar, escrutinio and intelligencia on the one hand, and on the other: enmendar adelante, pedir venia y pardón, acusar, guardar mandamientos, evitar peccados, while "falta" occurs a number of times in the singular and in the plural. The method is more an examination of conscience than prayer in the proper sense of the word. Interesting is the use of "mirar," which looks somewhat lost in this method. It occurs only once, and its object is "sus contrarios," that is, the seven capital virtues (245). The choice of the verb carries with it something of a nostalgic desire for virtue. So much about the first method, which falls outside the long retreat and, consequently, outside the scope of this study.

Second Method

A few facts concerning this method must be noted. The exercise is never to be omitted and the person, no longer called exercitant, will devote himself to it for some time ("de forma que por algún tiempo siempre se exercite en una dellas," 256). It is contemplative prayer. At the top of the page in the autograph text we find the expression "oración contemplando" twice. The verb is used in the title and in the third rule (249, 255), and the person practicing it is called "persona que contempla" (254). The subject matter of this contemplation is the meaning of each word of some prayer. Ignatius gives five prayers: the Our Father, Hail Mary, Creed, Anima Christi, and Salve Regina (253).

The exercise shows scant evidence of the type of contemplation with which we have become familiar during the four weeks. There are no points; Ignatius gives an explanation, three rules and two notes (252-57). There are no directions as to how often and at what time the contemplation has to be made, but its duration should be an hour (253). There are, however, some indications of importance. They can be gathered into four groups.

First, in contrast with what happened up till now, additions do not follow the contemplation, but one addition precedes it. Before entering on the prayer, the person will let his mind repose a little (reposar), and sitting or walking, according as shall seem best to him, he will consider where he is going and for what purpose (239). It is said to be the equivalent of the second addition of the second, third and fourth weeks: "Immediately on perceiving that it is the hour of the exercise which I have to make, before proceeding to it, I will place before my eyes whither I am going, before whom I am to appear, and I will briefly pass over in my mind the exercise which I am about to make" (131). The additions were always given as advice "in order to make the exercises better" (73), and undoubtedly Ignatius attaches great importance to them. In this second method of prayer, however, the aspect of advice appears to have gone. The fact that the addition precedes, implies that it is indispensable. This addition also shows that there is no exercise during the night or on rising: the word "resumption" is omitted. Evidently the hour of prayer takes place in the course of the day and in the midst of one's normal occupations. This is the conclusion to be drawn from the phrase "repose un poco el spíritu." Coming to rest or recollecting oneself presupposes that one is occupied with other matters. Rather relevant in this connection is that Ignatius prefers "considerando" to "poniendo delante de mí" and that he prefers the more businesslike "a qué" to the more personal "delante de quién." It is not easy to break away from everyday duties in order to devote oneself to an hour's contemplation.

The addition is made seated or walking, which seems to suggest that it will probably take some time. The prayer itself is made by the exercitant either kneeling or seated. Ignatius always attaches some importance to the posture to be adopted during and even before the exercise. He paid attention to this point before when he mentioned as possibilities: kneeling, prostrate on the ground, lying face upward, seated, and standing (76). It was not a matter of penance which posture was adopted: the guiding rule is to find better what one is seeking (*ibid.*). Why does Ignatius in this second method omit prostration, lying face upward, and standing, and because of its contrast with the preceding addition, also walking? Before replying to this question, we note that Ignatius has something else to add: the exercitant will keep his eyes closed or fixed on one place without allowing them to wander about (252). The presupposition here is that there is something to see, that there is something that might make the eyes wander about. There is hardly any possibility for this to happen in the cave of Manresa, a cell on Monte Cassino, or wherever the retreat is given, certainly not after spending some thirty days in such a place. The conclusion must be that this second method of prayer is employed somewhere in the open. This would at once explain why Ignatius confines himself to suggesting postures of sitting or kneeling; another reason will be given later in this chapter.

The fact that Ignatius singles out the second addition should not go unnoticed, for it emphasizes that the other nine are set aside. Hence, there is to be no short resumption the evening before nor in the early morning. There will be no review nor should the rest of the day be brought into harmony with the subject matter of the contemplation. There is no reason to keep silent and to observe a spirit of recollection nor is there any special reason for doing penance. In other words, life continues as usual. This is in sharp contrast with what the exercitant of the nineteenth annotation is asked to observe. Even though he cannot disengage himself from public affairs or necessary business, he is told to observe the ten additions. The exercitant of the nineteenth annotation makes the Exercises while he continues his working life, but the exercitant of the second method of prayer stands in the midst of life's activities and finds time for truly contemplative prayer "siempre por algún tiempo." The conclusion seems inescapable: some days of contemplating the meaning of the words of a prayer must be attached to the fourth week. This does not mean that at the same time he withdraws from normal life. The pattern of the four weeks has completely gone, and yet the retreat itself continues under totally different circumstances. In this respect it carries on what was begun in the contemplation to attain the love of God.

The second group of characteristics concerns the contents of this second method. There are indeed no preludes at all, but there is a preparatory prayer. It is quite different from what the exercitant has said at the beginning of each exercise so far. He does not ask God his Lord that all his intentions, actions, and operations may be purely directed toward the praise and service of the Divine Majesty (46). Now, "it should be made according to the Person to whom the prayer is addressed" (251). It reminds us to a certain extent of the third prelude, the introductory prayer, but no clue whatever is given by Ignatius as to what the contents of this preparatory prayer should be. One can only suppose that the exercitant, having been made familiar with preparatory and introductory prayers, will be influenced by them and that consequently petition will be the heart of this preparatory prayer.

The subject matter of the contemplation is the meaning of each word of the five prayers mentioned above. "Significación," however, does not stand for the meaning of a word as given in a dictionary. It is a question of comparisons, relish, consolation, and consideration (252). This is something new in the Spiritual Exercises. Indeed, in the second week the exercitant was taught to contemplate what the persons say (mirar, advertir y contemplar lo que hablan, 115), but from the structure of the contemplation on the Nativity, or for that matter, that on the Incarnation, it is clear that the primary object of the contemplation in this point is the person, or persons, whom he has seen in the previous point: the words spoken are mainly attended to as relevant as to what the person thinks, feels, undergoes, and so forth.

The end in view of *contemplando significación* is not a better and deeper understanding of the words used in any one prayer. The words "entendimiento" and "cognoscimiento" are not used. "Considerar" and "consideración" are found, but these mean little more than that the exercitant occupies himself with the words of the prayers. Once again, very significantly, there is no trace of "entender, conoscer, meditar." Ignatius does use the words "gusto" and "consolación," which leads us to the third group of elements that reminds us of true contemplation.

"Gusto y consolación" is a key expression in any context. It is used twice (252, 254). The word "devoción" has also found a place (252) and the triplet always points to a high degree of contemplative prayer. There is another expression closely associated with these words: it is "no pasar adelante," which is used twice in the fourth addition (76). The advice not to go on is inspired by Ignatius' anxiety that the exercitant should find rest (reposar) and satisfaction (satisfacer, *ibid.*). This in its turn recalls the second annotation, in which the exercitant is warned against a too intellectual approach to the exercises and is given the reason why: satisfaction proceeds from *gusto y fructo espiritual* and *sentir y gustar de las cosas internamente*. The second annotation and the fourth addition in a most intimate way touch upon the very heart of contemplative prayer, in which God is the main Agent, communicating Himself, disposing the exercitant and embracing him (15). The conclusion is clear: the few well-chosen words of this second method of prayer forge an indestructible link with the Spiritual Exercises: no one can properly practice the second method of prayer who has not made these Exercises in full.

We are now in a position to understand a few other points. The various elements of contemplation mentioned just now suggest a breath of peace and quiet, and at the same time one of deep reverence, reminiscent of the third annotation: in the acts of the will (more than those of the intellect) when we are conversing vocally or mentally, greater reverence is required on the part of the exercitant (3). Ignatius uses the expression "hablar vocalmente o mentalmente," which with a slight change we find again in the first rule of this second method (253). Above we referred to the posture of the body to be adopted by the exercitant and we drew attention to the fact that Ignatius now excludes the prostration, while he also does not want the exercitant to pray standing or lying down face upwards. These positions are now seen to be little conducive to, or even in harmony with, *devoción, gusto,* and *consolación;* they might entail *trabajos,* and this is not in keeping with the atmosphere of this prayer. It is only now that the first word of the title "oración contemplando" can be properly understood. The word is indeed used in a generic sense. We recall that every exercise opens with an *oración preparatoria.* It is found in this sense in the second method of prayer itself, when Ignatius writes of "cada palabra de la oración" in the title; in the first note he refers to "otras oraciones" (256). But it is also used in a more specific sense, and here Ignatius follows common practice of medieval writers. As meditation leads to contemplation, so contemplation will lead to *oración,* to *orar vocalmente y mentalmente.* The three forms of prayer are given in the first annotation, and in this classical order. In the twelfth annotation they recur, but there contemplation precedes meditation. The reason for this change is not far to seek. By far the greater number of exercises to be made by the exercitant are contemplations. It is with these that Ignatius is primarily concerned, as is clear from the text; meditation is rather rare, so is *oración,* but for a very different reason.[1]

The fourth set of elements that reminds us to a certain extent of an ordinary exercise concerns the end of the hour of prayer. The verb "acabar" is found no less than five times, and in the end it is not by any means crystal clear how this prayer of the second method should be ended. When the exercitant has spent an hour in *praying* (orar) the Our Father, he will say the other four prayers in the usual way (253). This is clear enough. It is possible, however, that he finds so much good matter, consolation, and relish in one or two words that these occupy him for the full hour; in this case, he will say the rest of the Our Father in the usual manner (254). Again, no difficulty. But the question should be asked why in the former case those other four prayers should be added and be said in the usual way? The answer seems to be that for Ignatius the exercise comprises a closely knit collection of prayers. This leads to the important conclusion that the one exercise, called the second method of prayer, does not last an hour, but lasts as long as it takes to contemplate all the words of these five prayers. It is one exercise spread over many days, and it is an exercise, be it repeated, in which the exercitant must exercise himself always for some time (por algún tiempo siempre se exercite, 256).

Ignatius again refers to the end of this prayer in the two notes. We quoted just now from the first, in which he says that, when he has finished the Our Father (acabado el Pater noster), the exercitant should turn to the other prayers (256). In the second note the exercitant is asked *acabada la oración* to turn to the person to whom the prayer was directed, and in a few words ask for the virtues or graces which he needs most (257). There can hardly be any doubt that "acabada la oración" does not stand for the end of the *hour* of prayer: we have been told that the exercitant should then say the other four prayers. So it must mean the end of the contemplation of each word of the Our Father or any of the other four prayers. But now it is rather strange that he should turn to the person to whom the prayer is directed. One would think that in contemplating the Hail Mary, one is praying to Our Lady; why, or how, turn to her at the end of many hours spent in praying to her? The question itself makes clear that *devoción, gusto,* and *consolación* are the characteristic features of this second method of prayer, and how incidental and subsidiary is the part which is played by the source of them, in this case, the contemplation of each individual word of a prayer.

The final note of Ignatius shows clear indications of the colloquy. In the first week the text has "hablar" and "pedir alguna gracia" (54); in the third week there is the desire to have this virtue or that and its petition for what is more earnestly desired with regard to some particular interest (199). The words "pedir, gracias, virtudes" are now found again, and instead of "hablar" we find "en pocos palabras." Why "in a few words"? And we might add another question: why not a proper colloquy and why not a Pater Noster at the end? Why this deviation from normal practice? The answer is that having contemplated one of those five prayers, the exercise is over. What follows is only a short petition. The petition is founded upon and entirely inspired by what has never been mentioned before in any colloquy or anywhere else (with the exception of the third point of the contemplation on the Nativity, where, however, the context is totally different) and what now comes most unexpectedly: the need of the exercitant (pida las virtudes o gracias, de las quales siente tener más necessidad). One would think that the exercitant had been taken into the seventh heaven, that he did not lack anything at all. Evidently, at the height of contemplation, he feels more than ever his own insufficiency; he realizes how he falls short in virtue and is in dire need of special help. Close union with God goes hand in hand with a profound sense of one's own unworthiness and even helplessness. We shall soon see, in the third method of prayer, how Ignatius will fall back upon the word "baxeza." Hence, "in a few words"; there is no need to use many words now. We are reminded once again of *humildad amorosa*.

Third Method

In the third method of prayer, which consists in a rhythmic recitation (por compás, 258), there is no trace of prelude, colloquy, or points. There is no mention of consolation or devotion. No precise duration is given; normally, the method will not take very long: a few minutes only. What remains and reminds us of a normal exercise is the brief moment of recollection which precedes the prayer, the equivalent, Ignatius calls it, of the second addition. It is the same as in the first and second methods (239, 250).

With each breath or respiration a single word of a prayer is said. Not of any prayer. It is the same five prayers of the second method that are thus said very slowly. There is a slight change in the order of the five prayers: the Creed and the Anima Christi have changed places, but we cannot see how any importance should be attached to this. The five are again kept close together so that, the Our Father having been said rhythmically, the other four are added in the usual manner (258). The five prayers have been contemplated before. Each word has been savored and relished. Each word has become known interiorly and is now charged with meaning, consolation, and devotion.

It is not the meaning of the words, not even the consolation or spiritual fruit with which they have become associated, that is of the essence of this method. The verb used is "mirar," which we have come across so frequently. Its object is the meaning of each word (significación de la tal palabra), but at once it is extended to embrace the person to whom the prayer is addressed (la persona a quien reza), the exercitant's own lowliness (la baxeza de sí mismo), and the difference between the greatness of the person to whom the prayer is addressed and his own lowliness (la differencia de tanta alteza a tanta baxeza propria). Clearly, the meaning of each word is of relatively slight importance. The exercitant in reciting those prayers is occupied with the person to whom he prays, with himself as praying, and the great discrepancy between this person and himself. The conjunction *o* (or) is used three times, as if Ignatius does not want to overburden the exercitant. At the same time, there can be no mistaking the direction which his prayer should take: the twofold use of "baxeza" and the explicit reference to the distance between himself and the person to whom he prays take away any doubt or hesitation. This does not come quite unexpectedly: the very end of the second method of prayer showed the shape of things to come.

After the contemplation to attain the love of God, which in all likelihood occupies the exercitant for some days, followed by some time spent on the second method of prayer, one would expect the exercitant's composition, that is one-ness with God, to be drenched in love. Why should lowliness be stressed explicitly and suddenly at this point? Ignatius sets aside the word "humility" and confines himself to "lowliness," which again is rather remarkable, if one recalls the three kinds of *humility* and the part played by the third kind in the third week. One would have thought that the word itself contains a special charm for Ignatius. "Baxeza" occurs in the contemplation on the Last Supper, where St. Peter objects to the Lord washing his feet, considering the Lord's Majesty and Peter's own lowliness (289). In the first kind of humility the verb "baxar" is used by the side of "humiliar" (165). Rather relevant is its use in the eleventh rule for the discernment of spirits. Ignatius is writing of a person in consolation; he advises him to humble and lower himself as much as possible (procure humiliarse y baxarse quanto puede, 324).[2] The motive given by Ignatius is that a person in consolation must not lose his head but should rather think of how little he is able to do in time of desolation, when such grace and consolation have been withheld. The same danger is signalized in the ninth rule, where Ignatius chooses the image of building one's nest in another man's house to clarify the same point (322).

It is these two rules that make for a better understanding of the third method of prayer. No one can afford to lose sight of the fact that the third method proceeds from the second: prayers are now recited that have been contemplated before and have been savored in great consolation. If at any time a reminder to be humble in the midst of consolation is most profitable (324), it is certainly not out of place when a person slowly recites prayers that by themselves cannot but bring into consciousness the sweetness of intense consolation. The exercitant must remain level-headed; he must keep both feet on the ground, he must always be a realist, with an undimmed vision of the actual situation in which he finds himself.

To achieve this aim, Ignatius avoids everything that might possibly enhance or intensify the consolation: devout postures, concentration of the mind by keeping one's eyes closed or even fixed on one spot, preludes, colloquies, and so on; even "reflectir a mí mismo" is omitted. On the contrary, the exercitant is to do nothing out of the ordinary. There is hardly even question of setting aside any special time for this third method. He is to take himself as he is, with those five prayers that now come to him almost automatically, and try to join the praying man to the breathing man, or more accurately the other way about: take the breathing man that he is and gently make him into a praying man as well.

But there is more. Consolation is a matter of motions and agitations, and these are quite often very intense. Thus Ignatius writes of "tanto estipendio de consolaciones y crescidas gracias," of "devoción crescida, amor intenso" (322), while the word "lágrimas" occurs quite frequently throughout the Exercises.[3] It looks as if Ignatius considers consolation to be normally a matter of *mucho hervor, crecido amor y gracia intensa* (320). Apparently the danger is that the exercitant will not be able to handle such motions and agitations.

One cannot shake off their effect as soon as the hour of prayer is past, and Ignatius himself tells the exercitant to learn how to distinguish the exact period of consolation from the time that follows (336). Indeed, he is dealing with consolation directly and without any preceding cause given by God, but the principle seems to allow for a much wider application. One is reminded of the quarter of an hour's review after each exercise in order that there might be a gradual transition between the time of motions and agitations and the period that follows. The exercitant, then, should train himself to keep such vehement motions in check, not to permit himself to be overwhelmed, let alone swept away by them. He has to direct them into certain channels to prevent them from running wild. Somehow, he has to live with them, and in no way should they make him unfit for life. Ignatius is once again very gentle in the way he suggests the handling of this problem. The motions and agitations must not be cut off, must not be suppressed: it would be equal to banishing God while He is working and communicating Himself. The exercitant should quiet his activity somewhat by bringing the motions of his heart into unison with the natural rhythm of his breathing. The means employed to achieve this is the group of five prayers that have been carefully contemplated before. The second method should always be practiced by the exercitant for some time. The third method does not contain such an injunction: the verb "querer" is used twice; it is left to the exercitant himself (259, 260).

Five prayers, and these five prayers: why these five, and why not more? The answer is not far to seek. The exercitant in his everyday life has to fall back upon prayers which come to him naturally, with which he is as familiar as with his breathing. Hence, it is the third method that imposes the quintet upon the second method, and not the other way about. There was little choice. The Our Father, Hail Mary and the Creed chose themselves. The Salve Regina, as is well known, was a great favorite with the Church of Spain in the late Middle Ages. The Anima Christi looks like Ignatius' own predilection. It must not be forgotten that the exercitant has been saying this prayer throughout the first three weeks some four or five times a day, for the triple colloquy of both the first week and of the meditation on Two Standards contains this prayer. There is nothing in the prayers themselves that forced Ignatius to choose them. The choice was mainly the result of familiarity and accessibility. The conclusion from this is as clear as it is practical: if today the exercitant is familiar with another set of prayers—and one spontaneously thinks of psalms—there is no objection to his using these according to the second and third methods. Ignatius took the prayers that occurred to him as the most familiar. The number happened to be five.

The *Directorium Granatense* calls the third method the easiest of the three and adds that it is meant "más para los simples" (*Dir.*, 561). If this were true, Ignatius would undoubtedly have mentioned it in the eighteenth annotation, where he provides exercises for the simple and unlettered. The cause of this misinterpretation lies in an overstressing of "por compás" and a misunderstanding of the correct meaning of "orar." What we said above about the meaning of "oración" holds good of the verb as well. The third method is not the same as a spirit of recollection floating, as it were, upon the rhythm of one's breathing. It is not a device to occupy oneself in light prayer. It is the Spiritual Exercises re-lived for a few brief but precious moments to the extent of their being integrated into the quiet and tranquillity of one's breathing. It is *orar* and *oración* at a very high level.

Ignatius explicitly states that the third method, just as the second, forms part of the Spiritual Exercises in the proper sense of the word. They may not be a part of the fourth week, but they definitely belong to the long retreat. The contemplation to attain the love of God, the second method of prayer, and the third show a gradual loosening of bonds with the four preceding weeks, and parallel with this, an ever-increasing occupation with the duties of the exercitant's normal life. The ultimate purpose of these three exercises, and especially of the second and third methods of prayer, is to carry the order and harmony achieved in the four weeks of the retreat into everyday existence and to prevent the manifold fruit of the Exercises from getting lost in the hustle and bustle of life. They are meant to prevent the thirty days' retreat from becoming a strange sort of oasis in anyone's life, which is like a desert. It is regrettable that this essential function of the three exercises following the four weeks has been neglected. Ignatius lived in a time when the danger of isolating the long retreat was considerably less than nowadays. The exercitant quite often had a long way to come in order to make the Spiritual Exercises: by itself a golden opportunity of preparing himself properly. Quite often he had as long a way to go back again, another golden opportunity of giving himself to the contemplation to attain the love of God and to the second and third methods of prayer. Once we understand these three exercises, ways and means will be found to adapt them to a quite different set of circumstances.

EPILOGUE

The Spiritual Exercises are first and foremost a school of prayer; this is clear from the opening paragraph of the book of Ignatius, the first annotation. They are a time for seeking and finding the will of God, and, consequently, for removing inordinate attachments; but they are mainly a time for praying. The dominant form of prayer is not meditation but contemplation, and the contemplation is of an ever-increasing perfection. It means that God will communicate Himself more and more intimately. This will not take place without the exercitant's experiencing various motions and agitations. These do not always find their origin in God. There will be temptation and desolation, and there is the possibility, indeed the probability, of Satanic deceits, frauds, and snares. It is not by any means easy to distinguish where the motions come from, not even consolation. One of the main duties of the director, therefore, is to sort out such motions; hence, he should be faithfully informed of them by the exercitant (17). Ignatius gives two sets of rules for distinguishing the activities of various spirits: we have mentioned them repeatedly. They are not an appendix but form an indispensable part of the Spiritual Exercises. Without them it would be highly dangerous to give or make the Exercises.

In a similar way, the rules for thinking with the Church belong to the Exercises. They are not added merely or mainly as useful warnings in turbulent times. If there always is a danger of being deceived by the devil as an angel of light, of attributing to God what really proceeds from one's heart and mind, it will be considerably reduced so long as the exercitant moves with great constancy within the framework of the Church. The word "framework" is not used by Ignatius, but it is suggested by the choice of "iglesia militante" in the title (352). Ignatius, however, quickly moves away from any idea of the Church as an institution and in the first rule he prefers "vera sposa de Christo nuestro Señor, que es la nuestra sancta madre Iglesia hierárchica" (353). The exercitant is supposed to let himself be guided by his love for the Church and by her Spirit; this Spirit is the same as the Spirit of Christ, her Spouse (365).

An exposition and analysis of the rules both for the discernment of spirits and for thinking with the Church do not belong to this study, which has been concerned with the exercitant described by Ignatius in the twentieth annotation. But the exposition of the Exercises would be incomplete if the attention were not directed toward safeguards, drawn up by Ignatius, to ensure that the exercitant, wishing to make as much progress as possible, may become closely united with his Creator and Lord (20).

A close study of the text of the *Spiritual Exercises* will make any exposition lean heavily toward the Exercises as a school and time of prayer, and not toward asceticism. The growth in the exercitant of a disposition leading more and more toward perfection is far more dominant than any occupation with the election of a state or way of life. In the end, the fruit of the tree is not to be judged so much by the resolutions made as by the exercitant's *abandon*, resignation, and the highest spiritual poverty. This may not, in every respect, be in line with what might be called the more traditional approach and interpretation. But the name of Lallemant from the distant past and that of Louis Peeters from only a few decades back are sufficient guarantees that the Spiritual Exercises as a school of prayer have always had a legitimate, if not always comfortable, place within the tradition of the Society of Jesus.

When Roothaan published his literal translation in 1834, he pleaded most earnestly in an accompanying letter for *studium diligens*. If the results of this study are here and there different from those of Roothaan, it is because "diligens" has been taken more strictly than intended. It is the results that must justify the method followed, or in a more homely expression, the proof of the pudding is in the eating. We make no pretense of having discovered and laid bare all the riches the Spiritual Exercises contain. We are convinced that we have in no way exhausted the mine. Taking the book of Ignatius in hand should always mean *buscar*, to go in search, because it is a book written by a great mystic about his own most profound mystical experiences and revelations. It will always result in *hallar*, in new discoveries. We make no other claim than to have shown the way and to have given proof enough that it is a safe way to travel.

NOTES

preface

1 That the Spiritual Exercises should be approved by the Holy See was one of the three wishes Ignatius wanted to see fulfilled before he died, the other two being the approbation of the Society of Jesus, and time and energy to write the *Constitutions* of his order. This information is given by Nadal in his preface to Ignatius' own *Pilgrim's Story,* as dictated to Luis Gonzâlez de Câmara. The text of what is usually called Ignatius' autobiography has been published in *Obras Completas de S. Ignacio de Loyola,* edited by I. Iparraguirre, S.J. Madrid, 1963, pp. 69-159 (English translation: *St. Ignatius' Own Story as Told to Luis Gonzalez de Camara,* by William J. Young, S.J. Chicago, 1956); it will be referred to as *Autobiography,* followed by a number indicating the paragraph. Cfr. *Autobiografía,* no. 1* in *Obras Completas,* p. 84.

2 "Todos los primeros Padres hicieron los exercicios exactamente y apartados" reports Gonzâlez de Câmara in his *Memoriale.* (*Fontes Narrativi de S. Ignatio de Loyola et de Societatis Iesu Initiis,* Vol. I-IV, Monumenta Historica S. I., Romae, 1943-1965. This work will be referred to as *F.N.*, followed by a Roman numeral indicating the volume.) Cfr. *F.N.*, I, p. 704.

3 *Exercitia Spiritualia Sancti Patris Ignatii de Loyola.* Taurini - Romae, 1928. *Exercitia Spiritualia Sancti Ignatii de Loyola.* Monumenta Ignatiana, series secunda, tomus I, Romae, 1919. Directoria Exercitiorum Spiritualium (1540-1594). Monumenta Ignatiana, series secunda, tomus II, Romae, 1955.

4 J. Morris, *The Text of the Spiritual Exercises of Saint Ignatius.* London, 1936. J. Rickaby, *The Spiritual Exercises of St. Ignatius*, Spanish and English, with a continuous commentary. Second edition, London, 1923. L. J. Puhl, *The Spiritual Exercises of St. Ignatius.* A new translation. Eighth revised printing, Westminster (Maryland), 1963. Th. Moore, *The Spiritual Exercises of Saint Ignatius of Loyola.* (Newly translated from the original Spanish "autograph"). New York, 1948. Th. Corbishley, *The Spiritual Exercises of Saint Ignatius.* A new translation. London-New York, 1963. A. Mottola, *The Spiritual Exercises of St. Ignatius.* Garden City (N. J.), 1964. Fr. Courel, *Exercices Spirituels.* Collection Christus No. 5, Paris, 1960. E. Raitz v. Frentz, *Ignatius von Loyola, Geistliche Übungen.* 10. Auflage, Freiburg, 1950. H. Urs von Balthasar, *Ignatius von Loyola, Die Exerzitien.* Luzern, 1946. Adolf Haas, *Geistliche Übungen.* Übertragung aus dem Spanischen Urtext. Erklärung der 20 Anweisungen. Freiburg, 1967. The *classical* English translation is generally considered to be that made by John Morris, S.J. A year before he died, the second edition had appeared (1892). Since then there have been five revised editions, but all

the revisions do not amount to very much. Although the editor of the fifth edition attributes the translation to "Fr. John Morris and others," the work of others is negligible. Language and style, and even the format have remained the same throughout the almost eighty years since its first publication. There was no cogent reason to set aside the fourth revised edition which we had been using for years in favor of the fifth revised edition: the sixteen years in between do not make any difference (1936 to 1952).

one

1 St. Ignatii de Loyola Epistolae et Instructiones. Monumenta Ignatiana, series prima, tomus I-XII, Matriti, 1903-1911. This collection will be referred to as Ep., followed by a Roman numeral indicating the volume. Cfr. I, p. 111.

2 *Autobiography*, 27; 20-21.

3 *F.N.*, II, p. 150; III, pp. 360, 690.

4 Morris, Puhl, and Mottola translate "to inflame." The autograph, however, clearly reads "abrazândola"; the reading "abrasândola" should be rejected. Moreover, if Ignatius had wished to use the image of love as a fire, he would have used "inflamar," as he does in the third rule for the discernment of spirits, second group (316).

5 "Alombrado" does not occur in the text of the Exercises; Ignatius prefers "ilucidado" (2) and "iluminado" (363). "Dechar" occurs a number of times, as for instance in the fifteenth annotation: the director should *allow* or *permit* God to work directly in His exercitant. From the photographic copy of the autograph text (Roma, 1907), it appears that in the fifth annotation "dechando" has been changed by Ignatius himself to "ofreciendo."

6 I. Iparraguirre, *Practica de los Ejercicios de San Ignacio de Loyola en vida de su autor* (1522-1556). Bilbao-Roma, 1949, pp. 98-101.

7 A comparison between what Polanco and Cordeses write and what we read in the official *Directory* some thirty years later is very instructive. Cfr. *Dir.*, 276, 540-46, 588-99.

8 From the first annotation it is clear that "exercise" has no military connotations. Fortunately, the English translations yield no difficulties in this respect. Cfr. L. Hertling, "De Usu Nominis Exercitiorum Spiritualium ante P. Ignatium." *Archivum Historicum S. I.*, 1933, pp. 316-18.

9 The twentieth annotation presupposes that the Spiritual Exercises are given to the individual exercitant. Where the collective retreat has become unavoidable, the strong tradition of the Society of Jesus, insisting on solitude and silence, deserves to be maintained as the nearest approach to the indispensable *apartar*.

10 Cfr. H. Rahner, *Ignatius von Loyola und das geschichtliche Werden seiner Frömmigkeit.* Salzburg-Wien, 1947, pp. 54-60. A very striking example is given in the letter which Ignatius wrote to those who were taking part in the Council of Trent (*Ep.*, I, pp. 386-89).

11 The German translation by Raitz v. Frentz has "Regelung" for "disposición," that of von Balthasar "Einrichtung"; Courel translates "disposition." Mottola and Puhl have "disposition," Morris prefers "ordering," Rickaby has chosen "laying out," while Corbishley falls back upon the verb "to regulate." Our objection to these translations is that they do not make clear who is the person that orders or regulates or lays out; in fact, the almost irresistible suggestion is that the exercitant is doing it.

12 Apparently, not much attention is given to the famous "affección desordenada," although it occurs in what might be called key positions: the first annotation, the

title, the sixteenth annotation, and a number of times when the election is dealt with. Moreover, "affectar, affecto, affectado, aficionado" are by no means rare. Ignatius simply accepts the fact that many attachments are inordinate and he does not ask the exercitant to discover what they are. He is much more interested in bringing them to order, and this involves, as has been stressed in this chapter, the work of God and of the exercitant in close cooperation. A preoccupation with inordinate attachments might easily give rise to the impression that the Spiritual Exercises aim merely or mainly at removing what is wrong and evil, and thus obscure their true purpose, namely, to achieve order and harmony.

13 Throughout this study, evidence will be accumulated showing that the Spiritual Exercises do not primarily aim at a sound election of a state of life. We are well aware of objections and of historical difficulties. Regarding the latter, the *Memoriale* of Luis Gonzâlez de Câmara, to whom Ignatius dictated his own *Pilgrim's Story,* says with reference to the Spiritual Exercises that they "are better for those who have not yet made an immutable choice of state of life," and the reason added is "because they will be more moved by divers spirits" (*F.N.*, I, p. 676). In the *Directory* dictated to Vitoria we read something similar: Ignatius seems to exclude from the Spiritual Exercises "casados o religiosos," apparently suggesting that they are meant only for those who are not married and do not belong to a religious institute, consequently, for those only who have not yet made an immutable election (*Dir.*, 91). With these and similar texts before us, we must make allowances for the fact that frequently Ignatius had no choice but to restrict himself to such as, in rather turbulent times, wished to make an immutable election, and this in keeping with the needs of the Church in those days. Quite often it was impossible to help all those who wished to make the Exercises in full: it did not mean that Ignatius excluded them or thought them unfit. This is clear from the *Directory* from which we quoted just now. In the *Constitutions* of his order he nowhere indicates that the Spiritual Exercises are only for people who wish to make an election. He does say that they should be given to few, "rari homines," or, so he adds, "to those who wish to decide about their state of life" (P. VIII, c. 4, n. 8 F; P. IV, c. 8, n. 5 E.).

two

1 An exception is made by Ignatius for the first method, which should be given to the exercitant of the eighteenth annotation. This is not surprising as this first method aims at what may be called a thorough and systematic examination of conscience. Ignatius appears to have been somewhat apprehensive of calling it prayer and of joining it to the second and third methods. "This manner of praying," he says, "is not meant so much to provide a form and method of prayer properly so called, but rather to supply a way . . . by which the soul might prepare itself . . . so that its prayer may be acceptable to God" (238). The reason why he placed this method here is that he wished to keep the three methods together. We return to this subject in our final chapter.

three

1 Faber, de Villanueva, and Doménech, and in this order; Estrada was good at giving the first week (*F.N.*, I, p. 658).

2 Cfr. Memoriale of Gonzâlez de Câmara, *F.N.*, I, p. 677; a clear echo is found in a letter to Francis Borgia (*Ep.*, II, pp. 233-37).

3 This is a deduction from the seventeenth annotation. In his *Directory* Ignatius is more emphatic (*Dir.*, 70). Polanco and the author of the *Directorium Granatense* give the same advice (*ibid.*, 297, 544). See also the *Directorium Breve,* the *Directory* of 1591 and the official *Directory* of 1599 (*ibid.*, 452, 664, 665).

4 *Sp. Ex.*, 72, 205, 227. The fourth annotation explains that some exercitants are slower, or more diligent, or more deeply moved and tried by various spirits, and hence the need for lengthening or shortening the various weeks.

5 Polanco: *Dir.*, 283, 296 and 334; Cordeses: 543; Gonzâlez Dâvila: 505; official *Directory:* 383 and 296.

6 Instructor: *Dir.*, 857 and 907; director: 948; retreat-master: 922; exercitant: 951 and 988.

7 "He who gives the Exercises": *Sp. Ex.*, 6, 7, 8, 9, 10, 12, 14, 15, 17, 18, 22. "He who receives the Exercises": 5, 7, 8, 10, 12, 14, 15, 17, 18, 22; cfr. also 11. "He who exercises himself": 6, 9, 10, 13, 72, 89, 130, 133, 205.

four

1 This is not immediately clear with regard to the third and fourth exercises, which are, respectively, a repetition (62) and a resumption (63). But as these belong to the first day, the director will have to explain what is meant by a repetition, and he will have to instruct the exercitant about the triple colloquy. In order to make the resumption properly, the exercitant must be told what is meant by "discurrir por la reminiscencia de las cosas contempladas en los exercicios passados."

2 Entrar en el exercicio: 5, 76, 131, 228, 239; pasar adelante (to proceed): 76, 254; discurrir (to wander about): 64; cfr. 3, 50-52, 180; hacer pausa, pausar, reposar: 62, 76, 227; estar delante de Dios: 151, 232.

3 Ignatius appears to have had a predilection for "mirar." Instructive is its use in the contemplation on the Ascension, where it is twice predicated of the apostles (312). Sometimes there is a subtle shift from "mirar" to "considerar," as in the second exercise of the first week: in the midst of a sevenfold use of "mirar" there is a sudden change to "considerar" when the object is God against whom man has sinned (56-59). The same is found in the exercise on the Kingdom: how the king addresses his subjects is the object of *mirar*, the reply made by good subjects is the object of *considerar;* again, in the second rule to arrive at a safe choice, "mirar a un hombre" is followed by "considerar" with as its object "advice given to the man." Latin and English translations leave little trace of this predilection.

4 This is not entirely accurate. In contemplations, the preludes belong to the exercise and are not merely introduction to it.

5 An exception is apparently given in the meditation on Two Standards. The exercise has two parts, and each part has three points, and yet each of these points is introduced by "considerar," its choice being no doubt strongly influenced by the whole character of this meditation, which is very much an investigation (135). Further light is shown on this matter by the text of the second method of making a good choice in the third time. Ignatius now speaks of rules, not points (184-88). Each of these rules contains a number of points, that is, different activities. This is very clear in the second rule, where "mirar," "desear," "considerar," and "guardar" (la regla) are found in succession.

6 From early times there has been a certain hesitancy in finding a correct rendering of "traer la historia." Leaving out the *Directories* and confining ourselves to the *versio prima* and the *versio vulgata*, we notice that the former has: proferre in medium contemplandae rei historiam (102), praeambulum ex historia dependet (111), sumitur ex historia (191), est iuxta historiam (201), accipitur ex historia (219), and historica quaedam consideratio (137); the latter has: proponere historiam (102), adducere historiam (191, 201, 219), adducere historiam in medium (111), and continet historiam (137).

7 Barcelona, 1857, p. 348.

8 The three quotations are found, respectively: *F.N.*, I, p. 540, *Dir.*, 94 and *Ep.*, II, p. 344.

9 The explanation of an "elleptica oratio" as given by the editor of the Exercitia Spiritualia in the Monumenta Historica Societatis Jesu must be rejected (pp. 186-87); the omission of "lugar" is too systematic for it.

10 "Imaginar" occurs four times. In the case of those who go on sinning, the devil proposes apparent pleasures, causing them *to imagine* sensual gratifications and delights (314). In the meditation on Two Standards, the exercitant is *to imagine* the chief of all the enemies (140) and similarly *to imagine* the sovereign and true Leader (143). The first colloquy reads: "He will *imagine* Christ before him and placed upon the cross" (53). A proper understanding of both the meditation on Two Standards and the first meditation of the first week will show how accurate the use of "imaginar" is.
The absence of this verb where it might be reasonably expected is also instructive. It is not used in the contemplation on the Nativity, where the first point is almost an invitation to imagine oneself present in the cave, helping Mary and Joseph in their needs; its use here would have meant the end of the mystery, which has been made present to the exercitant by means of the three preludes.

11 In the composition of the consideration on the Kingdom, which is made "viendo el lugar," the expression "con la vista imaginativa" is used (91), as is the case in the composition of the contemplation on the Nativity (112). The expression also occurs in the first point of the application of the senses, which exercise is introduced by "el pasar de los cinco sentidos *de la imaginación*" (121). In the composition and the first point of the meditation on hell, "con la vista de la imaginación" has been chosen. More often than not, either expression is reduced to a simple "ver" (103, 138, 151, 220, 230) or "considerar" (192, 202). With other senses than sight, neither *imaginativa* nor *imaginación* is used.

12 Regarding the translation of this expression, the *versio prima* always reads "compositio loci"; the *versio vulgata* has "ratio quaedam componendi loci (47), constructio loci (91, 138, 151, 192, 202), compositio loci (65, 103), and consideratio loci" (112). Roothaan has gone back to a very literal rendering "videndo locum." Peter Faber prefers "compositio loci," but the copy of the Exercises of the Englishman, Helyar, shows a great variety: "compositio circa locum est videre . . .; primum praeludium est compositio seu consideratio inferni. Hic erit imaginari longitudinem, . . .; compositio loci erit contemplari planitiem terrae" (*Ex. Sp.*, 627, 630, 631, 633).
The subject has received a good deal of attention from the time of the first commentators on the Exercises. Its purpose is said to be "ne vagetur in incertum animus" and "ut attenta sit oratio" by Dávila (*Dir.*, 503), its result, "que se halla presente a todo" (*ibid.*, 509). The *Breve Directorium* makes the composition into an act of the imagination: "quia multi in compositione loci multum laborant, et vim magnam capiti inferunt, moneantur qui minus apti ad eam comperiantur, ut revocent sibi in mentem historiam aliquam pictam . . . . Hoc enim praesidio facilius compositionem imaginariam conficere poterit" (*ibid.*, 449). Mirón, a commentator of the generation immediately following Ignatius' death, writes: "In compositione loci homo constituit se quasi presentem loco ubi res gesta fuit . . . . Sed in huius loci compositione non est nimis immorandum ne caput defatigetur . . ." (*ibid.*, 394).

13 Cfr. 48, 55, 62, 91, 101, 105, 110, 118, 121, 136, 149, 159, 190, 200, 204, 218, 231.

14 As a rule, Ignatius writes "el preámbulo es demandar lo que quiero" or "será aquí pedir . . ." (55, 65, 91, 193, 221; 139, 152). The contemplation on the Incarnation has "demandar" twice, which is also used throughout the third week; it is accompanied by "pedir" in the fourth week. Explaining this prelude in the first exercise, Ignatius writes "demandar gozo con Christo gozoso, demandar pena con Christo atormentado, demandar vergüenza y confussión" (48). There does not seem to be much difference between the two verbs; "demandar" has a certain

urgency, while "pedir" brings out humble begging. This could well explain why in the contemplation to attain divine love the former verb is not used at all; the exercitant confines himself to "pedir."
When dealing with this prelude for the first time, Ignatius speaks of "lo que quiero *y deseo*," to ask what I want *and desire*. However, throughout the four weeks this reference to desire is omitted.

15 A note on its meaning is given in the Marietti edition of the *Spiritual Exercises* (p. 199), in Puhl's translation (p. 187), and in the glossary of *Ejercicios Espirituales, Directorio y Documentos de S. Ignacio de Loyola,* by José Calveras. Barcelona, 1944; p. 488.

16 The warmth and intimacy conveyed by the use of "hablar" is easily discerned in what has come to us of Ignatius' diary (*Obras Completas*, pp. 301-386). At times the intimacy became so intense that he lost his power of speech (*ibid.*, pp. 307, 318, 331, 337). The diary is steeped in *acatamiento y reverencia,* which in the third annotation is closely associated with *hablar vocalmente o mentalmente.*

17 Cfr. *Sancti Ignatii de Loyola Constitutiones Societatis Jesu.* Monumenta Ignatiana, series tertia, tomus I. Roma, 1934; p. 392.

18 Polanco uses "meditation" for the exercises of the second and third weeks. When he deals with the matter of giving points, only "meditation" is found (*Dir.*, 320, 337). The official *Directory* practically substitutes meditation for contemplation, so that every difference between these two forms of prayer becomes obliterated (*Dir.*, 671, 673, 675, 677, 679, 681). Faber, as is to be expected, is faithful to Ignatius in the use of "contemplation"; he shows a predilection for "considerar" when giving points (*Ex. Sp.*, pp. 579-623).

19 *Op cit.*, pp. 99 ss., 245, 250, 253; cfr. *Ex. Sp.*, pp. 95-121.

20 Ignatius adds "desolation." It sounds rather strange, perhaps even heroic, to turn to those parts of the exercise where the exercitant experienced desolation. It has little to do with heroism. Ignatius had no choice. For desolation may be the work of God just as much as consolation is; and as consolation is not always the work of God, similarly desolation is by no means always the result of Satan's activities. At least two of the reasons why the exercitant may find himself in desolation are attributable to God Himself, who brings the exercitant to a clearer knowledge of the situation in which he finds himself as His creature and child (322).

21 In the *Constitutions* of his Order, Ignatius uses "meditation," sometimes in conjunction with "oratio" (P. III, c. 1, n. 20; P. IV, c. 4, n. 2; P. VI, c. 3, n. 1). One cannot very well prescribe contemplation, as if it were an effort by means of memory, understanding, and will, as meditation is.

five

1 "Exercitia plene non nisi paucis, iisque huiusmodi ut ex eorum profectu non vulgaris ad Dei gloriam fructus speretur, vel qui de vitae suae statu deliberare velint, tradenda sunt" (*Directorium* of Father Mirón; *Dir.*, 371). Ignatius himself writes to his followers in Portugal: "Si diese todos los Exercicios, daríalos a muy pocos, y letrados o personas muy deseosas de perfección . . . (*ibid.*, 111). Even when an election has to be made, Ignatius appears to be somewhat hesitant in giving the Exercises; in the same letter he writes: "En dar elecciones sería rarísimo, y con personas muy deseosas de letras" (*ibid.*, 112). That he is referring to an election made in the Spiritual Exercises, is clear not merely from the two preceding paragraphs of this letter, but also from his reference to the Exercises immediately following the quotation just given.

2 Francis Xavier made the long retreat in September 1534, a month after he had taken his vows, together with Ignatius and the other companions. By then he had known Ignatius for four years. (*F.N.*, I, p. 705; cfr. Iparraguirre, *Practica*, p. 5).

3 The verb "platicar" is used with reference to the First Principle and Foundation (19). Ignatius prefers "declarar" where in the second annotation the object is the history or the meaning of the history of a meditation or contemplation, and in the eighteenth annotation, where the object is the Commandments, capital sins, works of mercy, and so on; it is this word which is found in the *Directory* dictated to Father Vitoria (*Dir.*, 100-02).
"Platicar" is also found in the eighth annotation, where its object is the rules for the discernment of spirits, which in Ignatius' own words "contain matter that is too subtle and too high for him (that is, for one making the first week of the Exercises) to understand" (9). The verb suggests conversation during which a subject is considered (Cfr. also 362; see Calveras, *op. cit.*, p. 484).

4 "Resignation" is found in Ignatius' *Directory* dictated to Vitoria, and is preferred by Polanco, Doménech, and González Dávila (*Dir.*, 99, 285, 183, 493, respectively). Pereyra, in his commentary, explains indifference in terms of resignation: "Esta indifferencia es una resinación con la quel el hombre se pone en las manos de su Dios" (*ibid.*, 149-53).

5 This explains and justifies the traditional way of opening the retreat with meditations, not with instructions, on the First Principle and Foundation. From the early Directories it is abundantly clear that the first and second generation of directors linked this preliminary statement with those annotations that concern the initial disposition of the exercitant. Later tradition has given this statement a rather independent position, calling it the foundation upon which the whole edifice of the Spiritual Exercises is to be built, which represents only a small part of the truth.

6 Doménech mentions among the elements of the exercitant's disposition not only resignation but also "libertas filiorum adoptionis" and "laetitia spiritualis" (*Dir.*, 183); the *Directorium Granatense* finds room for both "joy" and "love" (*ibid.*, 538), while "love" and "peace" are words used by González Dávila (*ibid.*, 538).

7 Mottola has: "All things are created for man to help him fulfill the end . . ."; Corbishley reads: "Everything else on earth has been created for man's sake, to help him achieve . . ."; more literal is Morris' rendering: "The other things on the face of the earth were created for man's sake, and in order to aid him . . .," which corresponds to Rickaby's translation. Courel translates: "Les autres choses sur la face de la terre sont creées pour l'homme, pour l'aider . . .," omitting the translation of *y*. Raitz v. Frentz has: "Die übrigen Dinge auf Erden aber sind des Menschen wegen erschaffen, und *zwar* damit sie ihm . . . behilflich seien." The insertion of *zwar* in italics is explained by the translator in a note. Urs von Balthasar translates: "Die andern Dinge auf Erden sind zum Menschen hin geschaffen, und um ihm . . . zu helfen."

8 "Quitar" and "quitarse" occur more than twenty times in the text. The fundamental meaning is: to remove, to move away from. Ignatius wants Christians to avoid talking about grace in such a way that liberty is completely *removed* (quitar la libertad, 369); God and His angels *take away* sadness and confusion (329) just as the wicked spirits try *to remove* peace and rest (333, 315). There is a difference between *quitar* and *lanzar;* in the fifth rule for the distribution of alms, we read that the inordinate attachment must not only be *removed* but *cast off* (342). From other instances it is clear that *lanzar* stands for a complete break (35, 171, 313, 343), which is not always possible when "quitar" is used. One cannot always do away with one's inordinate attachments because one would like to be rid of them. But man must keep at a distance from them, leave them alone, not pay attention to them, and certainly see to it that he is not led or influenced by them. This meaning of "quitar" and "quitarse" occurs a number of times in the meditation on Three Classes of Men (153-55), in the rules for food and drink (213-17), and in those for doing penance (83, 84).

9 Misinterpretation of the word "indifference" may have contributed to its being only sparsely used. González Dávila points out: "Quoniam quae hic dicuntur de

indifferentia ex schola Pyrronis ad nos devenisse quidem iniqui censores perperam interpretati sunt, declaranda sunt" (*Dir.*, 501).

10 Rickaby: "solely desiring and choosing those things which may better lead us to the end . . ."; Morris: "and so in all other things, desiring and choosing only those which most lead us to the end . . ."; Mottola: "and so in all things we should desire and choose only those things which will best help us to attain the end . . ."; Courel: "mais que nous désirions et choisissions uniquement ce qui nous conduit davantage à la fin . . ."; Raitz v. Frentz: "indem wir einzig das verlangen und wählen, was uns mehr fördert zum Ziel . . ."; Urs von Balthasar: "einzig das ersehnend und erwählend, was uns jeweils mehr zu dem Ziele hin fördert . . . ."

11 For further instances of the use of "más" in this meaning: 18, 50, 78, 212, 217, 313, 314, 318, 319, 328, 362, 363. It is noteworthy that whereas we think the pronoun "nos" preceded by "más" to be very important, it is completely overlooked or left untranslated by some authors. Thus it has disappeared in Puhl's translation, which we quoted in the text; cfr. also L. Peeters, *Vers l'Union divine par les Exercises.* Louvain, 1923, p. 144; L. de Coninck, "Adaptation ou retour aux origines? Les Exercises spirituels de S. Ignace." *Nouvelle Revue Theologique*, 70, p. 929; H. Rahner, *op. cit.*, p. 12.

12 No word is more frequently used than "Señor"; by itself it occurs about forty times, in combination with "Dios" over sixty times, while Christ is called "el Señor" more than fifty times. God is "Criador" about twenty times, and "Divina Majestad" is found as often. It is always of importance to take careful note of when and where these words and expressions are used, as will be pointed out in the closing paragraph of this chapter.

13 In the *Examen Generale* and the *Constitutiones*, Ignatius remains true to this accurate use of "service, praise, glory." To give a few examples taken from the *Examen Generale:* when the total dedication of the Jesuit is mentioned, the correct combination "servicio y gloria" is found twice, together with "mayor" (C. III, n. 6, 14). When dealing with the right disposition toward Christ suffering on the cross, Ignatius speaks of "gloria y alabanza" (C. IV, n. 45, 46); he uses "divino servicio y alabanza" when he tells the Jesuit not to shirk begging from door to door, immediately adding "dando gloria a la su divina majestad," because the begging is done "por amor de Dios" (C. IV, n. 27). When an unsuitable candidate has to be dismissed, the text is more businesslike and reads: "quando el superior viesse que dellos no se ayuda para el mayor servicio divino." The sentence is, however, preceded by "mayor gloria de la divina majestad" when he is speaking of those who wish to live and die in his Society (C. VI, n. 8). When the Jesuit is told to strive after profound humility, Ignatius consistently speaks of "servir y laudar," of "amor y reverencia"; he does not mention the divine glory (e.g., C. VI, n. 7, C. VIII, n. 1 and 2). These examples must suffice. The subject is of importance for the light it sheds on the Ignatian *maior Dei gloria;* a detailed examination falls outside the scope of this book.

14 ". . . l'intention de S. Ignace n'est pas qu'on prenne les terms *'louer, révérer et servir'* dans leur sens propre et particulier, mais dans un sens commun et vague que rendraient également d'autres expressions, differentes de celles-ci" ("Étude sur le texte des Exercises de Saint Ignace." *Bibliothèque des Exercises*, 73-74, p. 121).

six

1 Cfr. *Dir.*, 80, where a survey is given of various possibilities of distributing the exercises of the first week.

2 Wisdom 9, 15; Hebrews 11, 13.

3 In the points of the exercise, "con el entendimiento" and "con la voluntad" are found; the activity of the will and the intellect are stressed in order that the exercitant might better understand how ashamed he ought to be. Ignatius uses the expression "discurrir con el entendimiento" three times, followed by "moviendo más los afectos con la voluntad" in the first point only, but he refers to it in the second and third points. Due emphasis should be given to the two verbs "discurrir" and "moviendo"; it is the reason why Ignatius adds "con el entendimiento" and "con la voluntad," which otherwise are rather ludicrous additions. Cfr. *Ex. Sp.*, pp. 143-44.

4 Cfr. *Ex. Sp.*, 121, 132, 159, 204, 207.

5 There is no question of Ignatius opening the exercises with a rather easy form of prayer called meditation "by means of the three faculties" for pedagogical reasons, gradually leading the exercitant to more advanced forms of prayer. The exercitant of the twentieth annotation is by no means a beginner. Besides, it would be impossible to have a contemplation on himself, let alone on his sins. The confusion is caused by misreading and misinterpreting the expression "by means of the three faculties."

6 Confession is mentioned in the eighteenth and nineteenth annotations in immediate connection with receiving Communion, as is done in the instruction immediately preceding the first exercise (44). In some cases we know of, a general confession preceded the long retreat. Ignatius himself made his before he went to Manresa and Faber confessed during the time of preparation. Cfr. Iparraguirre, *Practica,* pp. 7, 169. Most of the *Directories* make the general confession part of the first week (*Dir.*, 104, 452, 236, and so forth).

7 The generally accepted translation of this phrase is "series, or procession, of sins." Another translation is "indictment." We refer the reader to a note on the use and meaning of "processo" given by Puhl in his translation (*op. cit.*, p. 174). The whole phrase recalls the addition in which the exercitant is asked to consider himself as a guilty man, about to appear before the judge (74).

8 "Pecado mortal" stands for "capital sin" in the eighteenth annotation and the first method of prayer; the numeral *seven* takes away any trace of doubt (18, 138, 224, 244, 245). Cisneros, St. Teresa, St. John of the Cross, and other spiritual writers use the expression in this sense. (Cfr. Los Confessionales y los Ejercicios, *Archivum Historicum Societatis Jesu,* XVII, 1948, pp. 51-101, passim). "Capital sin" is the translation when the expression is used in the first rule for the discernment of spirits. Persons "que van de peccado mortal en peccado mortal" are not persons who go from mortal sin to mortal sin: such people are left alone by Satan; he need not worry about them—in his view they are safe. But those who go from capital sin to capital sin, who, in other words, are not concerned about their own evil dispositions, are carefully led on from faults to very serious sins (314). Hence, Ignatius writes "para mejor conoscer las faltas hechos en los peccados mortales" (245). In this case, the translation "mortal sin" would make no sense. In the first exercise the exercitant considers the case of the poor man who for one "pecado mortal" goes to hell (52). For one mortal sin? Or for one capital sin? Polanco did not like the very stern tone of this third point of the first exercise, and holding on to the translation "mortal sin," he inserts "forte," "perhaps." Not satisfied yet, he fastens on the second part of this point, namely, "forte multi ob peccata nostris pauciora aeternis poenis addicti sunt" (*Dir.*, 331). We prefer the translation "capital sin" in the second prelude and the third point of the first exercise.
The translation "mortal sin" is demanded in 25, 33, 41, 349.

9 In defense of this interpretation, the phrase quoted in the previous note and found in Ignatius' short treatise of prayer on the seven capital sins (245) might be adduced.

10 Amazement is frequently expressed in the exercises of the first week, *e.g.*, "por mis *tantos* peccados" (48, 74), "*tantas* maldades y ponzoña *tan* turpíssima" (58), "*tanta* piedad y misericordia" (71).

seven

1 "The offerings of greater value and of more importance" (98) is not called a colloquy, and is no colloquy. It is part of the third point. It is an oblation made by those who are moved by love rather than by any other motive.

2 The Our Father is mentioned at the end of each of the exercises of the first week (54, 61, 63, 71), at the end of the contemplations on the Incarnation and the Nativity, in their repetitions and the application of the senses (109, 117, 118, 126). It is found again at the end of the meditation on Two Standards (147) and it is not forgotten at the conclusion of the contemplations of the third and fourth weeks (198, 225) nor at the end of the contemplation to attain divine love (237). The exception seems to be the meditation on Three Classes of Men. As the exercitant is told, however, to make the triple colloquy of the preceding meditation, that is, of Two Standards, it is obvious that Ignatius wants to see this meditation ended in the same way, with an Our Father, that is.

3 No exercise is called a consideration by Ignatius; the only one that can make a claim to be one is the exercise on three degrees of humility, where in the introduction the word "considerar" is used twice. The verb and the noun occur quite frequently. A good illustration of the meaning of a consideration is given in the description of the third time, "tiempo tranquilo, considerando" (177; cfr. 181, 185, 186, 187) and in the advice given concerning desolation: "el que está en desolación, considere" (320). It is often used in the meditation on Two Standards, which is intended to give some insight into the reality of life as influenced by Satan and by Christ (141, 142, 144, 145, 146). Other instructive examples are found in 38, 39, 248, 275 and 340.

4 Tradition has been very strong here. As early as 1554 Nadal writes that the dedication of Ignatius to help souls stems from "dos ejercicios, scilicet, del Rey y de las Banderas" (*F.N.*, I, p. 307). There is no trace of this in the *Autobiography* of Ignatius. It must be observed that Nadal joins the exercise on the King and that on Two Standards. Provided that these two exercises are kept joined together, one might agree with Nadal, as the meditation on Two Standards really contains all the important points found in the exercise "del Rey." But even in this case a very clear distinction must be drawn between the contents and the form of the meditation on Two Standards, the contents being the experience of various spirits influencing the exercitant's soul, the form being the imagery of battle, contestants, banners, and so on. The *Autobiography* leaves no doubt about the way in which Ignatius was moved by various spirits and how he learned to discern these movements (6-12, 20-33).

5 Thus in the composition of the contemplations on the Incarnation and the Nativity (103, 112), on the Last Supper and the Agony (192, 202), and on the risen Christ (220). In the composition on Two Standards, the verb in the present tense is used, as was done in the explanation of the first week (138, 47). The composition of the meditation on Three Classes of Men, which looks rather similar to the prelude of the contemplation to attain divine love, will be examined more closely in a later chapter (151, 232).

6 The expression "hacer contra" occurs elsewhere. In the first exercise the third sin is described as "hacer contra la bondad infinita" (52), and in the examination of conscience the object of the expression is "tan pias exhortaciones y comendaciones de nuestros mayores" (42). In neither case is there any suggestion of deadly strife, which is often found in explanations of the exercise "del Rey." Ignatius in that case favors "hacer per diametrum contra" (351) or "hacer el oppósito per diametrum" (325).

eight

1 Cfr. 127, 130, 206, 208, 209, 226 and 261-312.

2 The application of the senses, which Ignatius never fails to mention (132, 133, 159, 204, 226, 227), is introduced by "aprovecha" (121). There does not even appear to be need for "mucho," which in other contexts precedes the main verb (*e.g.* 5, 17, 100, 157, 168, 217, 228).

3 The application of the senses has been dealt with in Bibliothèque des Exercises, Nos. 61-62, by J. Maréchal: "Note sur la méthode d'application des sens dans les Exercises de St. Ignace" (pp. 50-64). Cfr. also F. Wulf, "Grundzüge ignatianischer Frömmigkeit." *Geist and Leben, Heft 3,* pp. 167-84.

nine

1 In the margin of the autograph text is written: "como suele ut in pluribus." Cfr. *Ex. Sp.*, 350, 351.

2 The autograph text has: "para que más fácilmente vengan a vano honor del mundo." In the third point Ignatius speaks of "honor mundano," where the opposite is said to be "deseo de opprobrios y menosprecios"; it is opposed to "deshonor" in the First Principle and Foundation (23) and in the explanation of the second kind of humility (166).

3 The combination "vicios y peccados" is found in the first rule for the discernment of spirits (314).

4 Roothaan here briefly comments on the use and meaning of "crescida." The word occurs in the prelude of the second exercise of the first week, in which the exercitant will ask for *crescido y intenso dolor* (55), and again in the fifth point where he is amazed at what has taken place in his life *con crescido afecto* (60). It is also found a number of times in the rules for the discernment of spirits, where Ignatius speaks of "crecido amor" (320), "crescidas gracias, devoción crescida" (322), and of the "ferocidad crescida, crecida malicia" of the evil spirits (325).

5 "Haciendo el oppósito per diametrum" is found in the last rule concerning scruples (325). Ignatius is writing about devout souls, not scrupulous souls, in that rule.

6 The prelude, called the history, is introduced by "será (or: es) aquí, cómo" (102, 111, 137, 191, 201, 219). Here the text reads: "la historia, la qual es de tres binarios de hombres . . . ."

7 There is a somewhat similar composition in the contemplation to attain divine love: "composición, que es aquí ver cómo estoy delante de Dios" (232). Here Ignatius does not use the word "lugar," nor does he ask the exercitant to see himself.

8 The purpose, or perhaps better, the function of the exercise is fairly regularly indicated in the exercises concerned with the election or reformation of life (170, 175, 178, 189). A rare, but very clear instance is given in the contemplation "to attain divine love" (230).

9 Roothaan refers to the reading "melius servire" in a note when he is dealing with this exercise.

ten

1 The mysteries for these eight days are given after the meditations on Two Standards and Three Classes of Men (158, 161). The question of lengthening or shortening is dealt with in a note immediately following this division of the week into days (162). The examples of how to lengthen the second week all belong to the first half of this week.

2 The inference that the particular examination of conscience is made once a day during the first week and the first four days of the second week is unwarranted. Although Ignatius does not refer to the examination of conscience as explained in the instructions that precede the first week (24-31), he presupposes that the

exercitant is acquainted with it; there it is said to be an exercise that is made twice daily.

3 "Sometimes it will be profitable, even when the exercitant is strong and well disposed, to make some changes *from the second to the fourth day inclusive*, making one contemplation on rising, the second about the time of Mass, with one repetition about the time of Vespers and the application of the senses before supper," states a note at the end of the second day (133). For those who are not so strong, the third note holds good, allowing them to omit the night contemplation, but the number of contemplations is thereby not reduced, as they will now make a contemplation on rising, at the time of Mass, before dinner, at the time of Vespers and before supper (129).

4 Ignatius remarks that usually three points are given in order to make it easier to meditate and contemplate on the mysteries (261). The verb "to meditate" appears scarcely defensible. When Ignatius refers indirectly to this note in his discussion of lengthening or shortening the second week, he only uses the verb "to contemplate." The difficulty disappears as soon as it is realized that, whereas contemplation is the form of prayer for the exercitant of the long retreat, there is no reason why he should not *meditate* upon the life of Christ afterward. It should be remembered that the series of points covering the life of Christ is placed outside the framework of the four weeks.

5 Cfr. *Examen Generale* C. 4 n. 44, C. 6 n. 7, C. 5 n. 8, C. 8 n. 2; *Constitutiones* P. VI, c. 1, n. 1, P. VI, c. 7, n. 4. In his *Diary* Ignatius writes: "dadme humildad amorosa," which is followed by "reverencia amorosa" and "acatamiento amoroso" (30 March, 31 March, 4 April).

eleven

1 Roothaan translates "multum iuvat," which is taken over by Morris, Rickaby, Puhl, Mottola, Courel, Raitz v. Frentz. More accurate is "iuvat, multum considerare." The argument in favor of this reading is that Ignatius puts "mucho" before "aprovecha", as, for instance, in the note following the exercise on three kinds of humility (cfr. also 17, 157, 228, 319). The combination "mucho considerar" has its parallel in "mucho declara" (2), "mucho advertir" (12), and so forth.

2 "Affectar" is also found in the sixteenth annotation, the second addition of the fourth week (229), in the exercise "del Rey" (97), and elsewhere (3, 50, 157, 166, 179, 234, 338, 342, 363). Nonell discusses its various meanings in his analysis of the Spiritual Exercises. (French translation: "Analyse des Exercises Spirituels de S. Ignace de Loyola," par Jaime Nonell, S.J., traduit par E. Thibaut, S.J. Bruxelles, 1924, pp. 304-06.)

3 We follow fairly common usage, which, not quite accurately, translates "deliberar" by "to deliberate." Cfr. Nonell, *op. cit.*, pp. 315-17; Puhl, *op. cit.*, pp., 183-84).

4 Ignatius writes: "La primera manera de humildad es necessaria para la salud eterna, es a saber, que así me baxe y así me humille quanto en mí sea possible, para que en todo obedesca a la ley de Dios nuestro Señor de tal suerte que aunque me hiciesen señor de todas las cosas criadas . . . ." Roothaan translates as follows: "Primus modus humilitatis est necessarius ad salutem aeternam, scilicet quod ita me demittam, et ita me humiliem, quantum possim, ut in omnibus obediam legi Dei Domini nostri, adeo ut, etiamsi me constituerent dominum omnium rerum creatarum . . . ." Roothaan inserts a comma before "quantum possum." The suggestion now is that the conjunction *ut* immediately following is consecutive, corresponding to the preceding *ita*. One might deduce from this translation that the limit of one's humility is the avoidance of mortal sin. This would not be humility at all but clear calculation, which smacks too much of escaping hell and leaves no room for the love of God. The correct translation should make it clear that in the first kind of humility the person humbles himself as much as he can, because only then will he be able to obey the law of God;

"para que" introduces a final clause. The consequence, or the result, is introduced by "de tal suerte que," and an accurate translation would fall back upon "with the result that." Clear examples of the use of this expression are found in the first note following the fourth week (226), in the general examination of conscience (40), and in the preamble for making a good election (169). Ignatius continues: "de tal suerte que aunque me hiciesen señor de todas cosas criadas en este mundo, ni por la propria vida temporal, no sea en deliberar de quebrantar un mandamiento, quier divino, quier humano, que me obligue a peccado mortal." This is an unwieldy clause compared with the simple phrase "no sea en deliberar de hacer un peccado venial" of the second kind of humility. Why did Ignatius not write: "no sea en deliberar de hacer un peccado mortal"? The expression "quebrantar mandamiento" does not occur elsewhere in the Spiritual Exercises; the verb occurs in the third week, where Christ is spoken of as "quebrantado" (203; cfr. 206). Roothaan translates "transgredi mandatum," which seems a little flat. Evidently, Ignatius did not mean the same thing as "hacer un peccado mortal." There is a great difference between infringing a very important Commandment, one that binds man under mortal sin, and committing a mortal sin. It is over-simplification to state that the first kind of humility stands for avoiding mortal sin, however difficult this at times may be.

5 The autograph text of the second kind of humility reads: "si yo me hallo en tal puncto que no quiero ni me afecto más a tener riqueza que pobreza . . . ." The sixteenth annotation has: "debe affectarse al contrario, instando en oraciones . . ., y pidiendo a Dios nuestro Señor el contrario, es a saber, que ni quiere el tal officio o beneficio ni otra cosa alguna, si su divina majestad . . . no le mudare su affección primera."

6 The text of the First Principle and Foundation reads: "es menester hacernos indiferentes a todas las cosas criadas . . . en tal manera que no queramos de nuestra parte más salud que enfermedad, riqueza que pobreza, honor que deshonor, vida larga que corta" (23). The text of the first method for making a good choice reads: "y con esto hallarme indiferente sin affección alguna dessordenada, de manera que no esté más inclinado ni affectado a tomar la cosa propuesta que a dexarla" (179).

7 It is of importance to notice that the second kind of humility does not differ from the first because now a person will not even deliberate about committing a venial sin. We made this clear in the fourth note. The second kind of humility comprises two parts, which are joined together by means of "y con esto." This expression posits a juxtaposition and nothing more (cfr. 71, 179, 234, 367), and is consequently not identical with "de suerte que," "de manera que," or "por consiguiente" (23, 94, 169). The translation of "y con esto" by "deinde" in Roothaan's text of the first point of the contemplation to attain the love of God is not entirely accurate.
The juxtaposition does not mean that the two parts are unrelated. There must be some relation if together they make up the second kind of humility. The relationship seems sufficiently indicated by the verbs "quiero" and "affecto", followed by the infinitive forms "tener" (riqueza), "querer" (honor), and "desear" (vida larga) on the one hand, and "deliberar de hacer un peccado venial" on the other. The first part refers to man's disposition with regard to the good things of this life on earth, the second part has for its object a concrete situation in which a decision one way or the other must be taken. Hence it is that in the first part the phrase "siendo igual servicio de Dios nuestro Señor y salud de mi ánima" suggests an abstract, not to say fictional, situation. The opinion that the second part is contained in the first or that it is a conclusion from the first is untenable. There is no parity, for in the second part there is question of *inigual servicio:* otherwise the very mention of venial sin would be meaningless. Similarly, it cannot be held that the second part is a step back compared with the first part. A sound disposition is no guarantee that consequently the act will be in harmony with this disposition.

8 Love is not satisfied with a good disposition only. It demands action. So Ignatius writes "quiero y elijo," whereas in the second kind of humility he was contented with "no quiero ni me afecto." Further examples of Ignatian accuracy are given in the use of the verbs "tener," "querer," and "desear," each with its appropriate object in the second kind of humility. In the third, we find the same verbs and the same objects, except that "vida larga" has disappeared; it can never be the object of "elijo."

9 From the autograph text: ". . . quiero y elijo más pobreza con Christo pobre que riqueza, opprobrios con Christo lleno dellos que honores, y desear más de ser estimado por vano y loco por Christo . . . que por sabio ni prudente en este mundo": thus in the third kind of humility. The third prelude of the contemplations of the third week reads: "demandar lo que quiero, lo qual es proprio de demandar en la passión, dolor con Christo doloroso, quebranto con Christo quebrantado" (203), and the second addition has: "esforzándome . . . en entristecerme y dolerme de tanto dolor y de tanto padescer de Christo nuestro Señor" (206).

10 The introduction to the meditation on Two Standards has: "en qualquier estado o vida que Dios nuestro Señor nos *diere* para eligir" (135). In the third point of the same meditation we read: ". . . traerlos a summa pobreza spiritual, y si su divina majestad . . . los *quisiere eligir*" (146), which is followed by "si su divina majestad . . . me *quisiere eligir y rescibir*" (147) in the colloquy of the same meditation; the note following the meditation on Three Classes of Men contains: "pedir en los coloquios que el Señor *le elija* en pobreza actual" (157), and finally, "pidiendo que el Señor nuestro *le quiera eligir* en esta . . . mejor humildad" (168).

twelve

1 This is Puhl's translation of "según la edad, disposición y temperatura." Morris has: "according as age, disposition, and temperament help the exercitant." The same expression occurs in the note following the meditation on hell (72). The reader is referred to two notes given by Puhl (*op. cit.*, pp. 176, 187).

2 Ignatius uses "ver" in all contemplations of the second week (103, 112). It returns in the fourth week (220) and in the contemplation to attain the love of God (233). In the contemplations on the Nativity and the Resurrection it is accompanied by "considerar" and "mirar," respectively. In the other exercises "ver" is used (47, 65, 91, 138, 151), while it is followed by "considerar" in the explanation of the composition of the first week (47).

3 In a note Roothaan explains his translation as being the equivalent of "colloqui ratiocinando." Cfr. Nonell, *op. cit.*, pp. 324-25. We refer the reader to what was said in the fifteenth note of the fourth chapter.

4 "Actual" is used by Ignatius in the sense of "now taking place" when he speaks of "actual consolación" (336) and "dolor actual" (44). Roothaan translates here "magis actu," which is the basis of the translations of Courel (effectivement davantage), Raitz v. Frentz and Urs von Balthasar (ihm in der Tat ähnlicher zu werden) as well as of the translation of Morris, Rickaby, Moore and others.

5 In the first prelude of the contemplation on the Incarnation, Ignatius has "miraban" followed by "se determina"; this present tense is explained by the phrase attached to it, namely, "en la su eternidad" (102).

6 For further examples of "delante de" cfr. the first colloquy of the retreat (53), the exercise "del Rey" (92, 98), the composition of the meditation on Three Classes of Men (151) and of the contemplation to attain the love of God (232).

7 The third prelude has: "demandar dolor con Christo doloroso, quebranto con Christo quebrantado, lágrimas, pena interna" (203); the second addition: "entristecerme y dolerme de tanto dolor y de tanto padescer de Christo" (206); the

sixth addition: "induciendo a mí mismo a dolor y a pena y quebranto" (*ibid.*), while we read in the notes following Ignatius' remarks on penance: "llorar mucho sobre las penas y dolores de Christo" (87) and in the first explanation of the colloquy: "demandar pena, lágrimas y tormento con Christo atormentado" (48).

8 How strongly Ignatius felt on this point is evident from two passages in the diary of Luis González (*F.N.*, I, pp. 676-77, 644).

thirteen

1 In the third note of this fourth week, the exercitant is bidden to foresee (coniecturar) and determine the number of points of his contemplation (228). The noun "coniectura" is found by the side of "razones probables" when two ways are discussed in which it is permissible to speak of the sins of others (41). Cfr. *Sp. Ex.*, p. 189.

2 Cfr. additions 6, 5, 16 and 20; the rules concerning scruples (348-51), the instructions dealing with the election (175, 177), and the rules for the discernment of spirits (316, 326, 330).

3 In the rules for the discernment of spirits, it is much more frequently used in the second series than in the first. The question might be asked whether in the second set "ánima" is not used in the primary sense of the word. There is, however, a significant change from "ánima" to "persona" as soon as there is question of temptation and deceits by Satan, adversely affecting a state of spiritual delight and joy (334). Besides, the fifth rule contains a clear enough indication that it is more likely that "ánima" in all these rules stands for "persona." It might be pointed out that in the last rule Ignatius also uses "persona" where there is question of consolation. Reading carefully, one notices that Ignatius is actually dealing with a person whose period of consolation has just ended; he calls him "persona espiritual," and speaking of fervor, he employs "ánima" again (337).

4 The standard expression "the salvation of one's soul" is found a good number of times. In the contemplation on the Incarnation, God's intention is said to be to save mankind (salvar el género humano, 102) and to redeem mankind (hacer redempción del género humano, 107). The Incarnate Word is called "Señor" (104, 116).

fourteen

1 "La oración preparatoria solita" occurs in 65, 91, 101, 110, 136, 149, 190, 200, 218; "oración la misma" is found in 55.

2 Cfr. 48, 55, 65, 104, 139, 152, 193, 203, 221.

3 Cfr. 72, 99, 105, 127-31, 148, 157, 168, 204-07, 209, 226-29.

4 The exercise on Three Classes of Men seems to be similar in this respect. This exercise, however, is a meditation, and in fact a very special kind of meditation, which makes a considerable difference.

5 Other instances are found in the eleventh annotation, where the exercitant is told not to shirk toil in order to attain what he is seeking (para alcanzar la cosa que busca), and in the instruction about general confession, where the result desired is that a person should attain a greater knowledge of and sorrow for his sins (alcanzando más conoscimiento y dolor, 44).

6 Another example is given in the second prelude of the meditation on hell. The exercitant prays that, should he ever because of his faults forget the love of the eternal Lord, the fear of punishment will keep him from falling into sin (65). Notice: through his faults. Calveras takes "del Señor" to be a subjective

genitive, thus giving the meaning: "if he should ever forget that the eternal Lord loves him"; we do not agree (*op. cit.*, p. 387).

7 In a letter to Father Brandao, Ignatius writes about this subject; *those who are perfect* are not mentioned, but there is hope for those who make an effort to find the presence of God in all things (*Ep.*, III, p. 508).

8 The text of the *Constitutions* of the Society of Jesus removes all doubt: "apartando de sí el amor de todas la criaturas por ponerle en el Criador dellas, a él *en todas* amando y a todas en él (P. III, c. 1, n. 26).

9 When Ignatius speaks of the created universe, expressions such as "todo lo criado" or "todas cosas criadas" are used (23, 58, 165, 166, 189, 236). For the correct meaning of "creación" cfr. the paragraph dealing with the emendation and reformation of life (189).

10 The sixteenth annotation warns against *proprios provechos y intereses temporales;* in the exercise "del Rey" man is told to be on his guard against *propria sensualidad, amor carnal y mundano* (97). A general principle of spiritual progress is given in the section dealing with the reformation of life, where man is asked to turn his back upon *proprio amor, querer y interesse* (189).

fifteen

1 Possibly Ignatius became acquainted with these three forms of prayer through Cisneros' *Ejercitatorio*. Cfr. P. Philippe, O.P., "L'Oraison dans l'histoire," in *L'Oraison,* Cahiers de la Vie Spirituelle, Ed. du Cerf, Paris, 1947, pp. 8-59.

2 The combination is also found in the *Constitutions* of the Society of Jesus; the profession pronounced within the Society is called by Ignatius "professión de humildad y baxeza" (P. X, n. 6).

3 "Lágrimas" occurs in connection with contrition four times in the first week (55, 78, 87, 89), and it is called the fruit of the first week in the fourth annotation. The contemplation on the Passion should lead to tears (203, 48), but it is called a "gracia spiritual" (322) and it is found wedged in between "consolaciones" and "inspiraciones y quietud" as gifts of the good spirit (315). In the description of consolation, tears are mentioned as moving to the love of God (lágrimas motivas a amor de su Señor), whatever the reason for shedding them (316).

INDEX

The more important references under each topic are printed in italics.